The Tyndale Old Testament Commentaries

General Editor:
PROFESSOR D. J. WISEMAN, O.B.E., M.A., D.Lit., F.B.A.,
F.S.A.

1 CHRONICLES

This work is dedicated to those churches where I have learnt to love the Lord and his word:

Holy Trinity Parish Church, Wallington
Heath Evangelical Church, Cardiff
Stoneleigh Baptist Church, Epsom

1 CHRONICLES

AN INTRODUCTION AND COMMENTARY

by

MARTIN J. SELMAN, B.A., M.A., Ph.D.

Director of Postgraduate Studies, Spurgeon's College, London

INTER-VARSITY PRESS
Leicester, England
Downers Grove, Illinois, U.S.A.

InterVarsity Press
P.O. Box 1400, Downers Grove, Illinois 60515, U.S.A.
38 De Montfort Street, Leicester LE1 7GP, England

InterVarsity Press®, USA, is the book-publishing division of InterVarsity Christian Fellowship®, a student movement active on campus at hundreds of universities, colleges and schools of nursing in the United States of America, and a member movement of the International Fellowship of Evangelical Students. For information about local and regional activities, write Public Relations Dept., InterVarsity Christian Fellowship, 6400 Schroeder Rd., P.O. Box 7895, Madison, WI 53707-7895.

Inter-Varsity Press, England, is the publishing division of the Universities and Colleges Christian Fellowship (formerly the Inter-Varsity Fellowship), a student movement linking Christian Unions in universities and colleges throughout the United Kingdom and the Republic of Ireland, and a member movement of the International Fellowship of Evangelical Students. For information about local and national activities in Great Britain write to UCCF, 38 De Montfort Street, Leicester LE1 7GP.

UK ISBN 0-85111-847-X (paperback)
USA ISBN 0-8308-1431-0 (hardback)
USA ISBN 0-87784-260-4 (paperback)
USA ISBN 0-87784-880-7 (set of Tyndale Old Testament Commentaries, hardback)
USA ISBN 0-87784-280-9 (set of Tyndale Old Testament Commentaries, paperback)

Text set in Great Britain
Printed in the United States of America ♾

Library of Congress Cataloging-in-Publication Data

Selman, Martin J., 1947-
 1 Chronicles: an introduction and commentary/by Martin J. Selman.
  p.   cm.—(The Tyndale Old Testament commentaries)
  Includes bibliographical references.
  ISBN 0-8308-1431-0 (U.S.).—ISBN 0-87784-260-4 (U.S.: pbk.)
  1. Bible.   O.T.   Chronicles, 1st—Commentaries.   I. Title.
II. Title: First Chronicles.   III. Series.
BS1345.3.S45   1994
222'.6307—dc20   *94-26382*
                                              CIP

British Library Cataloguing in Publication Data
A catalogue record for this book is available from the British Library.

15	14	13	12	11	10	9	8	7	6	5	4	3	2	1
06	05	04	03	02	01	00	99	98	97	96	95	94		

GENERAL PREFACE

THE aim of this series of *Tyndale Old Testament Commentaries*, as it was in the companion volumes on the New Testament, is to provide the student of the Bible with a handy, up-to-date commentary on each book, with the primary emphasis on exegesis. Major critical questions are discussed in the introductions and additional notes, while undue technicalities have been avoided.

In this series individual authors are, of course, free to make their own distinct contributions and express their own point of view on all debated issues. Within the necessary limits of space they frequently draw attention to interpretations which they themselves do not hold but which represent the stated conclusions of sincere fellow Christians.

Though the two books of Chronicles are much neglected they have, as Dr Martin Selman skilfully shows, an abiding message of hope for today's church. Readers who study them with the aid of this commentary will surely come to a new appreciation of their place in the Old Testament canon.

In the Old Testament in particular no single English translation is adequate to reflect the original text. The version on which this commentary is based is the New International Version, but other translations are frequently referred to as well, and on occasion the author supplies his own. Where necessary, words are transliterated in order to help the reader who is unfamiliar with Hebrew to identify the precise word under discussion. It is assumed throughout that the reader will have ready access to one, or more, reliable rendering of the Bible in English.

Interest in the meaning and message of the Old Testament continues undiminished, and it is hoped that this series will thus further the systematic study of the revelation of God and his will and ways as seen in these records. It is the prayer of the editor and publisher, as of the authors, that these books

will help many to understand, and to respond to, the Word of
God today.

D. J. WISEMAN

CONTENTS

AUTHOR'S PREFACE

IT is the strange privilege of every commentator to recommend that the book his readers really ought to read is not the one he has written. In that sense, his role is not unlike John the Baptist's, whose ability to point away from himself to someone far greater ought to make him the patron saint of commentators.

My real desire, therefore, is that you come to read the books of Chronicles for yourself. That is the end for which this commentary has been written, in the hope that you will receive some guidance in understanding and praying over this part of the word of God.

Though the Chronicler has been my companion for several years, I have not ceased to be filled with admiration for the breadth of his vision and his extraordinary perception. His conviction that God's message is also essentially a hopeful one justifies his work being described as 'the good news according to the Chronicler'. I have been amazed too at the relevance of his work for the modern world, especially for Christians who form a minority in their society, perhaps even suffering for their faith, and with little hope of seeing positive change in the political context in which they live; those who have lost hope of ever seeing for themselves the glorious times experienced by Christians of former generations; those who are concerned for the spiritual health of their nation and would like to discover what role Christians could have in being an influence for good; those who want to have a broad vision of God's purposes for their lives and for the church; and those who want to understand what the Old Testament as a whole is about and why it is included in the Bible.

Maybe in the past you have been dissuaded from reading the books of Chronicles because of their length, or because they contain ancient history, or above all because of their lists of strange names, especially in the first nine chapters. None of these presents an insurmountable obstacle to enjoying Chronicles, however. Especially if you have never attempted to read Chronicles seriously before, may I suggest that you start at 1 Chronicles 10 and simply leave out the lists until you feel you are ready for them. It would be a shame to miss out on all that God has to say simply because of a problem about where to start.

The Chronicler's concern is that his readers should experience genuine healing, and what he has to say on the subject goes far deeper than most contemporary discussion and teaching. It is my prayer that each of you will receive something of this healing and restoration, and that in doing so you will discover more of God's own heart (*cf.* 2 Ch. 7:14, 16).

A special feature of this commentary is the information which occurs at the beginning of each section. First of all a quotation is given, selected from the section of biblical text which follows. This quotation is intended to summarize the thought of the section. It is remarkable how frequently the Bible itself crystallizes the theme of a passage in a succinct and apposite manner. The quotation is then usually followed by some biblical references, which may be quite extensive. These refer to passages which are in some way parallel with the passage under consideration. In fact, they probably indicate the sources which the Chronicler has used. Identification of these sources is an essential feature of this volume, since it is argued in the commentary that the Chronicler assumes that his readers are reasonably familiar with this earlier material. It seems as if the Chronicler is actually commenting on these earlier parts of Scripture, and that he does so by various methods. If the books of Chronicles are read with this perspective in mind, the modern reader will often find it useful to refer to the relevant parts of the Old Testament at the same time as reading the text of Chronicles. This will help considerably in illuminating the meaning of the biblical text, and will bring a much deeper awareness of the potential significance of God's word both then and now.

The basic version of the English Bible to which this commentary refers is the New International Version, which is usually quoted without any further details. However, other versions have been used extensively throughout, such as the New English Bible, the Revised English Bible, the New Revised Standard Version, the Revised Standard Version, the

Good News Bible, and the Jerusalem Bible. Readers should be able to use this commentary with whatever modern version is available to them, since the commentary is ultimately based on the Hebrew text of the Old Testament, usually known as the Massoretic Text. Since no single modern version can convey all the richness of the original Hebrew, the use of several versions in the commentary actually gives the reader a genuine advantage in understanding what God is saying.

Only those who have actually written a book can appreciate how much an author is indebted to others. Their contributions are a vital part of the whole enterprise, and I acknowledge with deep gratitude the help of everyone who has encouraged me, especially when it involved putting up with my absence from other activities. I am especially grateful to my colleagues at Spurgeon's College who have carried responsibilities for me at various times in order that the project might eventually be finished, and to the publishers for patiently waiting much longer than they originally expected. The Councils of Spurgeon's College and of Tyndale House, Cambridge, generously provided essential financial support. Previous commentators, and especially those who have written recent books and monographs on Chronicles, have constantly stimulated my thinking. A number of churches have had to suffer unexpected sermons on the Chronicler, and the commentary is dedicated particularly to those churches which first gave me a love of the Scriptures and have accepted me and my idiosyncrasies as part of their fellowship. Lastly, and above all, words of gratitude are quite inadequate to express the encouragement of my family who often have been deprived of my company, and who have endured my preoccupation with the Chronicler from beginning to end. I am deeply humbled by the support of all who have had a part in the production of this volume, and I have not the slightest doubt that it has been greatly improved by their involvement.

Easter, 1993   *Martin Selman*
                                        Spurgeon's College, London

11

CHIEF ABBREVIATIONS

AASOR	*Annual of the American Schools of Oriental Research.*
AB	Anchor Bible.
AHwb	W. von Soden, *Akkadisches Handwörterbuch*, 3 vols. (Wiesbaden: Harrassowitz, 1965ff.).
Albright	W. F. Albright, 'The chronology of the divided monarchy of Israel', *BASOR* 100, 1945, pp. 16–22.
ANET	J. B. Pritchard (ed.), *Ancient Near Eastern Texts Relating to the Old Testament* (Princeton: Princeton University Press, 1950).
AOAT	*Alten Orient und Alten Testament.*
Aram.	Aramaic.
Ass.	Assyrian.
BA	Biblical Archaeologist.
Barthélemy, *CTAT*	D. Barthélemy, *Critique Textuelle de l'Ancien Testament*, vol. 1, *Orbis Biblicus et Orientalis* 50/1 (Göttingen: Vandenhoeck & Ruprecht, 1982).
BASOR	*Bulletin of the American Schools of Oriental Research.*
BBET	*Beiträge zur biblischen Exegese und Theologie.*
Begrich	J. Begrich, *Die Chronologie der Könige von Israel und Juda* (Tübingen: Mohr, 1929).
Bib.	*Biblica.*
BTB	*Biblical Theology Bulletin.*
BZAW	*Beiheft zur Zeitschrift für die alttestamentliche Wissenschaft.*
CAD	A. L. Oppenheim, *et al.*, *Chicago Assyrian Dictionary* (Chicago: Oriental Institute, 1956ff.).

CBC	Cambridge Bible Commentary.
CBOTS	*Coniectanea Biblica Old Testament Series.*
CBQ	*Catholic Biblical Quarterly.*
Childs	B. S. Childs, *Isaiah and the Assyrian Crisis* (London: SCM Press, 1967).
ET	English translation.
Exp.T.	*Expository Times.*
FOTL	Forms of Old Testament Literature.
GK	E. Kautzsch and A. E. Cowley (eds.), *Genesius' Hebrew Grammar* (Oxford: Clarendon Press, 1910).
HAT	*Handbuch zum Alten Testament.*
HTR	*Harvard Theological Review.*
Hughes, *Secrets*	J. Hughes, *Secrets of the Times, JSOTS* 66 (Sheffield: JSOT Press, 1990).
IBD	*The Illustrated Bible Dictionary* (Leicester: IVP, 1980).
ICC	International Critical Commentary.
IDB	*Interpreter's Dictionary of the Bible* (Nashville: Abingdon, vols. I–IV, 1962; Supplement, 1976).
IEJ	*Israel Exploration Journal.*
Japhet, *Ideology*	S. Japhet, *The Ideology of the Book of Chronicles* (Frankfurt: P. Lang, 1989).
JBL	*Journal of Biblical Literature.*
JETS	*Journal of the Evangelical Theological Society.*
JQR	*Jewish Quarterly Review.*
Johnstone, 'Guilt'	W. Johnstone, 'Guilt and Atonement: the theme of 1 and 2 Chronicles', in J. D. Martin and P. R. Davies (eds.), *A Word in Season*, JSOTS 42 (Sheffield: JSOT Press, 1986), pp. 113–138.
JSNTS	*Journal for the Study of the Testament, Supplement Series.*
JSOT	*Journal for the Study of the Old Testament.*
JSOTS	*Journal for the Study of the Old Testament, Supplement Series.*
JTS	*Journal of Theological Studies.*
KB	L. Koehler and W. Baumgartner (eds.), *Hebräisches und Aramäisches Lexikon* (Leiden: Brill, [3]1967ff.).

Keil	C. F. Keil, *The Books of the Kings* (Edinburgh: T. & T. Clark, ²1883).
Kleinig, *Song*	J. Kleinig, *The LORD's Song: The Basis, Function and Significance of Choral Music in Chronicles*, JSOTS 156 (Sheffield: JSOT Press, 1993).
McKenzie, *Use*	S. L. McKenzie, *The Chronicler's Use of the Deuteronomic History*, Harvard Semitic Monographs 33 (Atlanta: Scholars Press, 1985).
Mason, *Preaching*	R. A. Mason, *Preaching the Tradition* (Cambridge: Cambridge University Press, 1990).
Mosis, *UTCG*	R. Mosis, *Untersuchungen zur Theologie des chronistischen Geschichtswerkes*, Freiburger Theologische Studien 29 (Freiberg: Herder, 1973).
NCB	New Century Bible.
NIDNTT	C. Brown (ed.), *New International Dictionary of New Testament Theology*, 3 vols. (Exeter: Paternoster Press, 1975–78).
OTL	Old Testament Library.
OTS	*Oudtestamentische Studiën.*
PEQ	*Palestine Exploration Quarterly.*
Polzin, *Typology*	R. Polzin, *Late Biblical Hebrew: Toward an Historical Typology of Biblical Hebrew Prose*, HSM 12 (Missoula: Scholars Press, 1976).
SBB	*Stuttgarter Biblische Beiträge.*
SBLMS	*Society of Biblical Literature Monograph Series.*
SVT	*Supplements to Vetus Testamentum.*
TB	*Tyndale Bulletin.*
TC	R. Le Déaut and J. Robert, *Targum des Chroniques*, 2 vols. (Rome: Biblical Institute Press, 1971).
TDOT	G. Botterweck and H. Ringgren (eds.), *Theological Dictionary of the Old Testament* (Grand Rapids: Eerdmans, 1974ff.).
Thiele	E. R. Thiele, *The Mysterious Numbers of the Hebrew Kings* (Grand Rapids: Eerdmans, ³1983).

Throntveit, *Kings*	M. A. Throntveit, *When Kings Speak*, Society of Biblical Literature Dissertation Series 93 (Atlanta: Scholars Press, 1987).
TOTC	Tyndale Old Testament Commentary.
VE	*Vox Evangelica.*
von Rad, *GCW*	G. von Rad, *Das Geschichtsbild des chronistischen Werkes* (Stuttgart: Kohlhammer, 1930).
VT	*Vetus Testamentum.*
WBC	Word Biblical Commentary.
Willi, *CA*	T. Willi, *Die Chronik als Auslegung* (Göttingen: Vandenhoeck & Ruprecht, 1972).
Williamson, *IBC*	H. G. M. Williamson, *Israel in the Books of Chronicles* (Cambridge: Cambridge University Press, 1977).
WTJ	*Westminster Theological Journal.*
ZAW	*Zeitschrift für die alttestamentliche Wissenschaft.*

TEXTS AND VERSIONS

Ar	Old Arabic version of the Old Testament.
AV	Authorized (King James) Version, 1611.
EVV	English versions.
GNB	Good News Bible (Today's English Version), 1976.
JB	Jerusalem Bible, 1966.
LXX	Septuagint (pre-Christian Greek version of the Old Testament).
LXX (A)	Septuagint, Codex Alexandrinus.
LXX (L)	Septuagint, Lucian recension.
MT	Massoretic Text (the standard Hebrew text of the Old Testament).
NEB	New English Bible, 1970.
NIV	New International Version, 1984.
NRSV	New Revised Standard Version, 1989.
OL	Old Latin translation of the Bible.
P	Peshitta (the Syriac translation of the Bible).

REB	Revised English Bible, 1989.
RSV	Revised Standard Version, 1952.
RV	Revised Version, 1881.
Tg.	Targum.
VSS	Versions, *i.e.* the ancient translations of the Bible, especially Greek (LXX), Aramaic (Tg.), Syriac (P), Latin (Vulg.).
Vulg.	Vulgate (the main, late fourth-century, Latin translation of the Bible by Jerome).

COMMENTARIES

Commentaries on 1 and 2 Chronicles (introductory commentaries are marked with an *)

Ackroyd	P. R. Ackroyd, *I & II Chronicles, Ezra, Nehemiah*, Torch Commentary (London, SCM Press, 1973).
Allen	L. C. Allen, *1, 2 Chronicles*, The Communicator's Commentary (Waco: Word Books, 1987).*
Bertheau	E. Bertheau, *Commentary on the Books of Chronicles* (Edinburgh, T. & T. Clark, 1857).
Braun	R. L. Braun, *1 Chronicles*, WBC 14 (Waco: Word Books, 1986).
Coggins	R. J. Coggins, *The First and Second Books of Chronicles*, CBC (Cambridge: Cambridge University Press, 1976).*
Curtis and Madsen	E. L. Curtis and A. L. Madsen, *The Books of Chronicles*, ICC (Edinburgh: T. & T. Clark, 1910).
de Vries	S. J. de Vries, *1 and 2 Chronicles*, FOTL 11 (Grand Rapids: Eerdmans, 1989).
Dillard	R. B. Dillard, *2 Chronicles*, WBC 15 (Waco: Word Books, 1987).
Japhet	S. Japhet, *I & II Chronicles*, Old Testament Library (London: SCM Press, 1993).
McConville	J. G. McConville, *Chronicles*, Daily Study Bible (Edinburgh: St Andrew Press, 1984).*
Michaeli	F. Michaeli, *Les livres des Chroniques* (Neuchâtel: Delachaux & Niestlé, 1967).

16

Myers, *1 Chronicles*	J. M. Myers, *I Chronicles*, AB 12 (New York: Doubleday, 1965).
Myers, *2 Chronicles*	J. M. Myers, *II Chronicles*, AB 13 (New York: Doubleday, 1965).
Rudolph	W. Rudolph, *Die Chronikbücher*, HAT (Tübingen: Mohr, 1955).
Wilcock	M. Wilcock, *The Message of Chronicles*, The Bible Speaks Today (Leicester: IVP, 1987).*
Williamson	H. G. M. Williamson, *1 and 2 Chronicles*, NCB (London: Marshall, Morgan & Scott, 1982).

Commentaries on 1 and 2 Samuel and 1 and 2 Kings

Anderson	A. A. Anderson, *2 Samuel*, WBC (Waco: Word Books, 1989).
Cogan and Tadmor	M. Cogan and H. Tadmor, *II Kings*, AB (New York: Doubleday, 1988).
Gray	J. Gray, *I and II Kings*, OTL (London: SCM Press, ³1977).
Hertzberg	H. W. Hertzberg, *I and II Samuel*, OTL (London: SCM Press, 1964).
Hobbs	T. R. Hobbs, *2 Kings*, WBC (Waco: Word Books, 1985).
Jones	G. H. Jones, *I and II Kings*, NCB (London: Marshall, Morgan & Scott, 1984).
McCarter	P. K. McCarter, *II Samuel*, AB (New York: Doubleday, 1984).
Nelson	R. D. Nelson, *First and Second Kings*, Interpretation (Atlanta: John Knox Press, 1987).
Šanda	A. Šanda, *Die Bücher die Könige* (Munster: Aschendorffscher Verlag, 1911–12).
Wiseman	D. J. Wiseman, *1 and 2 Kings*, TOTC (Leicester: IVP, 1993).

INTRODUCTION

THE English title of the books of 1 and 2 Chronicles has an unusual history. It originates neither from the original Hebrew, nor (despite the fact that 'chronicle' comes from a Greek word *chronikon*) from the Septuagint, the Greek translation of the Old Testament. It was not in fact until the fourth century AD that Jerome, the famous Bible translator, first applied the term 'Chronicle' to these books. He suggested in the prologue to his Latin translation of Samuel and Kings that in place of the Greek title *Paraleipomena* (see below) usually given to the work, 'we might more plainly call it the chronicle (*chronikon*) of the whole of sacred history'. Though Jerome wrote no commentary on Chronicles and retained the traditional Greek title, his proposal eventually became the basis of the title now used in the English Bible. The mediating influence came from Luther, whose German title, *Die Chronika*, passed into English when Bible translations proliferated during the Reformation period.

Despite its comparatively late appearance, 'chronicle' is a good idiomatic translation of the expression *dib^e rê hayyāmîm*, the accepted Hebrew title of the work. This phrase means literally 'the events of the days', *i.e.* 'annal, chronicle', and though it appears only once in the body of Chronicles (1 Ch. 27:24), it became associated with the work through its frequent appearance in Kings (*cf. e.g.* 1 Ki. 14:19, 29; 15:7, 23, 31). It may well have been used as a title for Chronicles from quite early on, judging by the similar usage of the phrase in other Old Testament books of the same general period (*cf.* Ne. 12:23; Est. 2:23; 6:1; 10:2). The Greek translators of the Old Testament, however, produced a quite different title, *viz.*, *Paraleipomena*, 'the things omitted', *i.e.* omitted from Samuel and Kings. This reflected a rather different understanding of the book from that implied by the Hebrew title, and it is the Greek approach which has had much the greater influence on the church's view of Chronicles down the centuries. Unfortunately it also contributed to the book's widespread neglect, since the Greek title implied that Chronicles was a kind of supplement or appendix and was therefore of only marginal value in the Old Testament.

The division of Chronicles into two parts, *viz.* 1 and 2 Chronicles, goes back to the Septuagint, though it is attested no earlier than the third century AD. In the Hebrew tradition, it is no older than the first printed edition of the Hebrew Bible in 1448 AD. This division was probably made for practical reasons, and has no other significance. On the contrary, the textual history of the Hebrew Bible as well as the contents and ideology of 1 and 2 Chronicles show that the two books are really a single unit. Once this is recognized, the length and scope of the work make clear that it is an extremely important part of the Old Testament. Its subject matter covers the whole of Israelite history from creation (1 Ch. 1:1) to near the author's own time (1 Ch. 9:2–34), and in terms of the number of chapters it is the third largest compilation in the Old Testament, after Psalms and Isaiah.

II. WHAT KIND OF BOOK IS CHRONICLES?

The existence of different titles for the book raises a fundamental question as to its nature and purpose. This issue must be considered at the outset, since the reader's expectations of the book are bound to have a direct effect on the way he or she interprets it. If people fail to grasp its real character, they are likely to miss the heart of what the author is saying. Out of the variety of alternative understandings that have been put forward, four will be examined here.

(a) First of all, Chronicles can be treated as a history book. This assumption is implicit in both the Hebrew and Greek titles, though each involves quite different understandings of what type of historical writing is involved. If the book is really a chronicle, for example, the reader is likely to expect a record of actual events in Israelite national life during the period under consideration. On this basis, Chronicles would be a parallel or alternative version of the historical record in Samuel and Kings. This approach to the interpretation of

Chronicles has long been followed by Jews and Christians alike, and on this basis Chronicles was frequently regarded until the late nineteenth century as an additional source for pre-exilic Israelite history.[1] Although in more recent times the Chronicler's contribution as a historian has sometimes been understood more in terms of the provision of an over-all framework of interpretation rather than in compiling an objective record of events, categorizing Chronicles as a work of history is still a frequent approach.[2]

However, it is doubtful whether this description is adequate, even allowing for differences in attitudes to historical writing in biblical as compared with modern times. One immediately obvious problem is that it is hard to see why a second historical account of the monarchy period is necessary alongside Samuel and Kings and the frequent references to the period in many prophetic works. More importantly, the selectiveness of Chronicles' content and structure does not support this approach. The extensive lists and genealogies, for instance, mark out Chronicles as distinct from Samuel–Kings and are inappropriate in a primarily historical work. More detailed comparison with the Deuteronomic History (a common term for Deuteronomy to 2 Kings) confirms this view, for it is clear that the Chronicler's concerns are more narrowly focused. In place of a history of Israel's monarchies, the Chronicler concentrates on the southern kingdom and on individual kings such as David, Solomon, or Hezekiah, though he also appears to adopt a more favourable attitude towards the north than the author of Kings. His preoccupation with specialist matters such as the temple, prayer, worship, and the Levites also indicates that his real interest lies outside the purely historical sphere.

If Chronicles is not an historical alternative to Samuel and Kings, then neither is it an historical supplement to these books in the sense implied by the Septuagint title, 'things omitted

---

[1] Classic examples of this approach are J. G. Eichhorn in the eighteenth century (*Einleitung im Alte Testament*, Leipzig: Weidmann, 1780–83, 3rd edn., 1803) and C. F. Keil in the nineteenth century (*Apologetischer Versuch über die Bücher der Chronik*, Berlin: Oehmigke, 1833; *The Books of the Chronicles*, ET, Edinburgh: T. & T. Clark, 1872 (1980)), though Keil specifically excludes the idea that Chronicles is annalistic.

[2] *Cf.* de Vries, pp. 15–16.

(from Samuel–Kings)'.[1] Though the Greek version rightly recognizes that Chronicles is dependent on earlier parts of the Old Testament, the implication that it relates only to Samuel and Kings is too limited. It is also erroneous to see it as filling in some of the gaps in the earlier books, as though it simply supplied extra information from sources otherwise unknown. In reality, the Chronicler omits as much material as he adds; he replaces and rewrites passages and restructures whole sections, and quotes a much wider range of biblical material than just Samuel and Kings.[2] He also has distinctive aims and emphases, reflected throughout the book in his own individual purpose, style, setting and theology.

These comments are not meant to imply that the Chronicler is not interested in what actually happened in Israelite history, though it is true that his historical reliability has often been questioned.[3] While the Chronicler's primary concern is not to record the story of Israel's past, it would be illogical to deduce from this that his presentation of historical matters is thereby suspect. In fact, the Chronicler treats what is written elsewhere in the Old Testament very seriously, and uses much of the history of Samuel–Kings as a basis for his own contribution. His own interest in historical method can be seen in his explicit reference to source material, the frequency with which he quotes various kinds of sources in their own style, and his willingness to retain the content of his additional sources even where it appears to create problems of inconsistency. Where the Chronicler has provided a fuller picture of particular incidents than Samuel–Kings, it has been recognized that the additional material has independent historical value, and that 'where we are able to check his record against extrabiblical data, the picture is that of a careful author.'[4] Two further comments may be added. The first is that where the Chronicler's material remains uncorroborated in other ancient sources, biblical or otherwise, a certain humility is appropriate on the part of the modern reader, given the large

---

[1] *Cf. e.g.* W. F. Albright, 'The Chronicler's method in redacting the Book of Kings was to supplement, not to rewrite', *JBL* 40, 1921, pp. 104–124 (quotation from p. 120).

[2] *Cf.* J. Goldingay, 'The Chronicler as a theologian', *Biblical Theology Bulletin* 5, 1975, pp. 99–126, especially pp. 99–108.

[3] *E.g.* de Vries, pp. 11–12; Coggins, pp. 4–5.

[4] Dillard, p. xviii; *cf.* Myers, *1 Chronicles*, pp. xv, xxx.

gaps in our knowledge of all ancient history. In fact, in quite a number of passages, the Chronicler is clearly developing aspects of earlier biblical texts which may not previously have received much attention. Secondly, all historical writing, modern as well as ancient, involves some element of interpretation. That the interpretative level lies closer to the surface in Chronicles than it does even in other biblical histories implies no necessary criticism of the Chronicler's historical method.

(b) If Chronicles' historical features are of secondary rather than primary interest, greater attention should perhaps be given to its theological emphases. Dillard, for example, has summed up the work as 'through and through a theological essay; ... it is a tract',[1] and the Chronicler has even been described as 'the first Old Testament theologian'.[2] The attraction of this approach arises from two factors in particular. The first is that the Chronicler seems to treat his historical material as a means to an end rather than as an end in itself. He shows greater interest in the underlying meaning of events than in the events themselves, as illustrated by his special interests. These include, for example, frequent speeches and prayers, the repetition of themes, an interest in the basic institutions of society such as the system of worship or the monarchy, and a concern for God's direct intervention in human affairs. Though each of these is present in Samuel and Kings, their theological role in Chronicles is much more prominent.

Equally important, however, is the context in which the Chronicler is writing, since it is notable that his total preoccupation with the past excludes any direct reference to his own time. This is all the more significant in that the author emphasizes features of Israel's former years that completely outshone anything that was achieved in his own era. Solomon's glorious temple and the divinely chosen monarchy are very much to the fore even though they no longer existed, and in contrast to the story of Israel's previous status as an independent nation or nations, by the time the work was compiled God's people had been reduced to nothing more than a cog in a vast imperial wheel.

All this indicates that the author was doing more than simply informing his readers about what had happened in the

---

[1] Dillard, p. xviii.
[2] P. R. Ackroyd, 'The Chronicler as exegete', *JSOT* 2, 1977, p. 24.

past, and intended to explain the meaning of Israel's history. Unfortunately, however, his precise purpose is never made explicit, so that readers are left to infer it for themselves. One obvious suggestion, given the prominence of the temple, is that he wished to show that the Jerusalem temple was the only legitimate place of worship for God's people.[1] This is to over-look, however, the considerable attention given to the Davidic monarchy, though commentators cannot agree about the exact significance of this emphasis. According to one view, 'the person and dynasty of David' are 'the heartbeat of all the Chronicler's theology', though another thinks that the interest in David indicates the Chronicler as 'the guardian of the messianic tradition'.[2] Other interpreters read the Chronicler's theological emphasis quite differently. Some of the more important proposals are that the book is an extended parable about the importance of seeking God,[3] that it presents a God-given way of atonement for Israel's deep-seated guilt,[4] or that it points to a way of restoration for Israel through exile and judgment.[5] More cautious approaches argue that no one theme is more important than any other,[6] or else that the author was content to underline the value of continuity with the past rather than advocate major changes.[7]

Such failure to agree on the book's aim suggests either that the author has not made himself very clear or that the nature and purpose of the book lie elsewhere. Though, therefore, the next two approaches agree that Chronicles is theological in character, they attach greater weight to other aspects of the book.

(c) The frequency of speeches or sermons in Chronicles has led some to the conclusion that the author was '"preaching" his people's history', or that he was 'a preacher of pastoral theology'.[8] More specifically, it is said that 'his whole work

[1] *Cf.* Braun, p. xxviii.

[2] R. North, 'Theology of the Chronicler', *JBL* 82, 1963, p. 376; G. von Rad, *Old Testament Theology*, I (London: SCM Press, 1962), p. 351.

[3] C. Begg, '"Seeking Yahweh" and the purpose of Chronicles', *Louvain Studies* 9, 1982, pp. 128–141; *cf.* G. E. Schafer, 'The significance of seeking God in the purpose of the Chronicler', Th.D., Louisville, 1972.

[4] Johnstone, 'Guilt', pp. 113–138.

[5] P. R. Ackroyd, 'The theology of the Chronicler', in *The Chronicler in his Age*, *JSOTS* 101 (Sheffield: Sheffield Academic Press, 1991), pp. 273–289.

[6] *Cf.* Williamson, p. 24; Japhet, *Ideology*, p. 7.   [7] *Cf.* Coggins, p. 6.

[8] Ackroyd, p. 27; Allen, p. 20.

takes on the parenetic character of a "Levitical sermon", warning and encouraging his contemporaries to a responsive faith which may again call down the mercy of their God'.[1] The idea of the 'Levitical sermon' is based on the observation that many of the speeches are homiletic in style, even though most of them are given by kings and prophets.[2] The teaching role ascribed to the Levites in 2 Chronicles 19:8–11 is also reckoned to be of special significance.

Though it is true that the speeches are fundamental to the structure of the work, it is questionable whether it is correct or helpful to describe them as sermons or preaching. For one thing, the Chronicler's written style is rather different from the practice of preaching today. Further difficulties include the lack of clear criteria for defining the Chronicler's concept of a sermon, and the wide variation in the form of these supposed sermons. Though the relevant passages show a genuine acquaintance with earlier Scripture, they are rarely based on a specific text, for example. What is even more damaging to this theory, however, is that the supposed 'Levitical sermons' are hardly ever spoken by Levites![3] It is therefore preferable to speak of 'speeches' or 'addresses' rather than sermons. The frequency of these speeches is also an insufficient basis for applying the term 'preaching' to Chronicles as a whole.[4]

(d) Finally, the Chronicler has been described 'as a person interacting with texts', or in other words he has produced a work of interpretation or exegesis.[5] Although this view shares some features with the previous one, it is more broadly based. Whereas the idea of the Chronicler as a preacher is effectively derived only from the speeches, this approach takes the whole work into account.

Though Samuel and Kings clearly provide the framework for Chronicles' main historical section (1 Ch. 10–2 Ch. 36), the author ranges much more widely over what we now call the

---

[1] Williamson, p. 33; *cf.* J. M. Myers, 'The kerygma of the Chronicler', *Interpretation* 20, 1966, p. 268.
[2] G. von Rad, 'The levitical sermon in 1 and 2 Chronicles', in *The Problem of the Hexateuch* (Edinburgh: Oliver & Boyd, 1966), pp. 267–280.
[3] *E.g.*, Mason, *Preaching*, pp. 133–144; *cf.* Throntveit, *Kings*, p. 127.
[4] *Cf.* Mason, *ibid.*
[5] Dillard, p. xviii; *cf.* Willi, *CA*, *passim*; P. R. Ackroyd, 'The Chronicler as exegete', *JSOT* 2, 1977, pp. 2–32; K. Strübind, *Tradition als Interpretation in der Chronik*, *BZAW* 201 (Berlin: De Gruyter, 1991).

Old Testament. The beginning and end of the work provide a good example of this. Chronicles starts with Adam, mentioned in the first book of the Old Testament (1 Ch. 1:1; *cf.* Gn. 2:20; 5:1), and ends with the edict of Cyrus in Ezra–Nehemiah, a book dating approximately to the Chronicler's own time (2 Ch. 36:22–23; *cf.* Ezr. 1:1–3). In between, quotations from and allusions to other parts of the Old Testament are frequent. Parts of the Pentateuch, for example, are found in the genealogies of 1 Chronicles 1–9, as in the use of passages such as Genesis 46:9–10, 12 and Numbers 26:5–6, 12–13, 19–22 (*cf.* 1 Ch. 2:3–8; 4:24; 5:3). The genealogies also contain excerpts from the historical books, such as the settlement lists from Joshua 21:4–40 (1 Ch. 6:54–81) or the summary of the reasons for exile in 2 Kings 17:7–23 (1 Ch. 5:25–26; *cf.* 2 Ki. 15:19, 29). The Psalms play an important role in Chronicles, especially in the use of parts of Psalms 96, 105, and 106 in 1 Chronicles 16:8–36 and the adaptation of some verses from Psalm 132 at a crucial point in 2 Chronicles 6:41–42. The prophetic books are also frequently mentioned, as in the use of parts of Ezekiel 18 to form the structure of the account of Joash (2 Ch. 24) and of the reigns of Jotham, Ahaz, and Hezekiah (2 Ch. 27–32). Key phrases in Chronicles can turn out to be quotations from almost any part of the Old Testament. For example, one of Chronicles' most important principles, that those who seek the Lord will surely find him, is found in both the law and the prophets (1 Ch. 28:9; 2 Ch. 15:2; *cf.* Dt. 4:29; Je. 29:13–14; Is. 55:6). Other examples include the use of Exodus 14:13–14 and Numbers 14:41 in the important prophecies of 2 Chronicles 20:17 and 24:20 respectively, or the quotation of Zechariah 4:10 in 2 Chronicles 16:9.

These somewhat random examples clearly demonstrate that the Old Testament as a whole plays a central role in Chronicles. In fact, it is the conclusion of this commentary that the Chronicler's overall aim was to offer an interpretation of the Bible as he knew it. More precisely, his guiding principle was to demonstrate that God's promises revealed in the Davidic covenant were as trustworthy and effective as when they were first given, even though the first readers lived centuries after almost all the events he recorded. The evidence on which this assessment is based will now be examined in more detail.

Any appreciation of the Chronicler's purpose must take account of the distinctive structure of the work. The author is an orderly thinker and an artist of considerable literary merit whose message can be properly grasped only by taking an over-all view of his achievement. The work has been constructed by combining the author's own contributions with extensive biblical and other sources, resulting in a series of clearly defined units woven together by means of a complex variety of patterns.

At the simplest level, three main sections can be identified:

1 Ch. 1–9	Genealogies from Adam to the post-exilic era
1 Ch. 10 – 2 Ch. 9	The United Monarchy of David and Solomon
2 Ch. 10–36	Judah under the Divided Monarchy

Though the central section is sometimes further subdivided into the reigns of Saul (1 Ch. 10), David (1 Ch. 11–29) and Solomon (2 Ch. 1–9), recent study has emphasized that these kings, especially David and Solomon, are presented as a single unit. Indeed, it is precisely in the combined account of David and Solomon that the main thrust of the entire work is to be found. The first section of the work containing lists and genealogies (1 Ch. 1–9) is clearly preparatory, emphasizing Israel's original unity and its preservation by God's grace. The third section looks back to the basic principles by which God deals with his people by tracing the varied responses of kings and people. The heart of the work is therefore the central section, which contains two words from God which are of fundamental theological significance. The first of these is generally known as the Davidic covenant (1 Ch. 17:3–14). By this, God promised that he would build an eternal house or dynasty for David and that one of David's offspring would build a house or temple for God. The second word is God's message to Solomon in response to his prayer at the dedication of the temple (2 Ch. 7:11–22). This is also in the nature of a promise, namely, that God is always ready to forgive and restore his people, though they will ultimately be removed from their land and see its temple destroyed if they fail to take

27

advantage of this gracious offer. The fact that both divine words are unparalleled in Chronicles in terms of both length and detail testifies to their significance, and indicates that the Davidic monarchy and the temple are central to the Chronicler's understanding of history. This view is confirmed by the development of both themes in the rest of the work.

In addition to this basic structure, the Chronicler uses a number of further refinements to amplify what he has to say.

(a) First of all, the second and third major sections are subdivided in various ways in order to highlight particular themes:

I. The United Monarchy of David and Solomon
(i)   1 Ch. 10–12   David becomes king over all Israel
(ii) 1 Ch. 13–16   David brings the ark to Jerusalem
(iii) 1 Ch. 17–21   God's promise to David and the final occupation of the land
(iv) 1 Ch. 22–29   David prepares for the temple
(v)   2 Ch. 1–9   Solomon builds the temple

II. Judah under the Divided Monarchy
(i)   2 Ch. 10–12   The patterns of repentance and resistance
(ii)   2 Ch. 13–16   The benefits of trust in God
(iii) 2 Ch. 17–23   An unholy alliance results in compromise and disaster
(iv)   2 Ch. 24–26   Three kings start well but finish badly
(v)   2 Ch. 27–32   Three contrasting kings
(vi)   2 Ch. 33–35   Three kings and humble repentance
(vii) 2 Ch. 36   Four kings, exile and restoration

These subsections can be identified by two distinct literary devices. One is the repeated use of key words and phrases, such as in 2 Chronicles 13–16 where 'to seek (God)' appears nine times and 'to rely (on God)' a further five times. The other, which is used in the account of the Divided Monarchy, is the way in which trios of kings are brought together according to distinct behaviour patterns, demonstrating in different ways the importance of individual responsibility for sin and the value of individual repentance (2 Ch. 24–35). Joash, Amaziah, and Uzziah all fall away after showing evidence of faith (2 Ch. 24–26), Jotham, Ahaz and Hezekiah each deliberately reject the ways of their respective fathers (2 Ch. 27–32), and Manasseh, Amon and Josiah illustrate contrasting attitudes to repentance (2 Ch. 33–35). This kind of patterning supports the view that the Chronicler's aim was to draw out spiritual and theological principles rather than produce an alternative history to Samuel and Kings.

(b) A second feature is the Chronicler's predilection for dividing history into periods. This characteristic has already been recognized in the division of Israel's history into three periods, before, during, and after the time of David and Solomon, and in the grouping of kings in 2 Chronicles 24–35. The same phenomenon is also evident within the reigns of individual kings. David's reign, for example, is divided into four sections marking his recognition as king and the various stages of his preparation for the temple. Another instance is Asa's reign. After periods of blessing (2 Ch. 14) and of reformation (2 Ch. 15), towards the end of his life he turns completely and abandons God (2 Ch. 16). Joash (2 Ch. 24) and Uzziah (2 Ch. 26) provide further striking examples. Joash totally changed his policies once his high priest and mentor Jehoiada had died (2 Ch. 24:17), while 'after Uzziah became powerful' (2 Ch. 26:16), the blessing he had previously known was replaced by divine judgment because of his pride.

(c) A further pattern is where persons or events are modelled on one another as examples to follow or avoid. The most obvious case is David's portrayal as a second Moses, and therefore worthy of the same kind of recognition as his illustrious predecessor. David received divine revelation as Moses did (*e.g.* 1 Ch. 28:11–19) and amended Moses' laws to the circumstances of later times (*e.g.* 1 Ch. 15:23). This is no rigid scheme, though, since Solomon also followed in the Mosaic tradition. Many details of Solomon's temple followed Moses' blueprint for the original Tent or tabernacle (2 Ch. 3–4) and the basic pattern of temple worship was faithful to Mosaic principles (2 Ch. 8:13). Joshua also functions as a model for David and for Solomon. Solomon formed a kind of team ministry with David just as Joshua had done with Moses (1 Ch. 22:6–9, 11–13, 16; 28:3, 7–10, 19–20), and David followed in Joshua's footsteps by completing the conquest of the Promised Land (*cf.* 1 Ch. 18–20). A variation on the same theme is the way in which Solomon continued David's work (*cf.* 2 Ch. 1:8–9; 6:16–17; 8:14–15), as though it was merely a further stage in the same era.

Other analogies are also evident, with Hezekiah as the focus of several comparisons. His reorganization of the temple and its worship mirror the Davidic-Solomonic era (2 Ch. 29–30), for example. Hezekiah's closest connections, though, are with Asa (2 Ch. 14–16; 29–32). Both kings prospered by seeking God from the heart and obeying his laws, and both invited Israelites from the north to participate in renewing the coven-ant (2 Ch. 15:9–15; 29:10; 30:1–5, 10–11). On the other hand, Hezekiah is clearly contrasted with Jeroboam I of Israel (as described by Abijah, 2 Ch. 13:8–12) and with his own father Ahaz (2 Ch. 28:22–24), especially in their attitudes towards idolatry. Further behaviour patterns to be avoided are those in which Ahaz followed Jeroboam I (2 Ch. 13:8–12, 16–17; 28:1–8, 22–25) and Manasseh followed Ahaz (2 Ch. 28:2–4, 25; 33:2–6). Even Josiah's death is modelled on that of Ahab, because both of them failed to listen to what God was saying (2 Ch. 18:19–34; 35:22–24).

Different events can also be associated with each other, of which the shadow cast over the whole work by the exile offers the most significant example. Exile is seen as a consistent punishment for unfaithfulness to God in both the northern and southern kingdoms (1 Ch. 5:25–26; 2 Ch. 36:14–20). On the other hand, the reversal of exilic-type judgments experi-enced by Saul (1 Ch. 10) and Ahaz (2 Ch. 28) shows that all was not lost even when the worst seemed to have happened (1 Ch. 10:14; 2 Ch. 29:5–11). The value of repentance in such situations is well illustrated by David. David's rebelliousness is indicated in Chronicles by his disastrous census (*cf.* 2 Sa. 11–12; 2 Sa. 24; 1 Ch. 21), but his simple confession, 'I have sinned', repeated from the famous Bathsheba incident (2 Sa. 12:13; 24:10; 1 Ch. 21:8), illustrates a path to forgiveness which becomes one of the Chronicler's regular principles (2 Ch. 7:14).

Several patterns are associated with the temple. Solomon's succession to David as the temple-builder is based on a genre of installation or commissioning previously illustrated by the handover from Moses to Joshua. The important feature is that neither the temple nor the occupation of the land can be attributed to the work of an individual but is the result of teamwork. The value of prayer is highlighted by the so-called 'request-response' pattern in the account of Solomon, con-firming that God regularly goes beyond human expectations when he answers prayer (2 Ch. 1:8–12; 6:14–42; 7:1–3, 12–22). This analogy even extends to the activity of providence in Solomon's exchange of letters with Hiram (2 Ch. 2:3–16). Finally, Israel's pattern of worship is revealed by a 'Festival schema' in which major celebrations are brought together according to a common format. In each case, details are given of the date, the participants, the detailed ceremonies, and the joy of each occasion of worship (2 Ch. 7:4–10; 15:9–15; 30:13–27; 35:1–19).[1]

These examples show that this use of models is both extensive and detailed, and individual analogies can sometimes share as many as half a dozen features in common. Their over-all effect is to underline that the principles by which God deals with his people remain consistent across the centuries, and the Chronicler's readers can take appropriate encouragement as a result. In all this, one example stands out above the rest, namely, that David, Solomon and the temple occupy a place in God's purposes that is equally foundational to that of Moses, Joshua, and the Tent (*cf.* 1 Ch. 17:10–14; 22:11–13; 28:8–10; 2 Ch. 7:12–22). The Davidic monarchy continues the work that God began under Moses, and is required to maintain the same standards. The message seems to be that if Israel seeks hope for the future, it must continue in the same tradition.

(d) A further structural feature is the way in which various speeches or addresses, including both prophecies and prayers, are used to bring out the special emphases of the work.[2] Some of the royal speeches for instance, are regularly located at the beginning of sections where they function rather like policy documents or manifestos.[3] A good example is David's first speech in Chronicles (1 Ch. 13:2–3), where David's plan for restoring the ark to its rightful place at the centre of Israel's life sets the tone for the whole of the following section (1 Ch.

---

[1] De Vries, pp. 264–265. Though de Vries' form-critical approach to Chronicles offers many more examples of literary schemes, genres, and formulae, few can be accepted with confidence.

[2] *Cf.* above, p. 23.

[3] The speeches by kings of Judah are as follows: 1 Ch. 13:2–3; 15:2, 12–13; 17:1; 22:1; 22:5, 7–16, 17–19; 23:25–26; 28:2–10, 20–21; 29:1–5, 20; 2 Ch. 2:3–10; 6:3–11; 8:11; 13:4–12; 14:7; 19:6–7, 9–11; 20:20; 28:23; 29:5–11, 31; 30:6–9; 32:7–8; 35:3–6. Speeches are also made by foreign kings (2 Ch. 35:21; 36:23), high priests (2 Ch. 26:17–18; 31:10), and by leaders in Israel (2 Ch. 28:11–13).

13–16). In the same way, David's encouragements to Solomon form a kind of ideological blueprint about God's purposes for the temple (*e.g.*, 1 Ch. 22:7–16; 28:2–10, 20–21). Speeches by some of the 'good' kings during the Divided Monarchy also fulfil a similar role. The main points of the Chronicler's message are summed up in Abijah's appeal to Jeroboam I of Israel, for instance (2 Ch. 13:4–12), where it is made clear what is expected of the kings who will follow Abijah. The same themes are also resumed in Hezekiah's messages to the priests and Levites and to the population at large, especially in his emphasis on the priority of worship in the temple at Jerusalem (2 Ch. 29:5–11; 30:6–9). What makes the addresses of these two kings particularly strategic is their context, for the very identity of the Israelite nation was under threat in both cases. Hezekiah's Judah was endangered by a combination of Ahaz' paganism and the fall of the northern kingdom of Israel, while Abijah's fledgling kingdom of Judah could have easily been obliterated by Jeroboam I. The speeches of Abijah and Hezekiah therefore rescued God's people from the consequences of apostasy and set them back on God's desired pathway. A final example of the importance of the addresses is the role played by Cyrus' edict at the end of the book (2 Ch. 36:23). Though like Hezekiah's letter (2 Ch. 30:6–9) it is in written form, it is really a royal manifesto for the next stage of the history of God's people. Cyrus' invitation to the exiles to return to the Promised Land is also a call to return to God's ways, and shows that the future with God is never closed.[1]

Prophecies and prayers are equally as important as the royal speeches. Both of them recur frequently and are located at strategic points.[2] The central significance of the prophetic words in 1 Ch. 17:4–14 and 2 Ch. 7:12–22 has already been mentioned, but the crucial role of prophecy is illustrated by several other examples. Sometimes the course of future events is changed by a particular prophecy, as in the case of Asa's covenant renewal or Josiah's reformation (2 Ch. 15:1–7;

---

[1] For a different view of the structural significance of the royal speeches, *cf.* Throntveit, *Kings*, pp. 113–120.

[2] The following may be regarded as prophecies, though they are not always identified as such: 1 Ch. 12:18; 17:4–14; 21:9–12; 2 Ch. 7:12–22; 12:5, 7–8; 15:1–8; 16:7–10; 18:7–27; 19:1–3; 20:14–19, 37; 21:12–15; 24:20; 25:7–9, 15–16; 28:9–11; 34:23–28. Prophecies are also described in summary form (*e.g.* 1 Ch. 11:2–3; 21:18–19; 25:1–3; 2 Ch. 24:19, 27; 35:26; 36:12, 21, 22), and as sources of further information.

34:23–28). By contrast, when the word of a prophet is rejected, a further prophecy can form the basis for God's judgment (2 Ch. 16:7–10; 2 Ch. 24:20; 25:15–16). The references to prophecy in Jehoshaphat's reign are particularly instructive. A kind of model prophecy given by someone who is not himself a prophet suggests that in principle the prophetic gift is available to anyone who is open to the Spirit's inspiration (2 Ch. 20:14–17). Prophecy is thereby democratized in Chronicles, though not for the first or only time in the Bible (*cf.* Nu. 11:29; Joel 2:28–29; 1 Cor. 14:1). Even more remarkably, in the same passage faith in the word of the prophets is regarded as the equal of faith in God (2 Ch. 20:20). There can be no clearer testimony to its significance.[1]

The prayers in Chronicles have an equal place with the prophecies in the structure of the work. The accounts of David and Solomon, for example, frequently include important prayers.[2] David shows the importance of responding to what God has said and done, by giving thanks for the ark's safe arrival in Jerusalem (1 Ch. 16:8–36), for God's promise of an eternal dynasty (1 Ch. 17:16–27), and for the provision of the necessary resources for the temple (1 Ch. 29:10–20). Prayer is often closely linked with the temple. The chain of events through which the temple was built arises out of David's prayer of confession (1 Ch. 21:8), the real source of the building funds is beautifully expressed by David's praise, and Solomon's prayer at its completion is doubly answered by fire from heaven and God's programmatic promise of restoration (2 Ch. 7:1–3, 12–22). The temple was certainly a house of prayer in the Chronicler's view (*cf.* Is. 56:7; Mt. 21:13, *etc.*). All the prayers in the record of the Divided Monarchy period illustrate the principles set out in 2 Chronicles 7:12–22.[3] Like the royal speeches and the prophecies, they tend to occur at critical points, such as the invasion in Jehoshaphat's day (2 Ch.

---

[1] On prophecy in Chronicles, *cf.* R. Micheel, *Die Seher- und Prophetenüberlieferungen in der Chronik*, *BBET* 18 (Frankfurt: P. Lang, 1983); I. L. Seeligmann, 'Der Auffassung von der Prophetie in der deuteronomistischen und chronistischen Geschichtsschreibung', *SVT* 29, 1979, pp. 254–284.

[2] The prayers of David and Solomon are found in 1 Ch. 14:10, 13; 16:8–36; 17:16–27; 19:13; 21:8, 17; 29:10–20; 2 Ch. 1:8–10; 6:1–2, 14–42.

[3] Prayers recorded from the time of the Divided Monarchy are found in 2 Ch. 14:11; 20:3–13; 30:18–20, 27; 32:20, 24; 33:12–13. The prayers mentioned in the genealogies follow these same principles (*cf.* 1 Ch. 4:10; 5:20).

20:3–13) or the decisive moment in Manasseh's conversion (2 Ch. 33:12–13).

There can be no doubt that the various speeches, prophecies and prayers summarize and expound essential elements of Chronicles' main themes. As with other structural features, they tend to concentrate on the Davidic covenant and the temple, underlining their priority in God's purposes and in Israel's national life.

(e) Finally, the Chronicler is fond of using what is known as the chiasmus or chiastic pattern. This is a literary structure commonly found in Hebrew literature where form or meaning is repeated with variation. In a chiasmus, the outer and inner parts of a literary unit are balanced with each other, and are usually focused on statements at the centre of the unit. There can, however, be considerable variation in the number of parts and in the nature of the balance, and none of the chiastic patterns in Chronicles are identical with each other. Indeed, it is this very creativity which stimulates the reader's interest.

A chiasmus can be found on a large scale, as in the account of Solomon (2 Ch. 1–9), or on a small scale, as in one of David's prayers (1 Ch. 29:10–13). The primary meaning of individual chiastic patterns can be based on the relationship between the inner parts (2 Ch. 2:2–18), on the relationship between pairs of sub-units (1 Ch. 11:1 – 12:40; 2 Ch. 14:2–16:12), on a large central section (1 Ch. 16:1–43), or even on one chiasm embedded with a large chiasm (1 Ch. 2:3–4:23). A chiastic structure can even imply a sense of movement. For example, 1 Ch. 11:1 – 12:40 confirms the increasing support for David by a momentum from the outer parts (11:1–3; 12:38–40) to the centre (12:8–15, 16–18), while the chiasm of Solomon's reign highlights the development towards the climax of the temple dedication (*cf.* the role of 2 Ch. 3:1 – 5:1 and 5:2 – 7:22 within the account of Solomon).

The books of Chronicles are clearly a carefully crafted work of literature. The author is equally skilled, however, in integrating into the patterns already described a large number of external sources, taken partly from other sections of the Bible and partly from extrabiblical documents. In order to appreciate the Chronicler's method more accurately, the next stage of investigation is to analyse the manner in which these sources have been transformed. In practice this means that only the biblical material can be examined, since unfortunately none of the extrabiblical sources are available for comparison.

This process has to be carried out in two stages. The obvious place to begin is the narrative framework of Chronicles which the author has derived from the biblical books of Samuel and Kings. The basic story from Saul's death (1 Ch. 10; cf. 1 Sa. 31) to the exile is the same in both works, but closer examination reveals that the Chronicler has made extensive adaptations.

(a) Substantial sections of Samuel and Kings have been omitted. The two most notable instances are the lack of direct interest in the northern kingdom and the omission of most of the personal details of individual kings. It is now widely recognized that the first of these is not the result of the author's prejudice against northerners, whether they belonged to the kingdom of Israel or the Samaritan community. Rather it reflects his preoccupation with God's long-term purposes for the representatives of David's dynasty who ruled in Jerusalem. It is for the same reason that many incidents from the personal lives of Judah's kings, especially David and Solomon, have also been left out. This omitted material includes not only the ups and downs of David's family life (2 Sa. 9–20), his adultery and murder (2 Sa. 11–12) or the murky details of Solomon's accession and his financial and marital excesses (1 Ki. 1–2, 11), but also the much more positive accounts of David's early anointings and rise to power (1 Sa. 16 – 2 Sa. 4) and his testimony to God's goodness (2 Sa. 22:1 – 23:7).

One of the reasons for omitting this material is that the reader is expected to have a working knowledge of much of Samuel and Kings, and also of many other parts of Scripture. Enough of the earlier text is included to identify particular incidents, but the author is sometimes liable drastically to reduce whole sections of Samuel or Kings, summarizing them even in a single phrase. 'The word of the LORD' which Saul failed to keep, for instance (1 Ch. 10:13), refers in fact to a series of messages given to Israel's first king, but only the reader who knows the record of Saul in 1 Samuel would be familiar with the underlying details. A quite different instance of an assumed awareness of the books of Samuel concerns the omission of David's adultery and murder (2 Sa. 11–12). In this case, the Chronicler includes sufficient hints to show he is well aware of the original story but wishes to interpret it in a fresh way. The beginning and end of the original story about Bath-sheba reappear unmistakably in 1 Chronicles 20:1-3, but other vital elements of the structure and vocabulary of the earlier account have been interwoven into the narrative about David's infamous census (1 Ch. 21; *cf.* 2 Sa. 24). In this way, readers who know something of 2 Samuel will recognize not only the creative way in which the author has combined the two narratives but also that David's sins have been highlighted rather than suppressed.

(b) On other occasions, the Chronicler has extensively sum-marized the text of Samuel and Kings. David's military vic-tories, for example, have been brought together from various parts of 2 Samuel into a single section but in a much reduced form (1 Ch. 18–20). The author's care in selecting those sections most relevant to his purpose while preserving the order of the original text shows his respect for the biblical text which had been passed down to him (*cf.* the chart in the commentary on 1 Ch. 18). The account of Solomon is also much shorter in Chronicles than in Kings. Anything that is not germane to the temple theme is clearly superfluous to the Chronicler's needs, even though that includes such achieve-ments as Solomon's wisdom, his administration, his wives and his wars (1 Ki.3:16 – 4:34; 11:1–40). A distinct method of summarizing has been employed for the final period before the exile (2 Ch. 36). The reigns of four kings have been presented almost as though they are one, and the increasing brevity of their descriptions most effectively underlines the increasingly unstoppable threat of exile.

(c) Small changes can be made in order to highlight par-ticular features already present in the earlier material. An important example concerning the theme of the kingdom of God is the change from 'your [*i.e.,* David's] house and your kingdom' to 'my house and my kingdom' (1 Ch. 17:14; *cf.* 2 Sa. 7:16). A related series of changes shows how God's promises about David (1 Ch. 17:10–14) have been developed and applied to various new circumstances. These include Sol-omon's role as the temple builder (1 Ch. 22:7–10), themes in 1 Chronicles 28:2–8 such as rest, election, and the kingdom of God, and thanks for the temple's completion in 2 Chronicles 6:4–11. A different set of important minor alterations involves the references to 'Israel' in 2 Chronicles 10:16–19 (*cf.* 1 Ki. 12:16–19). The Chronicler's point, which is absent from

Kings, is that under Rehoboam David's house has really been separated from Israelites in the south as well as the north, in contrast to the tribal unity experienced under David.

(d) Substantial portions of text can be added to Samuel and Kings. The most outstanding example concerns David's temple preparations (1 Ch. 22–29), where a brief passage in 1 Kings 2:1–12 has been expanded to include detailed instructions about Levites and priests and extended encouragements to Solomon and the people. Other important additions include details of Jehoshaphat's good deeds and of Ahaz' wickedness (2 Ch. 17; 19–20; *cf.* 1 Ki. 22:41–50; 2 Ch. 28:5–25; *cf.* 2 Ki. 16:5–18), and especially the information about Josiah's early life which has no parallel in Kings (2 Ch. 34:3–7). Each of these passages raises important questions of interpretation, but none more so than the inclusion of 2 Chronicles 7:12b–16a, a section which is at the heart of the Chronicler's theology. Its offer of undeserved forgiveness is significantly different from the call to obedience in the equivalent passage in 1 Kings 9:3, and understanding the reasons for this kind of change is essential if the Chronicler is to be correctly interpreted.

The Chronicler's additional material sometimes even appears to contradict earlier parts of the Old Testament, of which Manasseh's conversion undoubtedly presents the most taxing problem (2 Ch. 33). Having previously been described as the worst king in the Davidic line (2 Ki. 21:1–18), Manasseh is unexpectedly portrayed in Chronicles as an outstanding example of repentance. One aspect of this problem that has not always been recognized is that other instances of the same phenomenon also exist in Chronicles. A case in point involves Rehoboam, who according to Kings 'did evil in the eyes of the LORD' (1 Ki. 14:22), but who now illustrates the value of humble repentance (2 Ch. 11–12). Equally, the Chronicler's emphasis on Abijah's faithfulness is in direct contrast with the earlier assessment that 'he walked in all his father's sins' (1 Ki. 15:3). Closer examination of all three instances, however, suggests that Chronicles in each case does refer to the previous record. The Chronicler's point is that while recognizing the serious failures in the lives of these leaders, God always responds graciously to those who repent. No-one is disqualified, not even those who publicly commit serious offences. Though this kind of explanation makes no attempt to address all the issues raised by the Chronicler's apparent contradictions, it does at least show the author's respect for the earlier text, even where he makes significant alterations to it.

Having constructed his basic framework from Samuel and Kings, the Chronicler has incorporated into it a range of Old Testament sources. These wider references are used in two different ways. One small but significant group of them has been used to provide an outer framework, while the majority have been made part of the inner fabric of the text throughout the book. Taken together, the two approaches demonstrate conclusively that Chronicles' perspective is much broader than simply that of Samuel and Kings.

The outer framework comprises a summary of Genesis (1 Ch. 1) and a quotation from Ezra–Nehemiah (2 Ch. 36:22–23). The significance of this arrangement is greater than it appears at first sight. It must be remembered first of all that Genesis and Ezra–Nehemiah cover the earliest and latest stages respectively of Israelite history, and that apart from Chronicles, they form the first and last books in the present Hebrew Bible.[1] Secondly, a quotation from Ezra–Nehemiah also occurs at the end of the genealogies, that is, the end of the book's first main section. In other words, the extract from Ezra 1:1–2 in 2 Chronicles 36:22–23 has an analogy in the use of Nehemiah 11:3–19 in 1 Chronicles 9:2–17, 22. Even though Ezra 1:1–2 and Nehemiah 11:3–19 refer to different points in the post-exilic era, the fact that quotations from the same Old Testament book are found at the conclusion to two of the three major sections of the Chronicler's work is surely not accidental. Thirdly, the two passages borrowed from Ezra–Nehemiah are closely related to each other, in that they both refer to Israelites returning to the land of Israel. In fact, the invitation in 2 Chronicles 36:22–23 to go up to Jerusalem and rebuild the house seems to be fulfilled in 1 Chronicles 9:2–17, 22 by those who reinstated temple worship. In other words, God's purposes for the temple were transmitted via Cyrus' edict (2 Ch. 36:22–23) into the post-exilic period by the Levites and others in their concern for proper worship.

So far, the outer framework has hinted at a possible relationship between the Chronicler's work and the generations

---

[1] Ezra and Nehemiah were originally one book rather than two.

that immediately preceded his own era, which is the period to which 1 Chronicles 9:2–34 seems to refer. Is there any way in which that link can be further elucidated? A solution begins to emerge when one compares the beginning and the end of the genealogies. These two passages bring together the creation of the human race in Adam and the restoration of temple worship, a connection that also applies to the beginning and end of the book. In other words, the genealogies and the outer framework of the book demonstrate that the rebuilt temple represented in some way the continuation or the restoration of the work that God had begun in creating Adam. The temple could therefore be no optional extra, but was a central element in God's intentions for Israel and for humanity itself. When Chronicles is seen in this light, Samuel and Kings occupy no more than a chapter, albeit an important one, in a story that still remained unfinished in the Chronicler's day.

The material which has been woven into the body of the work is equally as significant as the outer framework. It too offers an interpretation of Samuel and Kings, but this time based on principles enunciated throughout the law and the prophets. This approach enables the author to show that what God had said and done during the monarchy period was consistent with the rest of the Old Testament, and that neither had been obscured by the disaster of the exile. This message is conveyed by a variety of methods which offer further evidence of the Chronicler's creativity.

(a) As with his treatment of Samuel and Kings, the Chronicler frequently summarizes other parts of Scripture. This is done either by the use of quotation or even by condensing the message of an entire section of Scripture into a single sentence. One example is the way in which the sections in Genesis which begin with the words, 'these are the generations of . . .' (Gn. 10:1–29; 25:1–4, 12–16; *etc.*), have been selected to form the structure of the main sections of 1 Chronicles 1. In this way, the whole of Genesis has been spectacularly reduced to a single chapter. Even though the original information has been converted entirely into genealogical lists, the underlying message of God's electing love in the associated Genesis narratives has been clearly preserved. An instance where a quotation has been used to summarize an even broader area of Scripture is found in Jehoshaphat's encouragement to 'have faith in his [*i.e.* God's] prophets and you will be successful' (2 Ch. 20:20). Though the identity of the prophets of whom the king speaks is not absolutely certain, it is probable that here, as elsewhere, the Chronicler is summarizing the message of the prophets as a whole (*cf.* 2 Ch. 24:19; 29:25; 36:16).

(b) The Chronicler's preferred method of referring to the rest of the Old Testament is by the use of allusions. His knowledge of a vast range of the Old Testament Bible and his fluency in incorporating its distinctive phraseology into his work reminds one of C. H. Spurgeon's assessment of John Bunyan, 'Prick him anywhere; and you will find that his blood is Bibline!'[1] Individual passages can contain references to several different biblical books, as in the case of David's census (1 Ch. 21). Though the underlying foundation of this chapter is based on a combination of elements from 2 Samuel 11–12 and 24, a whole variety of biblical allusions have also been incorporated. These include the destroying angel in the Egyptian Passover (v. 15; *cf.* Ex. 12:23), Abraham's purchase of a burial ground (vv. 22–25; *cf.* Gn. 23), Gideon's meeting with an angel (vv. 20–21, 26; *cf.* Jdg. 6:11–24), and fire from heaven in Aaron's time (v. 26; *cf.* Lv. 9:24)! Another example rich in biblical associations is David's prayer of thanksgiving and praise (1 Ch. 29:14–19). As well as containing passing allusions from the Psalms such as the idea that God's people are 'aliens and strangers' (v. 15; *cf.* Ps. 39:12) and that life itself is but a shadow (v. 15; *cf.* Ps. 102:11), it focuses on the known ways in which God deals with the human heart. Though he tests the heart (v. 17; *cf.* Je. 12:3), he looks for inner attitudes which are loyal to him (v. 18; *cf.* Gn. 6:5).

(c) Direct quotation is equally significant, and, though used more sparingly than allusion, two distinctive methods are evident. Sometimes a particular phrase or verse can sum up a whole section, as in the use of Exodus 14:13–14 in 2 Chronicles 20:15, 17 or Numbers 14:41 in 2 Chronicles 24:20. This practice has a loose analogy with a sermon text, though the differences of character and function between Chronicles as a piece of literature and an orally delivered sermon suggest this kind of comparison should not be pressed too far. On other occasions, the Chronicler borrows significant phrases from

---

[1] C. H. Spurgeon, *Autobiography*, 2 (Edinburgh: Banner of Truth, 1973), p. 159.

elsewhere in the Old Testament as a vehicle for his own message. Two examples of this stand out above all others. The first is the principle that those who seek God will find him but that God rejects those who forsake him. This is a fundamental tenet of the Chronicler's theology, and is based on phrases in both the law and the prophets to which only minor alterations have been made (Dt. 4:29; Je. 29:13–14; Is. 55:6). This is twice regarded as the explicit theological standard by which Israel's relationship with God is compared (1 Ch. 28:9 and 2 Ch. 15:2), and also frequently illustrates the contrasting ways in which God deals with his people. The other instance is Moses' famous encouragement to Joshua, 'be strong and courageous' (*cf.* Dt. 31:7, 23; Jos. 1:6–9). This phrase is spoken in Chronicles by David (1 Ch. 22:13; 28:20) and Hezekiah (2 Ch. 32:7) on three separate occasions, none of which is paralleled in the earlier texts, and a similar expression is also attributed to Joab (1 Ch. 19:13; *cf.* 2 Sa. 10:12). In this way, Moses' original words have become a model by which others are encouraged to exercise bold faith for themselves.

(d) Sometimes the Chronicler applies passages and concepts taken from other parts of the Old Testament as a pattern or paradigm for his own description of events. The major instance of this is undoubtedly the use of Moses' Tent or tabernacle as a blueprint for the building of the temple. This device occurs several times, and includes the revelation of the building plans to David (1 Ch. 28:11–19; *cf.* Ex. 25:9, 40), the fund-raising efforts (1 Ch. 29:6–9; *cf.* Ex. 25:1–7; 35:4–9, 20–29), the need for consecration to the task (1 Ch. 29:5; *cf.* Ex. 28:41; Lv. 8:33), the order in which the building is constructed (2 Ch. 3–4; *cf.* Ex. 36:1 – 39:32), and the appearance of God's glory at the opening ceremony (2 Ch. 5:13–14; *cf.* Ex. 40:34–35). Ezekiel's teaching about the need for individual repentance offers two further examples of the same process. Firstly, the description of a righteous person who departs from his former ways and commits sins (Ezk. 18:24–32) fits exactly the circumstances of Joash, Amaziah, and Uzziah (2 Ch. 24–26). The second example is furnished by Judah's next three kings, where the godly reigns of Jotham and Hezekiah are separated by the idolatrous Ahaz (2 Ch. 27–32). This matches precisely the scheme of Ezekiel 18:1–20, where three succeeding generations refuse to follow their respective father's righteous or wicked behaviour. The whole of 2

Chronicles 24:32 is clearly presented as a living commentary on the prophet's word.

(e) One especially fascinating feature is the author's ability to conflate passages from different parts of Scripture. The temple preparations provide a number of instances. The ark's arrival in the new temple, for example, combines aspects of David's bringing of the ark to Jerusalem with the dedication ceremonies for Moses' Tent (2 Ch. 5; *cf.* Ex. 40:34–35; 1 Ch. 13–16). The temple site is similarly associated with God's appearing to Abraham and to David (2 Ch. 3:1; *cf.* Gn. 22:2, 11; 1 Ch. 21:16). Such an approach underlines the continuity of God's purposes which the temple represented, an issue of great importance to the Chronicler. A similar point emerges from the way the length of the exile is described. The fact that the seventy-year period fulfilled both the law and the prophets (Lv. 26:34–35; Je. 25:11–14; 29:10) is intended to convey that the exile's end as well as its existence was part of God's known will. The Chronicler's first readers had no need to live in its shadow any more.

All these examples show very clearly the importance of the whole of Scripture to the Chronicler's task of interpretation. Though Samuel and Kings provide much of the raw material, his real context is the entire Old Testament. His work is in fact a good example of what has become known as 'inner-biblical exegesis', though the Chronicler's treatment is unparalleled in the Old Testament in terms of both scope and thoroughness.[1] While the development of earlier material is quite common in the Old Testament, as in the use of Israel's historical traditions in worship (*e.g.* Pss. 78, 105, 106) or the fulfilment of passages from both the law (*cf.* Jos. 23:14–15) and the prophets (Je. 26:18; *cf.* Mi. 3:12), Chronicles stands apart in its attempt to interpret the Old Testament from beginning to end. It is also appropriately placed at the end of the canon in the Hebrew Bible, as that book of the Old Testament which sums up the rest. Those who were responsible for arranging the order of the books of the Hebrew Bible perhaps understood more of its character than they are usually given credit for. Though this view is somewhat at variance with the usual approaches to

---

[1] See *e.g.* M. Weiss, *The Bible from Within* (Jerusalem: Magnes Press, 1984); M. Fishbane, *Biblical Interpretation in Ancient Israel* (Oxford: Clarendon Press, 1985).

Chronicles, the overdependence in contemporary Christian (though not Jewish) approaches to Chronicles on its place in the Greek Bible is part of the reason why its real nature is not always appreciated. Modern readers should not therefore be over-influenced by its position between Kings and Ezra–Nehemiah in translated versions, whether in English or any other language. The Hebrew Bible is a safer guide, in terms of its position as well as its structure and contents.

Detailed analysis of the Chronicler's approach to exegesis requires a distinction to be made between his secondary and primary methods. In the former category must be included those grammatical and lexical changes which do not affect the overall message of the book.[1] They include the updating of the spelling of proper names (*e.g.* Ornan for Araunah, 1 Ch. 21:15ff.; Abijah for Abijam, 2 Ch. 13:1ff.) or linguistic developments such as a tendency to turn nouns into verbs (*e.g.* 'to repair', 2 Ch. 34:10; *cf.* 2 Ki. 22:5; 'to tax', 2 Ch. 36:3; *cf.* 2 Ki. 23:33).[2] In the same category is the natural inclination to smooth out some of the difficulties and antiquated language of the original text. Examples range from simple alterations such as replacing an obscure word like 'tamarisk' (2 Sa. 31:13) by the better known 'oak' tree (1 Ch. 10:12) to a possible correction of the inexplicable reference to continual war between Rehoboam and Jeroboam I during Abijah's lifetime (2 Ch. 13:2; *cf.* 1 Ki. 15:6).

Though these adjustments to earlier texts are very important for a proper understanding of the Chronicler's over-all method, they are not of the essence of what the author is about. He is much more than a scribe and modernizer of ancient texts. He engages above all in theological exegesis, undertaken according to the principle of allowing Scripture itself to interpret Scripture. At the heart of this enterprise is a conviction that 'the word of our God stands for ever' (Is. 40:8; 1 Pet. 1:25). The word of God is both the subject which the author addresses and the method by which he addresses it.

This preoccupation with God's word leads the Chronicler to underline two distinctive features. The first is that God's word

---

[1] For the effect of the texts available to the Chronicler on his work, see below, p. 74.

[2] For further examples, see *e.g.* Willi, *CA*, pp. 78–91; Polzin, *Typology*, pp. 28–69. The same phenomenon is also evident in borrowings from American English into British English!

is the ultimate standard upon which his dealings with his people are based in every generation. The principles underlying his word are unchanging though the ways in which they can be applied to new situations are surprisingly adaptable. This is well illustrated by both the law and the prophets. God's laws remain valid, for example, in matters as varied as the transportation of the ark (1 Ch. 15; *cf*. Dt.10:8; 18:5) or the date of the Passover (2 Ch. 30:2; *cf*. Nu. 9:9–13). A particularly interesting illustration of the effectiveness of God's word is provided by two contrasting experiences in the life of Josiah. In one incident, the king takes very seriously a prophetic confirmation about the threat of divine judgment contained in a recently discovered scroll of the law, and even though the threat was real, judgment was delayed as a result (2 Ch. 34:14–31). Later, however, Josiah deliberately ignored what is fascinatingly described as 'what [Pharaoh] Neco had said at God's command' (2 Ch. 35:22), and paid for his negligence with his life. In the Chronicler's view, God's word, whether it is ancient or modern, written or spoken, is no dead relic of history but something that remains living and effective (*cf*. Heb. 4:12).

The second feature is the special emphasis given to the two 'words' from God which have already been identified as being at the heart of the Chronicler's work. Writing at a time when Israel's severely reduced circumstances seemed to have rendered God's word impotent, these two passages are interpreted in a fresh way for the Chronicler's generation. The author shows how God's covenant promises to David could take on new meaning even though the Israelites lived in a greatly diminished version of the Promised Land, the temple was neglected and they had no king of their own. By means of several small but significant amendments to the earlier version of the first 'word', God is shown to be eternally committed to his covenant promises and to Solomon as David's successor and temple builder (1 Ch. 17:1–15; *cf*. 2 Sa. 7:1–17). The second 'word' concentrates on the temple's potential significance for the Chronicler's readers, though the textual adaptations are more extensive in this case (2 Ch. 7:11–22; *cf*. 1 Ki. 9:1–9). The earlier association in Kings between the temple and obedience to God's word is replaced by an emphasis on God's promise of restoration through answered prayer and his personal presence in the temple (*cf*. 1 Ki. 9:3). This new message is established by directly linking Solomon's prayer with God's response (*cf.* 2 Ch. 7:13 with 2 Ch. 6:26, 28 = 1 Ki. 8:35, 37), and also by incorporating various scriptural promises about God's forgiveness (2 Ch. 7:14; *cf.* Lv. 26:41; Je. 30:17; 33:6). Between them, the two 'words' highlight God's continuing commitment to Israel and the central role played by the temple as a house of prayer and a symbol of God's eternal will to forgive.

A sign of the importance of these two 'words' in Chronicles is the recurrence of their main themes and the repetition of key phrases, often in passages unparalleled in the earlier books. Major references to the Davidic covenant appear in 1 Chronicles 22:6–13; 28:2–10; 2 Chronicles 6:4–11, 14–17; 13:5, 8; 21:7; 23:3; 36:23, while the restoration promise recurs in one form or another in 2 Chronicles 12:5–12; 13:13–18; 20:1–30; 32:24–26; 33:10–23, with its converse in 2 Chronicles 16:12; 24:17–26; 33:22–25; 36:15–20. The promise of restoration is dealt with in a programmatic way throughout 2 Chronicles 10–36, with a variety of illustrations of how the basic principles could be applied. Especially notable examples occur in the case of Rehoboam, the first king of the southern kingdom (2 Ch. 12:5–12), and of Manasseh, who according to Kings was the worst king of Judah (2 Ch. 33:10–23; *cf.* 2 Ki. 21:1–16). The themes of the two words are also often combined. The Davidic covenant, for instance, is much more closely tied in with the ideology of the temple than in Kings, as in David's temple manifesto (1 Ch. 22:6–13; 28:2–10), or in the Chronicler's view of the future. Though God finally pronounced a verdict of (lit.) 'no healing' (2 Ch. 36:16; *cf.* 2 Ch. 7:14) on Israel, meaning that they were apparently beyond redemption, a fresh start was still possible through Cyrus' allusion to the Davidic covenant and a new temple. The strategic importance of this reinterpretation of God's words is unmistakeable.

IV. THE CHRONICLER'S MESSAGE

(a) Covenant

According to Chronicles, the Davidic covenant is that element which most clearly expresses the meaning of Israel's continuing life as the people of God. Though this form of covenant is explicitly mentioned in only three passages (2 Ch. 7:18;

45

13:5; 21:7), it is frequently referred to, especially in relation to God's promises to David (*e.g.* 1 Ch. 17:18, 23, 26; 2 Ch. 1:9; 6:10, 15, 42; 21:7; 23:3). It is also the headstream out of which flow two of the major tributaries running through the books of Chronicles, namely the Davidic dynasty (1 Ch. 28:5; 29:23; 2 Ch. 6:10, 16; 2 Ch. 13:8; 23:3), and the Solomonic temple (1 Ch. 17:12; 22:6–11; 28:2–10; 2 Ch. 6:7–11). In its foundations and visible expressions, therefore, the Davidic covenant is clearly central to the thought of Chronicles.

The primary feature of Chronicles' presentation of the Davidic covenant is that its very existence depends on God's promise. Everything hangs on what God purposes, says and does. David's good intentions about building a temple, for instance, must be put aside because God's way and God's time have to take priority. God must first build a house for David (1 Ch. 17:10) and will also choose the temple builder (1 Ch. 17:12; 28:6). God too is the one who rescues and restores the covenant when its continuation is threatened, as happened even under David's leadership when the sword of God's judgment was dramatically drawn against Jerusalem (1 Ch. 21:15). Indeed, the Davidic line was in danger of being wiped out by a disastrous alliance between the dynasties of David and Ahab (2 Ch. 18–23; especially 21:6–7), had it not been that 'the LORD was not willing to destroy the house of David' (2 Ch. 21:7). God was committed to this covenant even through the exile, as the Chronicler shows by his statement that the LORD was behind Cyrus' edict 'to build a house' in Jerusalem (2 Ch. 36:23).

The idea of God as the inspirer and maintainer of the covenant is strengthened by an interest in divine election which is unparalleled outside Deuteronomy in the Old Testament. God's choice of people and places occurs directly in nine passages, only three of which have any kind of parallel in the earlier sources.[1] In addition to this, the election concept clearly undergirds the theology of the genealogies (1 Ch. 1–9), even though the verb 'to choose' does not appear. God's purposeful choosing is indicated by the way in which some lines are followed through rather than others, and by the special prominence given to the tribes of Judah and Levi.

---

[1] See 1 Ch. 15:2; 28:4–10; 29:1; 2 Ch. 6:5–6 (*cf.* 1 Ki. 8:16); 6:34, 38 (= 1 Ki. 8:44, 48); 7:12, 16; 2 Ch. 12:13; 29:11; 33:7 (= 2 Ki. 21:7).

Similarly, the direct link between the tribal genealogies and the post-exilic era (*cf.* 1 Ch. 9:2–34) is a clear sign of God's commitment to his original choice.

Election in Chronicles is very closely associated with the covenant, as in Deuteronomy and to a lesser extent elsewhere in the Old Testament. In contrast with the earlier texts, however, the objects of the Lord's choice are almost all associated with the Davidic rather than with the Mosaic covenant. In place of the Deuteronomist's interest in the election of Israel and of 'the place which Yahweh has chosen', the Chronicler is concerned with the choice of David's family, especially David and Solomon (*e.g.* 1 Ch. 28:4–10; 29:1; 2 Ch. 6:5–6), the city of Jerusalem and its temple (2 Ch. 6:6, 34, 38; 7:12, 16; 12:13, 33:7), and the priests and Levites (1 Ch. 15:2; 2 Ch. 29:11). The choice of David and Jerusalem and of Solomon as David's successor and temple builder particularly stand out. Even the choice of the priests and Levites is as much associated with David's adjustment of their role as with their original appointment (*cf.* 1 Ch. 15:2). The rejection of the houses of Saul (1 Ch. 10:6; 12:29) and Ahab (2 Ch. 21:6–7; 22:3–9) also confirms the election of the Davidic dynasty. This concentration on election and covenant is intended not only to highlight their intrinsic importance for Israel, but to confirm to the Chronicler's readers the continuing importance of David's line and the temple for their own generation.

God's guaranteed commitment to Israel is also expressed through a strengthened emphasis on the permanence and inviolability of the covenant. The well-known refrain from the Psalms, 'For his love endures for ever', often occurs, for example, though none of the quotations is paralleled in the books of Kings (*e.g.* 1 Ch. 16:41; 2 Ch. 5:13; 7:3, 6; 20:21). Its frequent appearance is an indication that the covenant's continuation depended on God's love rather than on Israel's achievements. The Chronicler's use of the phrase 'for ever' is also instructive. In some places, as in 1 Chronicles 17:23 or 2 Chronicles 33:4, it has been added to the earlier text to confirm the unchangeability of God's plans. In the Chronicler's own material, mention is often made of either the eternal nature of the covenant or the unchangeableness of God's purposes. God intends to dwell permanently in the Jerusalem temple (1 Ch. 23:25; 2 Ch. 30:8), where the priests and Levites are to minister to him for ever (1 Ch. 15:2; 23:13). The land has been promised for ever to Israel (2 Ch. 20:7), as long as they are obedient to his commands (1 Ch. 28:8). The kingship granted to David's family is an irrevocable gift, a promise that God personally guarantees (1 Ch. 22:10; 28:4, 7; 2 Ch. 13:5). Abijah's quotation of the phrase 'covenant of salt' (2 Ch. 13:5; *cf.* Nu. 18:19) is a particularly striking way of indicating that God always preserves and protects his relationship with Israel.

Abijah also mentions another very important and distinctive aspect of God's involvement in the covenant concept in Chronicles, namely, the kingdom of God. Apart from the Psalms and Daniel, Chronicles is the only book in the Old Testament which deals with the notion of the kingdom of God in any detail. Since the reality of this kingdom is revealed in Chronicles through the Davidic monarchy and the Jerusalem temple, it is clearly a covenant concept. The closeness of this association is confirmed by the change in God's promise from 'your house and your kingdom', referring to David, to '*my* house and *my* kingdom' (1 Ch. 17:14; *cf.* 2 Sa. 7:16). The point is not that these were different kingdoms in the Chronicler's view but that one was expressed through the other. The throne on which David and his successors sat is really God's throne and the kingdom over which they ruled is God's kingdom (see especially 1 Ch. 28:5; 29:23; 2 Ch. 9:8; 13:5, 8). The author repeatedly associates the temple with the kingdom of God, as in David's affirmation on completing his preparations for the new building, 'Yours, O LORD, is the kingdom' (1 Ch. 29:11). As with the interest in election, the new emphasis on the permanence of the Davidic covenant and the reality of God's kingdom demonstrated that the covenant and the kingdom were still very much alive, despite the devastation of the exile.

This is not to say that Chronicles has neglected the demands of the Sinai covenant or the need for human beings to acknowledge responsibility for their sin. Far from it, despite the Chronicler's widely acknowledged lack of direct reference to the exodus and the repeated demands of the Sinai covenant for Israel's obedience. The reason for this rather surprising situation is that in the Chronicler's thought the Sinai covenant is the foundation for God's promises to David. The Chronicler has in fact retained references to the exodus in several key passages, not least in the original promise of the Davidic covenant (1 Ch. 17:5; 21; 2 Ch. 5:10; 6:5; 7:22; 20:7). He has also retained from earlier texts requirements to obey the laws God gave to Moses (2 Ch. 6:16; 7:17; 33:8), and underlined in passages unique to Chronicles the need to keep God's standards (1 Ch. 22:13; 28:7; 2 Ch. 14:4).

The Chronicler also sees the positive value of covenant law as something which was continually relevant and effective rather than a relic left over from the past. The law, which is variously described as 'the law of the LORD (1 Ch. 16:40; 2 Ch. 31:3), 'the law of Moses' (2 Ch. 23:18; 30:16), or 'the word of the LORD through Moses' (2 Ch. 35:6; *cf.* 1 Ch. 15:15; *etc.*), often occurs in passages which have no parallel and is consistently regarded as God's ultimate expression of his authority in Israel. Though David and other kings exercise authority, their authority is dependent on God's gift and is subject to the requirements of the law, just as it is for everyone else. It is also a limited authority, in that David's interpretation of God's law is restricted to the specific areas of organizing temple rituals and personnel and establishing musical worship in the temple.[1] Though this has led to David being viewed as a second Moses, it only serves to underline the supremacy of the Mosaic law itself. It is the Mosaic law which is the basis of a succession of reform movements, which are given greater prominence as a succession of related events than in Kings. Though Josiah's reform is well known (2 Ch. 34–35 = 2 Ki. 22–23), the Chronicler mentions in addition a nationwide campaign under Jehoshaphat to instruct the population in 'the scroll of the law of the LORD' (2 Ch. 17:7–9; *cf.* 19:4–11), and a covenant renewal ceremony under Asa based on the tradition of the Sinai covenant (2 Ch. 15:12–15). A covenant also took place in Hezekiah's reign (2 Ch. 29:10) reinstating the pattern of worship required by the Mosaic law (2 Ch. 29:15–35) and David's supplementary instructions about the Levites (2 Ch. 29:25–26, 30). These various incidents clearly demonstrated that in the Chronicler's eyes the law remained a living concept which needed to be periodically restored to its rightful priority in Israel's life.[2]

Equally, the Chronicler's confidence in God's unshakeable purposes for David has not been achieved at the cost of ignoring the weaknesses of David and Solomon, though it is

[1] *Cf.* Japhet, *Ideology*, pp. 234–239.
[2] *Cf.* T. Willi, 'Thora in den biblischen Chronikbüchern', *Judaica* 36, 1980, pp. 102–105, 148–151.

often alleged that he has presented them as spotless kings who could do no wrong.[1] Those who point to the omission of such obvious failings as David's adultery and murder or Solomon's polygamy and financial extravagance have not fully grasped that he is much more interested in the way God's covenant purposes unfold in their lives. The major priority of the Chronicler's view of David and Solomon is that God has given their family his gift of kingship and confirmed it through Solomon's obedience in building the temple. In this context, the failings of David which the Chronicler does mention are all the more serious, since they concern his inability to discern what God was doing. He mistakes the real nature of God's holiness in the ark (1 Ch. 13) and his selfish pride prevents him from understanding the real nature of Israel as God's people (1 Ch. 21). The temple therefore becomes as much a means of atonement for David's sin as a sign of God's covenant faithfulness. The concentration on the temple in the account of Solomon merely confirms this view. Though the temple is a sign that God keeps his promise and of Solomon's obedience (*cf.* 1 Ch. 28:2–10; 2 Ch. 6:3–10, 14–17), it is also necessary for all in their need of forgiveness because 'there is no-one who does not sin' (2 Ch. 6:36).

The Chronicler's interest in the covenant is very much part of his interest in Israel's true identity, though it is remarkable that he concentrates on the Davidic rather than the Mosaic covenant to make the point. What is surprising is that in the Old Testament the Mosaic covenant is primarily concerned with the whole people of Israel whereas the Davidic covenant usually focuses on a single family within Israel. Chronicles' reason for preferring to apply the Davidic covenant to the people is not because of any deficiency in the Mosaic covenant, since it has already been pointed out that the latter has a distinctive role within Chronicles. A more likely explanation is that as the coming of the exile brought the monarchy to an end, the Davidic covenant began to be interpreted in a new way. This new interpretation is especially prominent in Isaiah 55:3, where the promise of an everlasting covenant for David is explicitly extended to the whole people – the *you* in the phrase 'I will make an everlasting covenant with you' is plural.

---

[1] *E.g.* Dillard, pp. 1–5; Michaeli, pp. 143–168; G. von Rad, *Old Testament Theology*, I (London: SCM Press, 1962), pp. 350–351.

Since the Chronicler uses this verse directly in an important passage in 2 Chronicles 6:42, it seems that it has had a major influence in his understanding of the significance of God's covenants for Israel.

The fact and quality of Israel's relationship with God was more important than their current political situation, and their status as God's people was of greater value than their citizenship of the Persian or the Greek empire. Whatever had happened to Israel in the past, nothing could change the fact of their relationship with God, and the Chronicler would certainly have agreed with Paul's statement that nothing 'will be able to separate us from the love of God' (Rom. 8:39). Although this view of covenant has some differences of emphasis from that of the prophets or the writers of the Deuteronomic History, the contrasts are the result of the different context in which the Chronicler was writing. Whereas the earlier authors stressed that the covenant was breakable and that Israel could be punished for disobeying God's laws, a view with which the Chronicler was still in full agreement (*e.g.* 2 Ch. 7:19–22), a new emphasis was needed now that the deserved punishment of the exile was past. Though God's standards had not changed, it was now clearer than ever that Israel's participation in the covenant could be preserved only through God's loving commitment to them. Israel had to start all over again in learning what it meant to be in covenant with God.

(b) Israel as the people of the covenant

What were the practical implications of being bound to God in a covenant relationship? The Chronicler's answer to this question was almost certainly different from that of most of his contemporaries and also from the work of Ezra–Nehemiah. Whereas many post-exilic Israelites tended to think of themselves as a rather dejected, unambitious, guilty, tight-fisted, defensive group of stragglers, the Chronicler was a theological optimist who wanted to bring fresh hope to his people.

The most crucial issue for the Chronicler's readers was their attitude towards other Israelites past and present. The author reminded them first that their ancestry did not go back just to David but could be traced to Adam himself (1 Ch. 1:1). The post-exilic community was part of what God has planned, not just for Israel, but from the very creation of the human race.

51

They enjoyed a special place among the nations of the world and were not therefore ultimately subject to the whims of foreign political and military decision-makers. Equally important, however, was that the Israelites recognized their true breadth, for they were not restricted to those members of Judah and Benjamin who formed the majority of the post-exilic community. According to the genealogies of 1 Chronicles 2:1 – 9:1, they were descended from all Jacob's twelve sons. In fact, the Chronicler goes out of his way to stress that the old divisions of north and south were really a consequence of a temporary judgment on Solomon's excesses, but that every opportunity should be taken to rebuild the whole community. Cyrus' invitation for the exiles to return is addressed, for example, to 'whoever among you out of all his people' (2 Ch. 36:23), offering the chance to anyone of Israelite descent to return to the land of Israel (*cf.* 1 Ch. 9:3; 11:1–3; 12:38–40; 2 Ch. 11:13–17; 15:9; 30:1–12; 34:9; 35:18).

The Chronicler never loses sight of the importance of Israelite unity. The phrase 'all Israel' appears more frequently than in his sources and with fresh significance, emphasizing that north and south are both truly Israel (*e.g.* 2 Ch. 10:16 – 11:3).[1] In the same vein, the Israelites are repeatedly called 'brothers' in passages without parallel in Samuel and Kings, particularly in contexts where real tension existed between various groups (*e.g.*, 1 Ch. 12:39; 13:2; 2 Ch. 11:4; 28:8, 11, 15). Representatives of the northern tribes are also commended when appropriate (*e.g.* 1 Ch. 5:1–2; 2 Ch. 11:16–17; 28:12–15), and a number of mixed marriages are mentioned without any form of censure (*e.g.* 1 Ch. 2:4, 17, 34–35; 4:18; 2 Ch. 8:11). Unity is not to be gained at any price, however. As well as underlining that the division of the monarchy was God's will (2 Ch. 10:15), Chronicles rejects any form of reunification that might result from violence and greed (2 Ch. 11:1–4; 13:3–20; 22:10 – 23:21; 28:5–11) or that was based on unholy alliances (2 Ch. 18:1 – 19:3; 20:35–37; 25:6–10). The only genuine basis for unity involved a fresh approach to the worship of the Lord, when north and south could join together before God's altar. This of course meant abandoning all forms of idolatry (*e.g.* 2 Ch. 11:15–17; 13:8–9; 28:1–5,

[1] *Cf.* the application of 'all Israel' to the north (2 Ch. 13:4, 15; 30:1, 6) and to the south (2 Ch. 12:1; 24:8; 28:23). See further, Japhet, *Ideology*, pp. 270–278; Williamson, *IBC*, pp. 87–131.

22–25) in favour of an acknowledgment that the Jerusalem temple was God's choice for his earthly residence. United worship could then take place, particularly on special occasions such as covenant ceremonies (2 Ch. 15:8–15) or the Passover (2 Ch. 30:1–20; 35:18).[1]

Chronicles therefore shows little evidence of an anti-Samaritan attitude, despite previous allegations to the contrary.[2] Such views have depended to a considerable extent on the acceptance of a close link between Chronicles with Ezra–Nehemiah, though in recent years scholars have identified substantial differences between the two works on this and a number of other issues. In fact, the Chronicler's neglect of the northern kingdom is to be explained more in terms of his positive convictions about the Davidic monarchy and the Jerusalem temple than because of any innate prejudice.

A distinctive feature of Chronicles' view of Israel is what has been termed a 'democratizing' trend.[3] Though this precise description might be questioned, it is clear that the Chronicler consistently highlights the role of the people as against that of the king. Incidents which in Samuel and Kings involved the king and a group of his associates are often attributed to the whole people (e.g. 1 Ch. 11:4; 13:5; 15:25; 2 Ch. 1:2–5). In the Chronicler's own material, a number of incidents concentrate on the part played by the people, including the contributions for the temple (1 Ch. 29:5–6; 2 Ch. 31:2–10), Jehoiada's revolt against Athaliah (2 Ch. 23:2–3) and Hezekiah's anti-idolatry crusade (2 Ch. 31:1). This interest is maintained even where the people did not support the king's reforms as the Chronicler would have wished, as in the reigns of Jotham (2 Ch. 27:2) and Hezekiah (2 Ch. 30:10). Perhaps most striking, however, is the regular mention of assemblies of the people and the frequent commendation of kings who entered into consultation. David was particularly fond of acting alongside the assembly, whether involving various types of leaders or the whole people (1 Ch. 13:2–5; 22:2; 23:1; 28:1; 29:1), and

[1] For the idea that the temple is presented as a focus of Israelite unity, see H. G. M. Williamson, in W. Horbury (ed.), *Templum Amicitiae*, *JSNTS* 48 (Sheffield: Sheffield Academic Press, 1991), pp. 15–31.

[2] *E.g.* von Rad, *GCW*, p. 24; Rudolph, p. IX; J. A. Soggin, *Introduction to the Old Testament* (London: SCM, [2]1976), p. 418. For the opposite view, *cf.* Williamson, *IBC*, pp. 87–140; Braun, pp. xxxv–xxxvii; R. J. Coggins, *Samaritans and Jews* (Oxford: Blackwell, 1975).

[3] Japhet, *Ideology*, pp. 417–427.

several kings followed his example (*e.g.* 2 Ch. 15:9–15; 20:5, 14, 26; 28:14; 29:4; 30:2). The same kings also made a point of consulting their subjects, including David (1 Ch. 13:1), Solomon (2 Ch. 1:2), Jehoshaphat (2 Ch. 20:21), and Hezekiah (2 Ch. 30:2; 32:3), though as a contrast some who sought advice from a limited range of biased supporters fell into deep trouble (2 Ch. 10:6–14; 25:16–17). Interest in the assembly undoubtedly reflects the practice of the Chronicler's own time (*cf.* Ezr. 10:1–5, 7–15; Ne. 7:73b – 8:18), but it was also a reminder that throughout Israel's history, the people could have a decisive impact on the nation's destiny. It is no accident that the main appeal for restoration is addressed to 'my people' (2 Ch. 7:14).

Certain attitudes were expected of Israel as God's covenant people, of which the most important in the Chronicler's terminology is that they should constantly 'seek' God. Passages in which the word occurs are given special prominence, often at the beginning of a king's reign in a way that sets the tone for what follows (*e.g.* 1 Ch. 13:3; 2 Ch. 1:5; 14:4, 7; 20:4; 34:3). It is a key emphasis in David's farewell speeches (1 Ch. 22:19; 28:8–9), and is a contrasting theme in the accounts of Rehoboam (2 Ch. 11:16; 12:14) and Asa (14:4; 15:12–13; 16:12). To fail to seek the Lord was to become liable to God's judgment (*e.g.* 1 Ch. 10:13–14; 15:13; 2 Ch. 12:14; 25:15, 20), whereas seeking God's face afresh was part of the process of restoration (2 Ch. 7:14). The term describes not a searching after God but a whole life orientation towards him. It was particularly reflected in worship that was faithful to the Lord (1 Ch. 13:3, 2 Ch. 1:5; 2 Ch. 15:12–13; 31:21), but could also include building activity (1 Ch. 11:8–9; 2 Ch. 14:7) and military success (*e.g.* 2 Ch. 20:22–26; 32:7). Despite the term's frequency and significance, however, there is insufficient evidence to support the claim that by itself it summarizes what the Chronicler's work is about.[1]

Those who made it their custom to seek God as a way of life could expect God's blessing in various ways (1 Ch. 14:10, 13; 28:9; 2 Ch. 14:7; 31:21), even in unfavourable circumstances (2 Ch. 7:14; 20:3–4; 30:18–19). The benefits might include God being 'with' his people (1 Ch. 22:11, 16; 2 Ch. 15:2, 9;

[1] Against C. Begg, '"Seeking Yahweh" and the purpose of Chronicles', *Louvain Studies* 9, 1982, pp. 128–141; *cf.* G. E. Schafer, 'The significance of seeking God in the purpose of the Chronicler', Th.D., Louisville, 1972.

17:3–4; 20:17), God's 'help' or support (1 Ch. 15:26; 2 Ch. 14:11; 26:7, 15), prosperity (1 Ch. 22:13; 2 Ch. 26:5), 'healing', that is, spiritual and physical wholeness (2 Ch. 7:14; 30:20; *cf.* 2 Ch. 36:16), a large family (1 Ch. 26:5; 2 Ch.13:21; 24:1–3), peace and rest (2 Ch. 14:7; 20:29–30; 23:21), and a recognition by foreigners of the reality of God's power (1 Ch. 14:17; 2 Ch. 20:29–30; 32:23). On the other hand, the fact that godly kings suffered serious trouble on several occasions (2 Ch. 14:9–11; 20:1–13; 32:1) indicates that faithfulness to God was no automatic assurance of success. Blessing was always treated by the Chronicler as essentially an undeserved gift, though God was always ready to be generous to those who were positively oriented towards him. The prayers especially bring out this sense of being dependent on God's grace, for even when the people had been generous, they could give only because God had given them something to give in the first place (1 Ch. 29:16)! In the same vein, David's bringing the ark to Jerusalem was acknowledged as 'what he [*i.e.* God] has done' (1 Ch. 16:8), and Solomon's throne and his temple were openly attributed to God's faithfulness to his promises (2 Ch. 6:10; *cf.* 2 Ch. 1:1–12). Post-exilic Israelites were being specifically reminded that as well as owing their very existence to God's faithful love, further blessing would follow as they sought him and his ways.

Two particular covenant blessings stand out in Chronicles, of which the first is Israel's presence in the Promised Land. The fact that the author updates the details of those who repopulated Jerusalem under Nehemiah confirms the importance of the land for the post-exilic community. There is also a sense that Israel's possession of the land and enjoyment of its 'rest' was something for each generation to experience afresh.[1] The whole issue of the land is traced back to God's covenant promise to Abraham (1 Ch. 16:15–18; 2 Ch. 20:7; *cf.* 1 Ch. 28:8), where Israel's presence in the land was seen from the beginning as a matter of gift rather than of right. Attention is also focused on tribal expansion into different parts of the Promised Land (especially 1 Ch. 4:24 – 5:26). Though the land had been given to Israel, it also had to be occupied with God's help, as is beautifully expressed in Jabez' simple prayer, 'O that you would bless me and enlarge

---

[1] *Cf.* Japhet, *Ideology*, pp. 386–393.

my territory' (1 Ch. 4:10). Similarly, David's completion of Joshua's task of occupying the land is vital, since it is a precondition for building the temple. On the other hand, threats to Israel's presence in the land are regarded as a challenge to God's declared purposes (*cf.* 2 Ch. 20:6–11; 32:9–20). The greatest threat was of course the exile, though its effects could be reversed by repentance (2 Ch. 30:9) and active faith (2 Ch. 36:23).

The second of these blessings is God's presence with his people. The Israelites were especially aware of this when they were under military attack, as when Hezekiah discovered for himself that the Lord is a God who intervenes to save and deliver his people (2 Ch. 32:22; *cf.* 32:10–17). This is by no means the only example, however, for God's presence ensured unexpected victory for Israel's armies on several occasions (*e.g.* 1 Ch. 14:9–16; 2 Ch. 14:8–15; 18:28–32; 20:15–17, 22–26). God's people could not take it for granted that he would always be on their side, however. There were occasions when God fought against both Israel (2 Ch. 24:23–26) and Judah (2 Ch. 28:5–8), and Abijah gave a blunt warning to Jeroboam I: 'Do not fight against the LORD, the God of your fathers, for you will not succeed' (2 Ch. 13:12). Nevertheless, God never abandoned his people to those who brought trouble on them, and though Israel did not always honour him, their cause was ultimately his cause. Not even the disaster of the exile could change that.

(c) The temple as the place of covenant-centred worship

The Jerusalem temple and its system of worship clearly dominates much of Chronicles. Most of David's reign is given over to temple preparations and the whole of Solomon's is designed around the temple's construction. The temple is also given a prominence in the reigns of Abijah, Uzziah, and especially Hezekiah that it does not have in the books of Kings (*cf.* 2 Ch. 13, 26, 29–31), and the Levites, who provided the temple personnel, receive frequent mention.

The Chronicler's interest in the temple, however, has less to do with its physical appearance than with its meaning, as illustrated by his abbreviation of Kings' account of the temple's construction (2 Ch. 3–4) and his expansion of the dedication ceremonies (2 Ch. 5–7). The Chronicler's view of the temple is not the same as in Kings, where the temple is the

Lord's chosen place for Israel's worship in contrast to the idolatrous sanctuaries throughout the land. Though this emphasis has been retained, the Chronicler has given a new priority to another theme present in Kings, namely, the link between the temple and the Davidic covenant. This association is repeatedly mentioned in a series of passages without parallel in Samuel and Kings concerning the two houses that God promised David (1 Ch. 22:6–13; 28:2–10; 2 Ch. 6:4–11, 14–17; 13:4–12). It is also confirmed by Solomon's testimony that God has kept his promise concerning both houses (2 Ch. 6:10). David's dynasty and Solomon's temple together represented 'the hub of the Lord's kingdom on earth'.[1]

The link between the temple and the royal family is maintained through the Davidic dynasty's continuing care for the temple and its services. In addition to David's detailed interest in the preparations for the building (1 Ch. 22–29), it is assumed that his successors would be faithful guardians of the worship of the Lord. Abijah, for example, demonstrated his commitment to God's intentions by his faithful adherence to the temple and its worship (2 Ch. 13:4–12). Kings such as Jehoshaphat, Joash and Hezekiah who conducted religious reformations were singled out for commendation, even though no details of these events are given in the Books of Kings (2 Ch. 24:1–16; 29:1 – 31:21).

The Chronicler was particularly concerned with the temple's personnel, its activities, and the attitudes of its worshippers. Among all the paraphernalia, it is the Levites' various roles in 'service' or 'ministry' that are singled out (*e.g.* 1 Ch. 23:2–5, 28–32), even above the activities of the priests. The main purpose behind this appears to be to underline the supreme importance of praise and sacrifice. Sacrifice is more prominent in Chronicles than in Kings, as indicated by the use of the post-exilic description of the temple as 'a house of sacrifice' (2 Ch. 7:12; *cf.* Ezr. 6:3). The Chronicler includes several summaries of the temple's sacrificial ritual in contrast to a single verse on the subject in Kings, so underlining the importance of regular worship (1 Ch. 23:11; 2 Ch. 3:4; 8:13; 13:11; 31:3; *cf.* 1 Ki. 9:25). The Levites' contribution to this pattern of worship was crucial (1 Ch. 9:28–32; 23:28–32; 2 Ch. 8:14; 13:10), and they were congratulated on more than

[1] Myers, *I Chronicles*, p. LXVIII.

one occasion for taking care about what the Lord required (*cf.* 2 Ch. 11:14; 29:34).

It is the Levites' role in the musical side of worship that is their most distinctive contribution, however (1 Ch. 6:31–32; 15:16–28; 16:4–6, 37–42; 25:1–31; 2 Ch. 5:12–13; 7:6; 20:19, 21; 29:25–30). David's organization of the Levites into three groups of musicians is repeatedly mentioned (1 Ch. 6:31–48; 15:16–22; 25:1–31; 2 Ch. 8:14; 29:25–30), as is their involvement in Israel's praise (*cf. e.g.* 1 Ch. 16:4–6, 37–42; 2 Ch. 5:11–14; 7:4–10). Their chief function is in fact to lead the people in praise, without which Israel's various dramatic sacrificial rituals were little more than a silent witness to the covenant. The Levites were 'chosen and designated by name to give thanks to the LORD' (1 Ch. 16:41), and the familiar refrain of the Psalms, 'for his love endures for ever', is frequently found in the praise which they led (1 Ch. 16:34, 41; 2 Ch. 5:13; 7:3, 6; 20:21), as though it were a kind of Levitical theme song. This praise was not for the Levites' own benefit, however, but for the people's (1 Ch. 15:16–28; 2 Ch. 7:4–10; 20:14–23). The Levites' task was to enable the people to become worshippers themselves and to be aware of what God could do through and for them. With the Levites' encouragement, the people restored the ark to its rightful place (1 Ch. 15:16–28), celebrated the appointed festivals (2 Ch. 7:4–10), and exercised collective faith in a time of national crisis (2 Ch. 20:14–23). Musical praise also maintained a form of prophecy, and one passage even uses 'Levites' where 'prophets' is found in the earlier text (2 Ch. 34:30; *cf.* 2 Ki. 23:2). As elsewhere in the Bible, prophecy in Chronicles is an umbrella term, including both the Levites' praise to God (1 Ch. 25:1–5) and their ability to bring specific words of direction (2 Ch. 20:15–17; *cf.* 2 Ch. 24:20).

These examples illustrate the central importance of the temple for each generation of Israelites. Their attitude to its worship was a kind of spiritual barometer of their commitment to God, as well as an opportunity through which God could bless them afresh (2 Ch. 7:10; 31:21; *cf.* 24:16). The Chronicler's concept of acceptable worship involved physical sacrifices alongside prayer and praise. Both were necessary, but if a conflict should arise between a person's intention to worship God and the demands of the ritual law, a right attitude of heart was clearly the higher priority before God

(2 Ch. 30:18–20). The Chronicler would certainly have approved of Jesus' instruction: 'the true worshippers will worship the Father in spirit and truth' (Jn. 4:23). Though proper observance of the ritual law provided the right framework for worship, the Chronicler's deepest concern was that worship should arise out a heart wholly committed to God. God looks for Israel to 'serve him with a whole heart' (1 Ch. 28:9; *cf. e.g.* 1 Ch. 29:9, 19; 2 Ch. 6:14; 11:16; 31:21; 34:31), just as the tribes came with a 'whole heart' and 'one heart' to acknowledge God's choice of David as king (1 Ch. 12:38). God answers those who pour out their 'heart's desire' to him (2 Ch. 1:11), and even sinners are accepted when they repent with all their heart and soul (2 Ch. 6:38; 29:10).

Wholehearted worship in Chronicles is characterized by joy, generosity, and unity. The notable emphasis on joy shows that the author is no grim and rigid ritualist, but one who stands in the tradition of Jesus' teaching that joy is a natural consequence of obeying the Father (*cf.* Jn. 15:10–11). Such rejoicing was usually a corporate experience in Chronicles, and was typically expressed at major festival celebrations, whether of a regular kind or on special occasions (1 Ch. 12:40; 15:25; 29:9, 22; 2 Ch. 7:10; 15:15; 20:27; 30:26). It was also sometimes accompanied by examples of unusual generosity which themselves encouraged further testimony to God's goodness (*e.g.* 1 Ch. 29:6–9; 2 Ch. 31:4–10).

The Chronicler saw in temple worship the best hope for restoring a sense of Israel's identity as the whole people of God. This was particularly true of the Passovers celebrated by Hezekiah and Josiah (2 Ch. 30:1–13; 35:17–18), but the same emphasis also comes through strongly on other occasions (2 Ch. 7:4–10; 11:14–16; 15:9–15). The temple expressed Israel's very essence as a gathered community of worshippers, including foreigners (1 Ch. 13:13–14; 2 Ch. 6:32–33), who acknowledged the Lord as their covenant King.

(d) The covenant as a basis for restoration
Although the Chronicler is keen to stress Israel's identity as God's covenant people, the nation consistently fell far short of her obligations. Israel's unfaithfulness is one of the most repetitive themes of Chronicles, and one of the main reasons for highlighting the Davidic covenant and the temple is the vital role they play in God's provision for restoration.

Attention is again centred on the two words from God, which in addition to their focus on the inviolability of the covenant also affirm God's commitment to forgive and renew his people.

Israel's failure is particularly expressed through two related Hebrew words *māʿal* and *maʿal*, meaning 'to act unfaithfully' and 'unfaithfulness' respectively. Their distribution throughout the work shows that from beginning to end, Israel is guilty before God (1 Ch. 2:7; 2 Ch. 36:14). Because of this unfaithfulness, both the northern and southern kingdoms were subject to the punishment of exile (1 Ch. 5:25–26; 2 Ch. 36:15–20). Individual kings who behaved in the same way suffered various fates such as personal exile (2 Ch. 33:19), the invasion of their land (2 Ch. 12:2; 28:19), or even the loss of their kingship (1 Ch. 10:13–14).

Unfaithfulness is clearly a key term in Chronicles. An attempt has been made to deduce its precise meaning from the Pentateuchal law concerning the guilt or reparation offering (Lv. 5:14 – 6:7) where it has the sense of depriving God of that which is his due.[1] Its use in Chronicles, however, seems to correspond more closely with Leviticus 26:40 and to a lesser extent the book of Ezekiel, where the guilt is that of a whole community rather than that of an individual. The passage in Leviticus 26:40–45 is particularly significant in view of its influence in key passages in Chronicles such as 2 Chronicles 7:14 and 36:21. *Māʿal* is also not restricted in Leviticus 26 to specific forms of sin, but refers more generally to acting sinfully against God. This is consistent with the Chronicler's use of it as a virtual synonym for the frequent expression, 'to forsake (God)' (Heb. *ʿāzaḇ*).[2] Personal rejection of God is more important in Chronicles than simply failing to meet his requirements, and this emphasis is confirmed by the use of *māʿal* in the context of marital infidelity (Nu. 5:12, 27).

The examples of Israel's infidelity and rejection of God are repeated so often that it seems nothing can deflect God's punishment. Each generation is implicated, even those of the so-called good kings. David fails to recognize the true nature of the ark (1 Ch. 13) and of God's people (1 Ch. 21), Solomon places a heavy yoke on the people (2 Ch. 10:3, 9–11, 14), Asa

[1] Johnstone, 'Guilt', pp. 113–138.
[2] *E.g.* 1 Ch. 28:9; 2 Ch. 7:19, 22; 15:2; 24:20, 24; 28:6; 29:6.

reverses his previous good policies (2 Ch. 16), and Jehoshaphat is involved in a disastrous alliance with the house of Ahab (2 Ch. 18:1 – 19:3; 20:35–37). Joash turns to idolatry once the restraining influence of his guardian Jehoiada is removed (2 Ch. 24:17–27), Hezekiah succumbs to pride in his own achievements (2 Ch. 32:25, 31), and Josiah fails to recognize God's guidance in the commonsense advice of a foreign king (2 Ch. 35:20–24). Quite apart, therefore, from the kings who were well known for their wicked ways, it is clear in Chronicles that Israel's guilt was due to even the so-called good kings (1 Ch. 21:3, 8; 2 Ch. 19:10; 24:18; *cf.* 2 Ch. 28:10, 13; 33:23). The result of their behaviour was that God was angry (1 Ch. 13:11; 15:13; 2 Ch. 19:2, 10; 24:18; 32:25–26; *cf.* 2 Ch. 25:15; 28:9, 25; 29:8, 10; 36:16) and inflicted a variety of punishments on them (*cf.* 1 Ch. 21:7–16; 2 Ch. 12:5; 16:7–10; 20:37). The most serious of these was the reality of the exile, which was seen as something much more than the single event of the fall of Jerusalem in 587 BC. The fall of the northern kingdom in 722 BC resulted in the experience of exile being shared with the citizens of the south (1 Ch. 5:25–26; 2 Ch. 29:9; 30:6). Despite the good intentions of Hezekiah and Josiah, that experience was never entirely removed, and the threat of final exile gradually gathered momentum during the last few decades of Judah's existence until the point came when there was no respite (2 Ch. 33:11; 34:23–24, 28; 36:4, 6, 10, 20). It is clear that following Judah's final demise, the whole experience entered deeply into Israel's psyche, and the effects were still felt long after some had begun to return (1 Ch. 9:1–2).

This summary of Israel's plight is significantly different from the explanation commonly associated with the theory of immediate retribution, an idea which has been held to be a central element of the Chronicler's thought since the time of Wellhausen (1878).[1] According to this view, 'reward and punishment are not deferred, but rather follow on the heels of the precipitating events'.[2] It is certainly true that, more than most Old Testament writers, the Chronicler affirms the

---

[1] *Cf.* J. Wellhausen, *Prolegomena to the History of Israel* (ET, Edinburgh: Black, 1885), pp. 203–210; *cf. e.g.* R. North, 'Theology of the Chronicler', *JBL* 82, 1963, pp. 369–381, especially, pp. 372–374; G. von Rad, *Old Testament Theology*, I (London: SCM Press, 1962), pp. 348–350; Dillard, pp. 77–81.
[2] Dillard, p. 77.

existence of a strong link between obedience and blessing and between disobedience and judgment in the lifetime of individuals, but this principle is neither simplistic nor automatic. Judgment can be cumulative, for instance, as in the case of the exile or in the way that kings rejected the teachings of the prophets as a whole (*cf.* 2 Ch. 24:19; 36:16). On other occasions, judgment that is threatened against an individual or nation often does not take place because of a repentant response to a prophetic warning (*cf.* 1 Ch. 21:15–19; 2 Ch. 12:5; 15:1–8; 36:15).[1] God often sends such warnings in an attempt to prevent his people experiencing greater trouble. Further, the Chronicler's confirmation that there is no-one who does not sin (2 Ch. 6:36) indicates that all deserve judgment. This conclusion has often been obscured by those who have described David as a 'spotless holy king who delivers solemn orations', or Solomon as 'completely without fault in his relationship to Yahweh',[2] but these latter assessments correspond neither with reality nor with the Chronicler's text.

It seems therefore that immediate retribution is too narrow a term to express adequately the Chronicler's theology of judgment and blessing, and it would be wise to revise substantially the use of the term. At least three separate aspects require fresh consideration. Firstly, the Chronicler's concern for correlating sin and judgment has more to do with the manner of judgment than the fact of it. He believes strongly in the well-known biblical principle that the punishment ought to fit the crime, as in the expression, 'If you forsake him, he will forsake you' (2 Ch. 15:2; *cf.* 1 Ch. 28:9; 2 Ch. 7:19–22), and provides several practical examples (2 Ch. 21:13–18; 24:21–26; 28:23). Judgment that does occur is directly related to the original offence. Secondly, one has to take account of the many occasions when people do not receive the punishment that is due to them. In contrast to the view that 'for the Chronicler sin always brings judgment and disaster',[3] the Chronicler's message is much better summarized in David's words: 'Let me fall into the hands of the LORD, for his mercy is very great' (1 Ch. 21:13). A number of David's descendants are treated more positively than in Kings, not because the Chronicler is any more lenient but because he sees in their

---

[1] *Cf.* Japhet, *Ideology*, pp. 176–191; Williamson, p. 32.
[2] G. von Rad, *op. cit.*, p. 350; R. Braun, *JBL* 92, 1973, p. 512.
[3] Dillard, p. 77.

lives explicit evidence of God's kindness to the undeserving. In fact, it is precisely because the Chronicler does not believe in automatic retribution that his account of rulers such as Solomon, Rehoboam (2 Ch. 11–12), Abijah (2 Ch. 13), and especially Manasseh (2 Ch. 33) differs so substantially from that of Kings.

Thirdly and most importantly, the Chronicler is concerned above all to emphasize the hope of restoration rather than the sad reality of retribution. The key text is undoubtedly 2 Chronicles 7:12–16, in which the temple is presented as the channel for divine forgiveness and restoration according to the principles of the Davidic covenant. The means by which this could take place primarily involved repentance and prayer. The Chronicler certainly believed in the power and reality of prayer, and he gives a number of instances of God's answering those who took their troubles to the LORD, in line with Solomon's basic request (2 Ch. 6:18–42). Those in various kinds of difficulty, even exile, who responded to God's invitation (2 Ch. 7:13–14), received God's forgiveness and his help in their time of need (*e.g.* 1 Ch. 21:13, 17; 2 Ch. 14:11; 20:1–13; 32:20, 24; 33:13, 19; Heb. 4:16). The Chronicler did not believe in faith without action, however, and confession of sin had to be accompanied by specific acts of humble repentance (*e.g.* 2 Ch. 12:6–12; 30:11; 33:12, 19; 34:27). Sometimes this took the form of a national ceremony of covenant renewal, which the Chronicler has interestingly made more prominent than has Kings (2 Ch. 15:12–14; 23:16 = 2 Ki. 11:17; 29:10; 34:31–32 = 2 Ki. 23:3). Such occasions provided the opportunity for the people to reform the practices of their faith on a nationwide scale and especially to restore the temple to its proper use (*cf.* 2 Ch. 14:3–5; 15:1–8; 24:4–16; 29:12 – 31:21; 34:3 – 35:19). Jehoshaphat also conducted a similar reformation based on the teaching of God's word, though he is not reported as having participated in a formal covenant renewal.

In all this, God is regularly portrayed as the source of forgiveness and restoration. It was he who planned that the temple should be a place of atonement (1 Ch. 28:11) and who answered prayers for forgiveness with fire from heaven (1 Ch. 21:26; 2 Ch. 7:1–3). He was also ultimately responsible for appointing the Aaronite priests to offer sacrifices and appear in the Holy of Holies for the atonement of Israel's sins, both on a regular basis (1 Ch. 6:49) and on special occasions (2 Ch. 29:24; 30:13–16). Moreover, he was never far away from his people, for the temple was the place of his earthly residence. It was his 'dwelling place' (2 Ch. 6:21, *etc.*) where he appeared in his glory (2 Ch. 5:13–14; 7:1–3), the house of prayer where he was accessible to all who called on him. It bore his Name, a frequent term in the Deuteronomic History which the Chronicler has borrowed extensively (*e.g.* 1 Ch. 17:24; 2 Ch. 2:1, 4; 6:5–10; 7:16, 20; 20:8–9). Any Israelite or foreigner who prayed to him could therefore be sure that God was waiting to listen, even if they were not physically in the temple (*e.g.* 1 Ch. 16:8; 2 Ch. 6:24, 26; 7:14; 14:11). One memorable passage even promises that God's very heart was located in the temple (2 Ch. 7:16).

What this indicates is that the temple was primarily a witness to the God who was worshipped there. It is through temple worship that he is acknowledged as the one who lives in heaven (2 Ch. 20:6) as well as on earth (2 Ch. 6:18). Everything in heaven and earth belongs to him (1 Ch. 29:11–12), for he cannot be limited by anything, either by the highest heaven or by the temple itself (2 Ch. 2:6; 6:18). He is unique (1 Ch. 17:20; 2 Ch. 6:14) and supreme over all possible rivals, including other gods (2 Ch. 2:5). His greatness is recognized even by foreigners (1 Ch. 16:18; 17:24; 2 Ch. 2:12; 9:8), for he saves his people from all forms of human power, however overwhelming they might have appeared (2 Ch. 32:7–8, 22).

It is worth noting in this context that the Chronicler is more concerned with the presence of God's kingdom in Israel than with its coming in the future. There is no evidence in Chronicles of a strong messianic hope, despite the views of some commentators who have stressed the significance of the Davidic covenant and the idealizing portrait of David and Solomon.[1] In reality, however, the Chronicler does not concentrate on the future but on the continuity between the distant past and the present or recent past. The three passages where the Chronicler's account comes nearest to his own time all stress this link rather than awaken any explicit hope for the future. The post-exilic continuation of David's line (1 Ch.

[1] *E.g.* von Rad, *GCW*, pp. 119–132; A. M. Brunet, 'La théologie du Chroniste: théocratie et messianisme', in J. Coppens (ed.), *Sacra Pagina* (Louvain: Universitaires de Louvain, 1959), pp. 384–397; W. Stinespring, 'Eschatology in Chronicles', *JBL* 80, 1961, pp. 209–219.

3:17–24), the account of the resettlement of Jerusalem (1 Ch. 9:2–34), and the summary of Cyrus' edict (2 Ch. 36:22–23) all indicate that God is still building his house and that he invites his people to go on participating in the task.

It would be a serious error, however, to conclude that the Chronicler has no interest beyond the present.[1] The post-exilic generations do not just continue the past but are caught up in the current of an ever-flowing stream. Despite Israel's current reduced circumstances and loss of the Davidic monarchy, the rebuilt temple is a visible sign that God is still at work. The community that worshipped in the temple therefore has a vital role to play in passing on their faith to future generations. They must take seriously the occupation of the land, and worship the God who promises eternal kingship to David's line. God's purposes remain incomplete, and the future lies open to all who believe that God will not abandon what he has started (*cf.* Phil. 1:6). He will yet keep his promise to set one of David's descendants 'over his house and his kingdom for ever' (1 Ch. 17:14).

V. THE ORIGINS OF CHRONICLES

(a) The relationship between Chronicles and Ezra–Nehemiah

Most of the major literary critical questions relating to the origins of Chronicles depend on one's view of its relationship with Ezra and Nehemiah. Ever since 1832, scholars from a variety of theological persuasions have accepted the hypothesis that Chronicles and Ezra–Nehemiah were originally a single work covering Israel's history from Adam to the time of Nehemiah.[2] It has even been argued occasionally that Ezra himself was the Chronicler.[3] This standard view reigned supreme for many years despite occasional challenges such as that by Welch (1935), and it was only after Japhet's fresh

---

[1] Against *e.g.*, Rudolph, pp. xiii–xxiv; O. Plöger, *Theocracy and Eschatology* (Oxford: Blackwell, 1968); Japhet, *Ideology*, pp. 493–504.

[2] Like 1 and 2 Chronicles, evidence clearly indicates that Ezra and Nehemiah were originally one book (*cf.* H. G. M. Williamson, *Ezra, Nehemiah*, WBC (Waco: Word Books, 1985), pp. xxi–xxiii. The notion that Chronicles and Ezra–Nehemiah were two parts of the same work was first proposed by L. Zunz, 'Dibrehajamim oder die Bücher der Chronik', *Die gottesdienstlichen Vorträge der Judea historisch entwickelt* (Berlin: Asher, 1832), pp. 13–26.

[3] *E.g.* W. F. Albright, 'The date and personality of the Chronicler', *JBL* 40, 1921, pp. 104–124.

assessment of the issues (1968) that scholarly opinion as a whole began to shift.[1] In fact, so much movement has taken place in the last two decades that although the traditional approach still has its defenders, Chronicles and Ezra–Nehemiah are now more likely to be regarded as separate compilations.[2]

The main factors involved in this debate are as follows.

(a) The last two verses of Chronicles (2 Ch. 36:22–23) are also found at the beginning of Ezra (Ezr. 1:1–3), though the situation is complicated by the fact that the link between the two is rather less obvious in the Hebrew Bible where Ezra–Nehemiah precedes Chronicles. The usual explanation of this overlap separates the issue of the compilation of the two works from that of their inclusion in the canon. Whereas the order of the English and Greek Bibles suggests that the story of Chronicles is simply continued in Ezra, the reverse order of the books in the Hebrew Bible is regularly explained as the result of Ezra–Nehemiah being accepted into the canon first as a proper continuation of the history in Samuel–Kings. Chronicles was then added as a supplement to the main account, as implied by its Greek title, 'the things omitted'. This reconstruction lacks conviction, however. It is hard to avoid the impression that the fact of the different order of the books in the Greek and Hebrew Bibles has been conveniently adapted to address separate problems without proper consideration of the overall picture. Since direct evidence about why and how Chronicles and Ezra–Nehemiah were admitted to the canon does not actually exist, proper methodology suggests that prior attention should be given to the Hebrew rather than the Greek arrangement. It is noticeable in fact that support for the continuation of Chronicles in

---

[1] S. Japhet, 'The supposed common authorship of Chronicles and Ezra–Nehemiah investigated anew', *VT* 18, 1968, pp. 330–371; *cf.* A. Welch, *Post-Exilic Judaism* (Edinburgh: Blackwood, 1935). See also especially Williamson, *IBC*, pp. 5–82; R. Braun, 'Chronicles, Ezra and Nehemiah: theology and literary history'. *SVT* 30, 1979, pp. 52–64; and the commentaries by Braun, Dillard, and de Vries.

[2] Those who remain unconvinced by the arguments of Japhet and others include Mason, *Preaching*, p. 9; McKenzie, *Use*, pp. 17–25; Polzin, *Typology*, pp. 70–75. On the other hand, a comparison between P. R. Ackroyd's earlier and later writings on the Chronicler reveals that his own position has become distinctly more cautious (*cf.* the various articles in P. R. Ackroyd, *The Chronicler in his Age*, *JSOTS* 101 (Sheffield: Sheffield Academic Press, 1991).

Ezra–Nehemiah and for treating Chronicles as a supplementary account belongs to the Greek rather than the Hebrew tradition, and is not necessarily original. Furthermore, strong evidence exists to suggest that far from Ezra continuing the story of Chronicles, 2 Chronicles 36:22–23 is actually dependent on Ezra 1:1–3. The abrupt ending to Chronicles, 'and let him go up' (2 Ch. 36:23), makes much more sense as an abbreviation than if it were the original version. Also, the difference between the Hebrew for 'by the mouth of Jeremiah' in 2 Chronicles (*bpy*) and Ezra 1:1 (*mpy*) is more easily explained by secondary influence of 2 Chronicles 36:21 on 2 Chronicles 36:22, since the identical expression occurs in both verses.[1]

(b) A Septugintal work called 1 Esdras moves across the juncture between the two books without interruption and without repeating the overlapping material. This book is an historical narrative which begins at 2 Chronicles 35–36 and is followed by the whole of Ezra and by Nehemiah 7:72 – 8:13a, but which also includes limited additional material. Scholars are divided as to whether 1 Esdras is a part of an older translation of the original form of Chronicles + Ezra–Nehemiah or whether it is a secondary work. The majority opinion favours the latter view, since there is evidence that 1 Esdras is a derivative compilation and is paraphrastic in character.[2] Though the fragment view still has its defenders, it is worth noting that the contribution of 1 Esdras seems to be another issue which is more to do with the development of the Greek text than the original Hebrew form of these works.[3]

(c) Substantial similarities exist between the language of Chronicles and of Ezra–Nehemiah, and extensive lists of the common features were compiled in the nineteenth and early twentieth centuries.[4] More recent investigation, however, prefers to conclude from the same evidence that the two works belong to a distinct dialect now usually called Late Biblical Hebrew. Further complications arise because the amount of

---

[1] *Cf.* Williamson, *IBC*, pp. 9–10.   [2] *Cf. ibid.*, pp. 12–36; de Vries, p. 9.

[3] For a defence of the fragment view, *cf.* K. F. Pohlmann, *Studien zum dritten Esra* (Göttingen: Vandenhoeck & Ruprecht, 1970); R. W. Klein, 'Studies in the Greek text of the Chronicler', unpubl. Ph.D. thesis, Harvard, 1966; McKenzie, *Use*, pp. 18–25.

[4] Especially S. R. Driver, *Introduction to the Literature of the Old Testament* (Edinburgh: T. & T. Clark, [9]1913), pp. 535–540; Curtis and Madsen, pp. 27–36.

literature in this dialect is very limited, and because the non-synoptic material in Chronicles comprises by far the largest literary unit in Late Biblical Hebrew. The evidence therefore for assessing whether Chronicles and Ezra–Nehemiah might be attributed to a single author is actually quite restricted. Even Polzin, who argues for an 'amazing linguistic similarity' between the language of Chronicles, Ezra, and the Nehemiah Memoir, speaks only of similarity rather than identity of authorship.[1] Perhaps more significant is the view of Throntveit, who, while accepting that Chronicles and Ezra–Nehemiah both belong to Late Biblical Hebrew, believes that the weight of evidence is strongly against common authorship.[2]

(d) Chronicles and Ezra–Nehemiah clearly share a number of common interests. These include the temple and its worship, the Mosaic law, covenant renewal, and the sense of continuity between pre- and post-exilic Israel. The key question, however, is whether this common ideology is close enough to warrant treating them as different parts of the same work or not. Merely identifying similarities is not sufficient, and a comprehensive picture must investigate the contrasts between them. In fact, the two works exhibit significant differences in both the breadth and depth of their interests. Not only do they cover different topics, but more importantly they deal with the same themes in contrasting ways. The list of examples is surprisingly extensive, and includes David and the Davidic covenant, mixed marriages, the Sabbath and the Levites, the Chronicler's interest in the patriarch Jacob/Israel as against the exodus and conquest in Ezra–Nehemiah, the fall of the northern kingdom and the fate of its inhabitants, conflict with the northerners, approaches to prophecy and to historiography. The existence of these differences has been widely recognized, and their importance duly acknowledged.[3]

Less attention has been devoted to variations in the character of the two works. This has been partly the result of regarding Chronicles as an historical work, supplementary to Samuel–Kings as well as preparatory to Ezra–Nehemiah. If, however,

---

[1] Polzin, *Typology*, pp. 70–75. The quotation is from p. 75.

[2] M. A. Throntveit, 'Linguistic analysis and the question of authorship in Chronicles, Ezra and Nehemiah', *VT* 32, 1982, pp. 201–216.

[3] *E.g.* Williamson, *IBC*, pp. 60–69; R. Braun, 'Chronicles, Ezra and Nehemiah: theology and literary history', *SVT* 30, 1979, pp. 52–64.

as has been argued above, Chronicles is really an interpretation of earlier Scripture, including Ezra–Nehemiah, then they are much less likely to share a common purpose or a common authorship. This is well illustrated by the varying treatments of the resettlement of the land, which is a major preoccupation in Ezra–Nehemiah. The latter devotes much space to the question of who would return to the Promised Land and how it should be carried out, whereas the Chronicler seems to take the fact of the return more or less for granted. His concern is how the return fits into God's over-all purposes for Israel, especially in relation to God's dealings with Jacob and David. His whole outlook is quite different. Where Ezra–Nehemiah speaks of Israel as still in bondage (Ezr. 9:7; Ne. 9:36) and ends on a note of unfulfilled expectation (Ne. 13), the Chronicler emphasizes how God's intentions go on being fulfilled, whether through Cyrus' invitation or those who repopulated Jerusalem (1 Ch. 9:2–34; 2 Ch. 36:22–23).[1]

All these factors, and especially the different subject matter, suggest there are good reasons for treating Chronicles as a separate entity, unencumbered by conclusions about the origins and nature of Ezra–Nehemiah. In any case, it is important to examine Chronicles as a work that is complete in itself, with its own character and structure. In this commentary that distinctiveness is taken as a starting-point, as is the final form of the Hebrew text of Chronicles. Though many sources have been used in the compilation of Chronicles, and the date and precise contribution of the person generally referred to as the Chronicler remain unknown, the completed Hebrew text is to be regarded as the fixed objective standard for interpreting the work.

(b) The date and authorship of Chronicles

Any assessment of the date of Chronicles is inevitably tied up with issues relating to the composition and development of the work. If, for example, Chronicles is assumed to be linked with Ezra–Nehemiah, then the date of Chronicles cannot be earlier than the latest item in Ezra–Nehemiah. On the other hand, if the Ezra–Nehemiah issue is put aside and in addition the genealogies of 1 Chronicles 1–9 are treated largely as a

---

[1] See J. G. McConville, 'Ezra–Nehemiah and the fulfilment of prophecy', *VT* 36, 1986, pp. 204–22, and *cf.* W. J. Dumbrell, 'The purpose of the books of Chronicles', *JETS* 27, 1984, pp. 257–266.

supplement deriving from a later hand than that of the Chronicler, then the rest of Chronicles could conceivably be located as early as the restoration period towards the end of the sixth century BC.

It is no surprise therefore that assessments of the date of Chronicles have varied enormously, from as early as 529–515 BC (Newsome) to as late as 200 BC (Noth, Gressmann).[1] Even when the proposals are reduced to the main alternatives, the range is still very wide. They include the four options of the restoration period (*e.g.* Freedman, Cross's first edition), the post Ezra–Nehemiah period (*e.g.* Myers, Albright, Cross's third edition), the late Persian period (*e.g.* Ackroyd, Williamson), and the Greek period (*e.g.* Rudolph, Curtis and Madsen, Welten).[2] Chronicles itself offers few clues as to when it was written. The clearest evidence all occurs in the opening genealogies of 1 Chronicles 1–9, though it is disputed how much of this section belonged originally with the rest of the work. Two passages are of special interest. The first concerns the list of those who repopulated Jerusalem (1 Ch. 9:2–34), which is apparently dependent on a similar list in Nehemiah 11:3–19. On the basis of changes to some of the names and the Chronicler's small increase in the numbers of those settling in the city, the Chronicles version seems to belong to a period approximately half a generation later than Nehemiah's list. What is less certain is whether 1 Chronicles 9:2–34 is a little later than Nehemiah in the late fifth century BC or whether it depends on the reference to the great-grandsons of two of Nehemiah's contemporaries (Uzzi from Mattaniah's line, Ne. 11:22, and Jaddua the high priest, Ne. 12:11, 22) and therefore belongs to the first half of the fourth century. The second passage is the list of post-exilic Davidic descendants in 1 Chronicles 3:17–24, though again its interpretation is dogged by uncertainty. The list may extend for a minimum of five

[1] J. D. Newsome, 'Towards a new understanding of the Chronicler and his purposes', *JBL* 94, 1975, pp. 201–217; M. Noth, *The Chronicler's History, JSOTS* 50 (Sheffield: Sheffield Academic Press, 1987), pp. 69–75; H. Gressmann, *Die Schriften des Alten Testaments* (Göttingen: Vandenhoeck & Ruprecht, 1925).

[2] D. N. Freedman, 'The Chronicler's purpose', *CBQ* 23, 1961, pp. 436–442; F. M. Cross, 'A reconstruction of the Judean restoration', *JBL* 94, 1975, pp. 4–18; W. F. Albright, 'The date and personality of the Chronicler', *JBL* 40, 1921, pp. 104–124; Myers, *1 Chronicles*; Ackroyd; Williamson; Rudolph; Curtis and Madsen; P. Welten, *Geschichte und Geschichtsdarstellung in den Chronikbüchern* (Neukirchen-Vluyn: Neukirchener, 1973).

or a maximum of ten generations after Zerubbabel, who was governor in Jerusalem towards the end of the sixth century BC. It could therefore reach either to the end of the fifth century or to the late fourth century. On the evidence of both these passages, a date for Chronicles around 400 BC is more probable, but any date in the fourth century would be quite reasonable.

An early date has recently attracted fresh support, partly because of the obvious link between the Chronicler's interest in the temple and the rebuilding of the temple and because Zerubbabel's leadership would have awakened fresh interest in the Davidic dynasty. This view does suffer from a number of difficulties, however, not least the doubtful requirement of regarding 1 Chronicles 1–9, which refers to events of a later time, as a later addition. It is also questionable whether the Chronicler shared the same kinds of concerns about the temple as Haggai and Zechariah. Whereas the two prophets were preoccupied in seeing the second temple actually built, the Chronicler shows greater interest in the use and staffing of the temple. Similarly, the Chronicler's preoccupation with the Davidic dynasty does not necessarily mean that he was particularly interested in Zerubbabel as such, or that he looked for a political restoration under his leadership. Another difficulty is that the use in 2 Chronicles 16:9 of what would be a contemporary text from Zechariah 4:10 is unlikely when compared with other frequent quotations of the prophets in Chronicles. Finally, the earliest date for Chronicles is related to the mention of the Persian daric coin (1 Ch. 29:7), which was named after Darius I (522–486 BC) and is not known to have been minted before 515 BC. This factor in particular makes it difficult for a date in the late sixth century to command confidence.

As to who the author of Chronicles may have been, nothing can be concluded with certainty. There is some possibility that he may have been a Levite, and the adjustments made in 1 Chronicles 16:34–35 to parts of Psalm 106 may reflect his Levitical activity as one who was involved in the ministries of leading in praise and interpreting Scripture. It is also very likely that as a Levite he would have had access to some of the source material which lies behind the work. Like most biblical authors, however, he must remain anonymous, known to posterity only by his mysterious title, 'The Chronicler'.

(c) The development of Chronicles

The Chronicler has clearly made use of a variety of sources which have been incorporated into the final form of his work. Though the fact of this process is beyond dispute, the extent and nature of this material, and the manner in which it has been incorporated into the over-all composition, is widely debated. It is therefore necessary to comment on the sources which were available to the Chronicler and the use he has made of them as a means of understanding how Chronicles reached its present form.

The first task is to classify the Chronicler's sources. They can be divided into three categories, the biblical quotations and allusions, the sources mentioned in the Chronicler's citations, and other non-biblical material. Since it has already been explained that the main biblical material has been taken from Samuel–Kings and from other parts of the Old Testament, its use will not be explained further.

The sources which are explicitly cited were intended to provide the original readers with further information about individual kings. Two different kinds of formula are mentioned, some of a prophetic character and some of a political character. The political citations are familiar from the books of Kings, despite a number of changes to the wording. These were some kind of official records distinct from the biblical books of Kings, and some question must be raised as to whether they were still available in the Chronicler's day.

Both sets of citations reveal several important characteristics about the Chronicler's methods and interests. Firstly, all the political citations include 'Israel' in the title, even though this term was never used of Judean kings in the books of Kings. In place of 'the annals of the kings of Judah', the Chronicler has the following variations: 'the annals of the kings of Judah and Israel' (*e.g.* 2 Ch. 16:11), '. . . the kings of Israel and Judah' (*e.g.* 2 Ch. 27:7), or even '. . . the kings of Israel' (*e.g.* 2 Ch. 33:18).[1] This is one of the methods by which the Chronicler brings out the importance of God's people being always identified as Israel, whatever divisions and disasters they may have suffered. Secondly, the Chronicler has introduced prophetic citations, which are without parallel in Kings. They reflect the Chronicler's distinctive interest in prophecy, and according to

---

[1] The exception is 'the midrash of the book of kings' (2 Ch. 24:27).

the citations he made use of at least two different types of prophetic literature. Some of the references are to prophetic material in Samuel–Kings (*e.g.* 1 Ch. 29:29; 2 Ch. 9:29), suggesting that the Chronicler saw the latter as basically prophetic rather than historical works. Others, however, are included within the political sources known as the 'annals of the kings of Judah and Israel', *etc.* (*e.g.* 2 Ch. 20:34; 33:18–19), which indicates that these too were regarded as prophetic histories. Whether all the prophetic citations can be attributed to these two sources or whether other independent prophetic collections were involved is less clear. In favour of the former is the fact that all the passages where the Chronicler cites only a prophetic source are paralleled by reference to a political source in Kings (except for David, 1 Ch. 29:29). On the other hand, the mention of 'Isaiah the prophet, son of Amoz' as a source for Uzziah (2 Ch. 26:22) is not necessarily a reference to either the biblical books of Kings or Isaiah or the usual non-biblical annals. Neither Kings nor Isaiah contains very much at all about Uzziah, especially since the latter mentions the prophet's call in the year of Uzziah's death (Is. 6:1). The alteration from 'Book of the annals of the kings of Judah' (2 Ki. 15:6) to this prophetic source may therefore be an indication of independent material. Thirdly, the citations indicate the Chronicler's dependence on external sources, and his care in identifying them. Whereas only a few of these external sources are specifically mentioned in the citations, such as several letters (2 Ch. 2:11–16; 21:12–15; 30:6–12), many others are identifiable either by comparison with other parts of the Bible or by signs of distinctive style and content. These non-biblical sources include genealogies and other lists, military (1 Ch. 5:18, 26; 7:2–5) and tribal records (1 Ch. 4:34–43; 5:7–10), temple records (1 Ch. 16:4–7, 37–42), judicial sources (2 Ch. 19:5–11), and prophetic sources (2 Ch. 25:7–16). Though the existence of these sources from outside the Bible cannot be absolutely verified, the variety of styles and content, especially in passages which reflect a different outlook from the Chronicler's own time, is a strong point in favour of their authenticity.

In addition, the Chronicler himself was of course also responsible for a significant part of the material. His distinctive literary style, his structures and patterns, and his special vocabulary are often easily identified, especially in the various speeches, prophecies, and prayers of which he is so fond. What is more difficult is to separate his own contribution from the material which he found already to hand. Without the benefit of external controls, one can only speculate about the full extent of the Chronicler's use of source material, but his attention to detail in frequently pointing the reader to other sources of information suggests that he was careful to base his own contributions on a proper historical foundation.

The situation has become somewhat more complicated in the light of recent new evidence about the actual Hebrew text available to the Chronicler. Until comparatively recently, it was frequently assumed that any differences between Chronicles and its main biblical sources had resulted from the Chronicler himself. More recent study has indicated, however, that in addition to the Hebrew Massoretic Text, Chronicles has been influenced by other textual traditions, including the Lucianic LXX (L) and a manuscript of parts of Samuel found among the Dead Sea Scrolls (4QSamª). Though the precise relationship between Chronicles and 4QSamª is still being investigated, it has already become clear in the case of Samuel that where the Chronicler has relied on written sources he has usually kept fairly closely to them, whether the Massoretic Text tradition or that represented by 4QSamª. Textual factors must therefore be taken into account in explaining the variations between Chronicles and its known sources, and the evidence confirms the author's care in handling what was available to him.[1]

The question as to how the work has developed into its present form has spawned a particularly wide range of hypotheses. Indeed, the very variety probably indicates as much about the different starting-points of the scholars making the proposals as anything else. They can be reduced to three basic types of approach, including those who accept that the work as a whole is effectively the production of the Chronicler himself (*e.g.* Myers, Michaeli), those who argue for minor additions (*e.g.* Williamson, de Vries), and those who believe

---

[1] See especially F. M. Cross, 'The history of the biblical text in the light of the discoveries in the Judean desert', *HTR* 57, 1964, pp. 281–299; *idem*, 'The contribution of the Qumrân discoveries to the study of the biblical text', *IEJ* 16, 1966, pp. 81–95; W. E. Lemke, 'The synoptic problem in the Chronicler's history', *HTR* 58, 1965, pp. 349–363; McKenzie, *Use*, pp. 49–73; Braun, pp. xxi–xxiii.

that it is the result of extensive secondary reworking (*e.g.* Rudolph, Cross). Most of the major debate revolves around the role and provenance of the genealogies in 1 Chronicles 1–9 and of the material concerning the Levites in 1 Chronicles 15–16; 23–27. Certainly this material is very varied, and the editor has sometimes preferred to remain faithful to his individual sources rather than iron out superficial contradictions (*cf.* the confusing genealogies of Caleb in 1 Ch. 2:18–24, 42–55; 4:1–8, or the contrasting references to the high places in 2 Ch. 14:3, 5; 15:17; 17:6; 20:33). However, as de Vries has noted, the decision of a number of scholars to amputate the majority of the genealogies is a 'cheap surrender', often made because their purpose has not been fully appreciated.[1] In fact, the various lists and genealogies regularly prepare the reader for the following section of narrative.[2] They confirm how the actions of David or Hezekiah, for example (*cf.* 1 Ch. 15–16; 23–27; 2 Ch. 29:12–24), reflect their faithfulness to the Mosaic law or to God's purposes in choosing and preserving his people. They also frequently supplement the main themes of the Chronicler's narrative, such as all Israel, temple worship, the Levites, effective prayer, and Israel's unfaithfulness, either by the choice of particular lists or by the inclusion of annotations. If the lists and genealogies are read in this way, there is no major obstacle to accepting the work as a whole as the Chronicler's own composition.

[1] De Vries, p. 12.
[2] *Cf.* also M. Oeming, *Das wahre Israel*, BWANT 128 (Stuttgart: Kolhammer, 1990), ch. 7

ANALYSIS

F. Solomon prepares for the temple (2 Ch. 1:1 – 2:18)
    i. Solomon's splendour (1:1–17)
        a. Solomon's kingdom established (1:1)
        b. Solomon's worship (1:2–6)
        c. Solomon's wisdom (1:7–13)
        d. Solomon's wealth (1:14–17)
    ii. Solomon's preparations (2:1–18)
        a. Building instructions (2:1)
        b. Census of labourers (2:2)
        c. Solomon's letter to Hiram (2:3–10)
        d. Hiram's letter to Solomon (2:11–16)
        e. Census of non-Israelite labourers (2:17–18)

G. Solomon builds the temple (3:1 – 5:1)
    i. Beginning to build the temple (3:1–2)
    ii. The ground-plan and porch (3:3–4a)
    iii. The golden temple (3:4b–13)
    iv. The veil (3:14)
    v. The pillars (3:15–17)
    vi. The Temple equipment (4:1–22)
        a. The bronze altar (4:1)
        b. The Sea (4:2–6, 10)
        c. The ten gold lampstands and ten tables (4:7–8)
        d. The courtyards (4:9)
        e. Bronze work (4:11b–18)
        f. Gold objects (4:19–22)
    vii. Completion of the temple (5:1)

H. Solomon dedicates the temple (5:2 – 7:22)
    i. The ark and the cloud (5:2–14)
        a. Solomon assembles all Israel (5:2–3)
        b. The ark's final journey (5:4–6)
        c. The ark's final resting-place (5:7–10)
        d. God's glory and Israel's praise (5:11–14)
    ii. Solomon's praise and prayer (6:1–42)
        a. Solomon responds to God's glory (6:1–2)
        b. Solomon's testimony to God's promise (6:3–11)
        c. Solomon's dedicatory prayer (6:12–42)
    iii. God's answer to prayer (7:1–22)
        a. God's fire and glory (7:1–3)
        b. Israel's sacrifice and praise (7:4–10)
        c. God's promises (7:11–22)

I. Solomon completes the temple (8:1–16)
    i. Solomon's other building work (8:1–6)

COMMENTARY

I. THE TRIBES OF ISRAEL (1 Ch. 1:1 – 9:44)

A Jewish student was once asked by a fellow Gentile student to identify his favourite part of the Bible. 'The first eight chapters of First Chronicles,' he replied. The Gentile was amazed, but as his friend started to give his reasons, he began to understand something of the mysterious attraction of these chapters. 'From my (Gentile) point of view,' he reflected, 'I have often wondered why God allowed so much space in his Word to be "wasted" on such trivia. But to a Hebrew (and to many other kinship-oriented societies around the world), genealogical lists of this nature demonstrate in the clearest way the specificity of God's love and concern that lie at the heart of the gospel.'[1]

The Chronicler's first readers, however, are unlikely to have seen things quite so positively. Despite their Jewish heritage, they were too preoccupied with an overwhelming identity crisis and a deep sense of guilt and shame to give much attention to the meaning of God's love. Tucked away and often ignored in a far-flung corner of the Persian Empire, the largest empire the world had yet seen, they had nagging doubts about whether Israel could ever again really be God's people. Furthermore, many Jews felt that their present sad state of affairs was God's will, a punishment for past sins. And yet these seemingly intractable problems are almost certainly the kind of issues that the lists and genealogies of 1 Chronicles 1–9 are intended to confront. The sense of belonging and of continuity which they conveyed were clearly gospel or good news as far as the author was concerned. They show that the Chronicler's generation had not after all been cast off from

[1] Quoted in C. Kraft, *Christianity and Culture* (Maryknoll: Orbis, 1979), p. 229.

85

their historical, geographical, and spiritual moorings. If they would only look back, look around, and look up, they would see that they still belonged to 'Israel', and that their present predicament was not hopeless.

Three specific answers to their problems are revealed in chapters 1–9:

(a) A summary of the 'generations' of Genesis, from Adam to Edom/Esau, shows that all the nations were God's creation and therefore part of his special purposes for Israel (1:1–54);

(b) The present small Jewish community was still descended from Jacob's twelve sons and from 'all Israel' who had inherited the Promised Land (2:1 – 9:1);

(c) The exile had not cut the umbilical cord of the post-exilic community's life, for those who now lived and worshipped in Jerusalem remained heirs of the promises of God (9:2–34).

This basically simple framework of 1 Chronicles 1–9 contains various patterns of lists and genealogies. Names can be listed vertically, usually in descending order from the oldest (*e.g.* 6:1–15), though an ascending order starting with the most recent name is occasionally used (*e.g.* 6:33–47). Another variation, found in chapter 1, is a descending order where the key family in each generation (not necessarily related to the oldest son) is left to last. The forms of expression also vary considerably. The commonest formula is 'the sons of X: Y, Z, *etc.*' (*e.g.* 2:1–9), but one also finds bare lists of names (*e.g.* 1:24–27) as well as the famous 'begat' formula (*cf.* AV), though the latter is rare (*e.g.* 2:10–13, 36–41).

This variety is a strong indication that the lists are not the Chronicler's invention, but that he has fused together for his own purposes lists of varying character from different periods. Some are based on earlier Scripture, as in chapter 1 and in some of the shorter tribal lists in 4:24 – 5:26; 7:1–40. Others are taken from various official sources, such as temple and tribal records, some of them connected with military service. Most of the lists, with the major exception of 9:2–34, are pre-exilic in origin, though again there is much variety.[1]

The result appears to be a real hotchpotch, sometimes with quite obvious gaps (*e.g.* no details are given about the tribe of Zebulun, though *cf.* 2:1). Closer examination, however,

[1] On the origins of the lists, see *e.g.* J. P. Weinberg, 'Das Wesen und die funktionelle Bestimmung der Listen in 1 Chr 1–9', *ZAW* 93, 1981, pp. 91–114. For a helpful general introduction to OT genealogies, see Braun, pp. 1–12.

reveals the presence of certain connecting threads which give the patchwork a real sense of design:

(a) Israel belongs to the past, but must not live in it. The fact that the Davidic line (3:17–24) and the sketch of post-exilic Israel (9:2–34) come near, or even down to, the Chronicler's own generation shows that the lists are not intended to be a historian's delight. A proper sense of history involves understanding the ways of God in past days so that faith may be renewed in the present (*cf.* Phil. 1:16).

(b) Certain people have a special significance in the purposes of God. In the earliest period, Adam (1:1) and Israel (= Jacob; 1:34; 2:1–2) are the key names, as representatives of God's creative and redemptive work for and through humanity. God's purposes then continue through three tribes, Judah (2:3 – 3:24), Levi (ch. 6), and Benjamin (7:6–12; 8:1–40; 9:35–44), who occupy the lion's share of the tribal lists and form an over-all framework for them. David's continuing line in Judah (3:1–24) sustains a hope that Israel's kingship could reappear, while Levi's presence indicates ongoing provision for atonement, sacrifice and praise (6:1–81).

(c) Occupation of the Promised Land remains a priority. Much of chapters 2–8 is in fact concerned with showing how all the tribes had lived in the land, even though this sometimes involved both pain and prayer (*cf.* 4:9–10). The corollary of this for the Chronicler's readers was the need to go on committing themselves to the rebuilding of Jerusalem and its temple (*cf.* 9:2–34).

(d) The nations of the world belong to God. Though the list of nations is confined to chapter 1, the vital point is that their genealogy is also Israel's genealogy. There is no dividing line. All are part of God's sovereign purposes, with the nations having to acknowledge God's power (*cf.* 1 Ch. 14:17; 2 Ch. 20:29), and even mighty Cyrus fulfilling God's prophetic word (*cf.* 2 Ch. 36:22–23). Not only need Israel not feel threatened, they could even take a positive view, for Abraham (1:27–34) was God's promised source of blessing for the nations (*cf.* Gn. 12:2–3).

(e) All types of people have a place within the purposes of God. The good, the bad, and the ugly are all included in the lists. All the tribes are there, including both sides of the old north–south divide. Foreigners and those involved in mixed marriages are included (*cf.* 2:3, 34–35; 4:18). Ordinary people, totally forgotten apart from the record of their names, are placed alongside some of the great names of Israel's past. The people of God in all their variety and their failure are in fact the central subject of the lists. In the compiler's mind, these were certainly not dry old genealogies. They deal with real places and real people, who despite Israel's 'unfaithfulness' (see notes on 2:7; 5:25; 9:1) all have a role in God's continuing activity.

Has this kind of material any relevance for Christians? The answer must be yes, since each of the above themes has a Christian counterpart. The spiritual heritage of the church, for example, is an important issue, as is the reminder about the significance of spiritual geography. God is still working out his sovereign purposes throughout the world, and has a concern for every place where Christians live and work.

Two issues are worth pondering in more detail. The first is the truth that Christians as well as Israelites are in Adam (*cf.* 1 Ch. 1:1). Although Adam is often associated with the idea that the human race is under the bondage of sin and death (Rom. 5:12–19; 1 Cor. 15:21–22, 45–49), the Bible, and this includes Chronicles, also has another more positive view of him (*cf.* Lk. 3:38; Acts 17:26). Chronicles' reference to Adam alludes to the description in Genesis where he was created through God's personal will in God's image. Although that image was damaged by sin, it was not destroyed, and all Adam's descendants share something of his original dignity. But Jesus Christ too is a son of Adam (Lk. 3:38). This means not only that Jesus is real man, but that he is able to redeem those who have fallen in Adam's sin. Rather than separating Christians from their humanity or 'Adam-ness', therefore, Jesus enables them to fulfil the humanity for which they were created. Chronicles in other words starts with a family tree to which the people of all nations belong, but where only those who are in Christ can find their true heritage as sons of God and sons of Adam.

The second issue concerns the nature and purpose of the people of God. Israel's diversity offers an analogy for the variety that constitutes the church. The church is no homogeneous unit, but a mixture of 'all kinds and conditions of men'. Indeed, this is true in even greater measure than for Israel, since the church derives from many nations, not just one. Because it is like a body (Eph. 4:16) or a building (Eph. 2:21), the church has many parts, and has received many varieties of gifts (Eph. 4:7–8, 11–12). Unfortunately, it also, like Israel, has a record of 'unfaithfulness' (*cf.* Eph. 2:2; 2 Tim. 2:13). Chronicles' answer to this problem is found in the genealogies of Judah and Levi, for it is Jesus who now fulfils the royal and priestly functions represented by these tribes. As King he rules over the affairs of the nations, and as High Priest he assures believers that their sins have been put away for ever. Like Israel, therefore, the church need not be cowed by any threats, whether they be external or internal. God's intention today is still to restore his people on the basis of his age-long purposes, just as he did for the post-exilic community.

A. Adam to Esau (1:1–54)

The opening chapter has a majestic sweep, covering the entire period from *Adam* (v. 1) to *Esau* and *Jacob* (always known in Chronicles as Israel, v. 34; *cf.* 2:1). It is in effect a brief commentary on Genesis, structured around the famous recurring phrase of that book, 'These are the generations of . . .'. This phrase originally formed a heading to various lists which have now been brought together, apart from the passages associated with the first (Gn. 2:4) and last (Gn. 37:2) occurrences of the phrase. Chronicles has sometimes combined two lists in the interests of economy, particularly where one was originally quite short (*cf.* v. 4a and Gn. 6:9–10; 10:1; vv. 27–28 and Gn. 11:10, 27; v. 35 and Gn. 36:1, 9), but otherwise all the relevant passages appear in one form or another. The original lists have been stripped of all headings, summaries, and various personal details, and sometimes only the names themselves are preserved (vv. 1–4a, 24–27).

This chapter has therefore become a panoramic view of God's dealings with humanity in both creation and redemption. God's name does not actually appear, of course, but his activity is visible everywhere to the discerning reader. The Chronicler assumes that the basic story and personalities of Genesis are known. He has also made into pivotal points names that have great significance in the early history of God's people, especially *Adam* (v. 1), *Noah* (v. 4), *Abraham* (vv. 27, 28, 32, 34), and *Israel* (v. 34; 2:1). The sections are so arranged that the person providing the link from Adam to Israel is dealt with last in each generation. The structure can be represented as in the diagram on page 90.

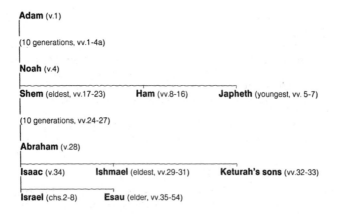

Adam (v.1)
|
(10 generations, vv.1-4a)
|
Noah (v.4)
|
Shem (eldest, vv.17-23)   **Ham** (vv.8-16)   **Japheth** (youngest, vv. 5-7)
|
(10 generations, vv.24-27)
|
Abraham (v.28)
|
Isaac (v.34)   **Ishmael** (eldest, vv.29-31)   **Keturah's sons** (vv.32-33)
|
Israel (chs.2-8)   **Esau** (elder, vv.35-54)

Holding back the key name in this way is unique in chapters 1–9, and draws attention to the final name of each generation. This does not always correspond with the order of birth, for sometimes the oldest child comes first (*e.g.* Shem), sometimes a younger one (*e.g.* Isaac, Israel). The hidden scarlet cord binding all these disparate names into one seamless robe is God's electing love, through which two emphases are brought out. Firstly, all the nations are presented in a kind of world map, clearly placing them inside rather than outside God's over-all purposes.[1] Secondly, and even more importantly, Israel lies at the centre of this scheme. The Israel of the Chronicler's day was not only united with the first Israel, but belonged to the nations as a whole and was even descended from the first man.

In contrast to the genealogies of chapters 2–9, many lines in this chapter are traced for only a generation or so. Only the line of Israel is continued throughout. But though the discontinued lines cannot transmit God's promises, they still have an important role in God's sovereign purposes. Interest in the nations is a typical theme in Chronicles, and two implications follow from it here. One is that the imperial powers of the exile and later are seen as direct descendants of God's creative

---

[1] *Cf.* M. Kartveit, *Motive und Schichten der Landtheologie in 1 Chronik 1–9*, *CBOTS* 28 (Stockholm: Almqvist & Wiksell, 1989), pp. 110–117.

activity in Adam. They are therefore still subject to his sovereign will (the Medes and the Greeks (*Madai* and *Javan*, v. 5) are mentioned explicitly, though not Babylon or Persia). The other is that the Gentiles have prospered too, whether indirectly in response to God's command to 'be fruitful and multiply' (Gn. 1:28) or in association with God's covenant promises (*Ishmael*, vv. 29–31, *cf.* Gn. 21:13, 18; *Esau*, vv. 35–37, *cf.* Gn. 33:9; 36:1ff.).

i. Adam to Noah (1:1–4a)

Cf. Genesis 5:1–32

This list of ten generations is extracted from Genesis 5. *Adam* appears only here outside Genesis. It is a bold theological statement to trace Israel's ancestry back not just to Abraham, but to creation itself. When one considers that the Chronicler was writing at a time of great Israelite weakness, it is difficult to conceive of a more magnificent association with which to begin his account. Luke traces his genealogy of Jesus to the same source (Lk. 3:23–38).

ii. The descendants of Noah (1:4b–23)

Cf. Genesis 10:1–29

This list, which is based closely on the Table of Nations (Gn. 10:1–29), gives the descendants of Noah's three sons, *Shem* (vv. 17–23), *Ham* (vv. 8–16), and *Japheth* (vv. 5–7). As is usual in this chapter, they are dealt with in reverse order, though in this case, it is the eldest who provides the continuity. The names are selective rather than comprehensive, with many lines not developed at all. It appears to cover the known world but without going into every detail. The Japhethites were basically Israel's northern and western neighbours (*e.g. Javan* = Greece, v. 5; *Kittim* = Cyprus, v. 7), the Hamites include northern Africa (*Cush* = Ethiopia, *Mizraim* = Egypt, v. 8) and Syria/Palestine (*cf.* vv. 13–16), and the Semites, or descendants of Shem, lived in the east (*e.g. Elam* = ancient Persia, *Asshur* = Assyria v. 17).

4. The Chronicler has not included a statement about the parentage of Noah's sons (see RSV, JB). This is almost certainly due to compression rather than carelessness, as the same thing happens twice more (vv. 17, 36), and is one indication that the author expects his readers to have some familiarity with his sources. Most EVV nevertheless supply *The sons of Noah*, with LXX.

7. *Rodanim,* probably Rhodes, is 'Dodanim' in Genesis 10:4, and is one of a number of small textual variations.[1] Several short notes from Genesis have been preserved (vv. 10, 12, 19), though the one about Nimrod is much abbreviated. They illustrate contemporary points of interest, but also demonstrate the extent of the Chronicler's faithfulness to his sources.

17. *The sons of Aram* is a further example of parentage omitted in MT but usually supplied in EVV (*cf.* v. 4). 'Mash' (NEB, *cf.* Gn. 10:22) is to be preferred to MT's *Meshech* (RSV, NIV, *etc.*). Expanding a name by adding a consonant (in Heb.) is unparalleled in this chapter, and MT here is probably influenced by verse 5.

iii. Shem to Abraham (1:24–27)
Cf. Genesis 11:10–32

These names are extracted from Genesis 11:10–32, and, as in verses 1–4a, ten generations are given. The Chronicler remains faithful to the bare details of his source, even though it produces an overlap with the previous section (*cf.* vv. 24–25 with vv. 17–19).

iv. Abraham (1:28–34)
1:29–31 – *cf.* Genesis 25:12–16
1: 32–33 – *cf.* Genesis 25:1–4

The Chronicler shows greater freedom with his sources in this part of the chapter than in any other section. Neither the heading (v. 28) nor the conclusion (v. 34) is directly paralleled in Genesis, and the source for the descendants of *Ishmael* (vv. 29–31) has been more extensively rearranged than usual. The section on *Keturah* (vv. 32–33) is also distinctive. It is based on Abraham's concubine rather than his son, it interrupts the order of the original genealogies, and it is not derived from a passage originally beginning with 'These are the generations of ...' (see above). All these features point to the fact that although *Abraham* (vv. 27, 28, 32, 34) is not perhaps the centre of attention in these chapters, he is still worthy of special

---

[1] Most of these variations concern the alternation of two similarly written letters, either *d* and *r*, as here (also Diphath, v. 6, NIV mg. and Gn. 10:3; Hamran, v. 41 and Gn. 36:26; Hadad, v. 50 and Gn. 36:39), or *w/o/u* and *y/i/e* (Ebal, v. 22 and Gn. 10:28; Zephi, v. 36 and Gn. 36:11; Homam, v. 39 and Gn. 36:22; Alian, v. 40 and Gn. 36:23; Shephi, v. 40 and Gn. 36:23; Pai, v. 50 and Gn. 36:39; Aliah, v. 51 and Gn. 36:40).

recognition. The extensive details about Esau and Edom (vv. 35–54) are probably also intended to show something of the blessing on Abraham's wider family.

v. Esau and Edom (1:35–54)

1:25–37 – *cf.* Genesis 36:10–14
1:38–42 – *cf.* Genesis 36:20–28
1:43–54 – *cf.* Genesis 36: 31–43

Four separate lists are combined, with *Esau* as the common denominator. Esau's descendants (vv. 35–37) are followed by their neighbours, the *sons of Seir* (vv. 38–42; *cf.* Gn. 36:9, 20), and by two lists of Edomite rulers, their *kings* (vv. 43–51a) and *chiefs* (vv. 51b–54). The unexpected extent of these names is partly explained by their relationship with Abraham, but is due even more to their being parallel with the descendants of Esau's brother *Israel* (v. 34 and chs. 2–8). Esau had indeed multiplied, though that was as nothing to the miracle that God had worked for his brother's family.

Timna (v. 36) is another case of abbreviation. She is actually *Amalek*'s mother (*cf.* v. 39; Gn. 36:12), as NIV suggests. The association of Edom (vv. 43, 51, 54) with Esau is a good example of the fluidity between individual and nation in this chapter (*cf.* also vv. 11–15). *Hadad also died* (v. 51a) is an addition to Genesis 36:40, and is probably the Chronicler's way of bringing that part of the list to a natural end.

B. The tribes of Israel (2:1 – 9:1)

Judah (2:3 – 4:23) heads the tribal genealogies, and receives more extensive treatment than any other tribe. The reason for this special prominence is to be found in the central position of *David*'s line (2:10–17; 3:1–24), which in turn arises out of the importance given to the Davidic covenant in Chronicles (1 Ch. 17, *etc.*). The line tracing God's purposes from Adam to Israel (ch. 1) is now narrowed down to the family of David. In other words, through this multitude of largely unknown names, the Chronicler points out that God's election purposes were still at work despite the vicissitudes of Judah's history (*e.g.* 2:3, 7) and the exile (*e.g.* 3:17–24).

To understand the Chronicler's method and message in this section, it must be read as a whole. The entire genealogy of Judah has a chiastic structure, that is, a framework in which the thought patterns and vocabulary of the outer and inner sections correspond with each other.[1] This pattern functions at two levels, the first of which concerns the period from Judah to Hezron, as follows:

a. Judah's five sons (2:3–4)
   b. The descendants of Judah's twin sons, Perez and Zerah (2:5–8)
      c. The descendants of Perez' son, Hezron (2:9 – 3:24)
   b_1. Further descendants of Perez (4:1–20)
a_1. Further descendants of Judah's son, Shelah (4:21–23).

A second chiasm is then developed for the sons of Hezron (2:9 – 3:24):

a. Sons of Ram, to David (2:10–17)
   b. Sons of Caleb, to Bezalel (2:18–24)
      c. Sons of Jerahmeel (2:25–33)
      c_1. Further descendants of Jerahmeel (2:34–41)
   b_1. Further descendants of Caleb (2:42–55)
a_1. Further descendants of Ram, from David (3:1–24).

The focus of the outer layer falls on the central section and on the two outer sections of the inner layer, in both cases of course pointing directly to David. This is not to divide his line artificially, as some have alleged, but to make him the watershed of his family. He thereby becomes a more important point of division than the exile, in contrast to the other tribes.

The sources for this section remain largely unknown. A few short passages concerning the earliest stages of the tribe and of David's family have been borrowed directly from other parts of the Old Testament (see the headings of each section). In addition to these and the royal line (3:1–16), lists from various periods and with differing characteristics seem to have been employed, resulting in a certain lack of smoothness. The relationship of the supplementary lists in chapter 4 to the list as a whole is not always clear, and further variation exists in the form and character of the names, which are partly personal, partly tribal, and partly geographical. Only the more important variations can be noted here, though for further

---

[1] H. G. M. Williamson, 'Sources and redaction in the Chronicler's genealogy of Judah', *JBL* 98, 1979, pp. 351–359.

refinements the larger commentaries can be consulted. Nevertheless, the details need not detract from the wider perspective which can be gained from an over-all view.

i. The sons of Israel (2:1–2)

2:1–2 – *cf.* Genesis 35:23–26

This brief list, which follows the pattern of chapter 1, is parallel with that of Esau's sons (1:35). It is a heading to chapters 2–8, not a conclusion to chapter 1, since the similar passages in 1:4, 28, 34 are all introductory in character. The Chronicler thinks on a large scale, historically, theologically, and in terms of literary design. In fact, this little passage is the chief link between the international perspective of chapter 1 and the development of the tribes of Israel. The order of names follows Genesis 35:23–26, with one exception. Dan is expected after Benjamin, and no convincing reason has been put forward for the change (*cf.* also Ex. 1:2–4). A different order is used in the following chapters.

ii. The tribe of Judah (2:3 – 4:23)

2:3b – *cf.* Genesis 38:7
2:10–12 – *cf.* Ruth 4:19–22
3:1–4a – *cf.* 2 Samuel 3:2–5
3:4b – *cf.* 2 Samuel 5:5
3:5–8 – *cf.* 2 Samuel 5:14–16

a. Judah to Hezron (2:3–8). This section, which gives the names of Judah's five sons (vv. 3–4) and the descendants of his youngest son *Zerah* (vv. 6–8), is based on the only two other genealogies of Judah in the Old Testament (Gn. 46:12; Nu. 26:19–22), both of which stop at *Hezron and Hamul* (v. 5). It highlights God's involvement in Judah's line in both judgment and election. The former is well illustrated by the abrupt ends of *Er, Onan,* and *Achar* (vv. 3, 7; *cf.* Gn. 38:6–10). Chronicles' first mention of 'the LORD' shows God's intolerance of sin even in a chosen tribe: 'Er, Judah's first-born, was wicked in the sight of the LORD, and he slew him' (v. 3, RSV = Gn. 38:7). It also reflects Chronicles' special interest in the fulfilling of God's purposes through the demotion of firstborn sons (v. 3; see further comment on 5:1–2; also 26:10). The mention of the twins *Perez and Zerah* (v. 4) hints at God's election or choice of a particular family. The unusual circumstances of their birth (v. 4; *cf.* Gn. 38:11–30) and the preservation of Perez' line signified the special workings of divine providence, through human actions that might be good, bad, or indifferent. It is notable that Chronicles faithfully records God's activity in several mixed marriages (v. 3; *cf.* also 2:12, 17, 34–35; 4:18).

According to 1 Kings 4:31, the last four of Zerah's sons (*Ethan . . . Darda/Dara*, v. 6) were famous wise men ('Ezrahite', 1 Ki. 4:31, is probably an alternative for 'son of Zerah'). *Carmi* (v. 7) is the son of *Zimri* (v. 6; *cf.* Jos. 7:1, 18), and a statement to this effect is sometimes added in EVV (*e.g.* NEB). 'Sons of Carmi' (v. 7, MT; *cf.* RSV, JB) is unexpected, since only one son is named. It is an example of a common problem in the genealogies, and ancient as well as modern translations vary (another example is the 'sons of Ethan', v. 8). The formula 'sons of . . .' was probably purely conventional, irrespective of the number of children listed. In this case, the son is a famous one, *viz.*, 'Achan' (*cf.* Jos. 7), called here *Achar* (= 'trouble'). This play on words is a deliberate development of Joshua 7:24–26, and places Achan in the same tradition as Ahab, also a 'troubler of Israel' (v. 7, NRSV, *etc.*; *cf.* 1 Ki. 18:17).

Achan was also guilty of 'unfaithfulness', a key term in Chronicles (Heb. *māʿal*) translated here as *violating* (NIV, JB, *cf.* NEB) or 'transgressed' (RSV). This word has the nuance of depriving God of his due, and is Chronicles' favourite explanation for the disaster of the exile. This example at the beginning of the tribal genealogies is analogous with the description of Saul at the beginning of the narrative section (10:13), and comparable instances occur at the end of both the genealogies (9:1) and the narrative (2 Ch. 36:14). Israel is clearly riddled with 'unfaithfulness', from their entry into the Promised Land until their destruction by the Babylonians.[1] The only real hope of recovery from this bad start to Israel's genealogies lies with David, who is the leading name in the next section.

b. The descendants of Ram (2:9–17). The entire section 2:10 – 3:24 is divided up between Hezron's three sons, *Ram* (2:10–17, 3:1–24), *Caleb* (called 'Chelubai' only in v. 9, *e.g.* RSV, JB; 2:18–24, 42–55), and *Jerahmeel* (2:25–33, 34–41), with

[1] See further Johnstone, 'Guilt', pp. 116–138.

verse 9 as a heading. Though not the eldest, Ram is placed first, since, in contrast to chapter 1, the most important son is now given priority.

Ram's importance derives from his descendant *David*, who forms the climax to this section (v. 15). Verses 10–12 are based directly on Ruth 4:19–22, with the addition of the statement about *Nahshon*'s status (v. 10; *cf.* Nu. 3:2). It is not clear why David is regarded as the *seventh* son here, but as the eighth in 1 Samuel 16:10–13; 17:12. David's *sisters* (vv. 16–17) are described as such only here, though *Zeruiah* and her three sons are well known elsewhere. The presence of an *Ishmaelite* in the family (v. 17) is another example of intermarriage (*cf.* v. 3), assuming this is a superior reading to 2 Samuel 17:25.

c. The descendants of Caleb (2:18–24). *Caleb* is a problem,

on two counts. His genealogy is in several parts (2:18–24, 42–55; 4:1–8) and the name could refer to one or two persons. In practice, the otherwise unknown Caleb son of Hezron is probably distinct from Caleb, a Kenizzite and son of Jephunneh, who is frequently said to have 'followed the LORD wholeheartedly' (*e.g.* Nu. 14:24; 32:12; Jos. 14:6, 13–14). The latter does seem to be listed separately (4:15–16), though there is some overlap in one section (2:42–50a). Mention of *Bezalel* (2:20), the Tent (or tabernacle) architect, also seems to support the existence of two Calebs. He was the great-grandson at least of Caleb son of Hezron but a contemporary of Caleb son of Jephunneh in the wilderness period. *Jerahmeel* son of Hezron, like his brother Caleb (2:9, 25, 33, 42), is otherwise unknown, apart from a brief geographical reference (1 Sa. 27:10; the 'Negev of Caleb' in 1 Sa. 30:14 is probably associated with the son of Jephunneh, since it is not far from the Hebron area).

The structure of Caleb's family tree is provided by his wives and concubines. There were at least four of them, his wives *Azubah* (vv. 18–19) and *Ephrath* (2:19, 24, 50; 4:4) who was probably his father's widow (see comment on v. 24), and his concubines *Ephah* (v. 46) and *Maacah* (v. 48). In addition, the mother of Caleb's sons in verses 42–45 is unnamed. *Jerioth* (v. 18) is more likely to have been his daughter (NEB, GNB) than yet another wife (NIV, RSV).[1]

---

[1] The singular suffix on 'her sons' (v. 18) suggests that only one wife is involved.

18–20. The first part of the genealogy is concerned with the Tent architect, *Bezalel* (*cf.* Ex. 31:2; 35:30). Though he lived in a very different period from David (v. 15), the two genealogies are juxtaposed to underline the early association between the Davidic monarchy and the Tent, in preparation for the building of the temple by David and Solomon.

21–23. The next section, about a connection between Judah and some Gileadites who lived in northern Transjordan, is unexpected. It might allude to a marriage in late patriarchal times, to David's marriage to an Aramean princess (*cf.* 1 Ch. 3:2 = 2 Sa. 3:3), or to the resettlement of some Judeans in Gilead after the exile. *Makir father of Gilead* (NEB, 'founder of') is the first occurence of a frequent formula, 'personal name, "father of" + place name'. The phrase combines genealogical and geographical data, and could reflect an interest in places well known in post-exilic times. *Havvoth Jair* (NIV, RSV, NEB) is to be preferred to 'villages of Jair' (GNB; 'Encampments', JB). It was a distinct area, comprising between thirty (Jdg. 10:4) and *sixty towns* or villages (Jos. 13:30; 1 Ki. 4:13; *cf.* v. 23).

24. Textual uncertainties here have obscured *Ashhur*'s status (*cf.* 4:5), but he is probably the son of Caleb and Ephrath (RSV, NEB, *etc.*, with LXX, Vulg.) rather than of Hezron and Abijah (NIV, as MT). 'His father' is to be preferred to *Abijah*, who is otherwise unknown.

d. The descendants of Jerahmeel (2:25–41). This section actually comprises two lists (vv. 25–33, 34–41), as indicated by the summary at the end of verse 33 and the different style in verses 36–41 in particular. None of these names is mentioned in the rest of the Old Testament, though they are twice mentioned in passing as a group (1 Sa. 27:10; 30:29). *Ahijah* (v. 25) is probably *Jerahmeel*'s first wife (v. 26) rather than his fifth son (as AV, NIV). *Ahlai* must be *Sheshan*'s daughter, if the statements about his family are meant to be harmonized (vv. 31, 34).

e. Further descendants of Caleb (2:42–55). This section continues 2:18–24. It contains at least two lists (vv. 42–50a, 50b–55), separated by the conclusion and heading in verse 50. Many names are unique, but those that can be identified contain a mixture of personal and geographical details. Several in verses 42a–50, for instance, are in the *Hebron* area (*e.g. Ziph, Mareshah*, v. 42; *Beth Zur*, v. 45), although those in verses 50b–55 seem to be scattered all over Judah. *Beth Zur* was on Judah's southern boundary after the exile, and since there are some more southerly names, this particular list is probably pre-exilic. *Hebron* (vv. 42–43) and Caleb's daughter *Acsah* (v. 49) are associated with Caleb son of Jephunneh, suggesting that the traditions of the two Calebs have become interwoven in verses 42–50a. *Mareshah* (v. 42) might be *Mesha*'s grandson (GNB, JB) or his brother (NEB, *cf.* Rudolph), or possibly Caleb's only son (RSV, *cf.* LXX). *Haroeh* (v. 52, = 'the seer') is sometimes equated with Reaiah (4:2). *The clans of scribes* (v. 55) is a possible but not a secure translation. They may be comparable with the guilds of 4:14, 21, 23, but others regard it as a gentilic expression, either 'Sophrites' (NEB, JB) or Siphrites, *i.e.* from Kiriath-Sepher (Rudolph).

f. The royal family of David (3:1–24) The Davidic line is the centrepiece of Judah's genealogy. It continues 2:10–17 and contains three distinct stages: David's own children (vv. 1–9), the kings of Israel (vv. 10–16), and the post-exilic generations (vv. 17–24). The last section is the only part of Chronicles to continue for several generations after the exile, and presumably reaches down, or nearly so, to the Chronicler's own time, though textual problems in verse 21 unfortunately make it impossible to be certain of actual dates. Interest centres on the family line as a whole rather than on any individual. Though the Chronicler clearly believed that God's promise to David (especially 1 Ch. 17:10b–14) remained effective in his own day, he did not identify any individual who might restore the kingdom to Israel. Jesus' own genealogies trace David's line through different sons of Zerubbabel, neither of whom is listed in verses 19–20 (*cf.* Mt. 1:13; Lk. 3:27).

1–8. The list of David's children has a few variants compared with 2 Samuel 3:2–5; 5:14–16. *Daniel* (v. 1) appears for 'Chileab', and *Eliphelet* (v. 6) and *Nogah* (v. 7) are additional, though the total *nine* (v. 7) suggests their inclusion is no accident. *Bathshua* (v. 6; NIV fn.) is probably an alternative pronunciation for *Bathsheba*, perhaps influenced by 2:3, though *Solomon* is described unexpectedly as her fourth son (*cf.* 2 Sa. 12:24–25).

10–16. The list of kings is a very mixed bag, and in comparison with the dynastic changes in the northern kingdom, it is a miracle that the line was preserved at all. All the Davidic kings are here, and only Athaliah, Ahab's daughter (*cf.* 2 Ki. 11), is missing. Kings' spelling of *Azariah* is used (v. 12; *cf.* 2 Ki. 15:1–7), though he appears in 2 Chronicles 26 as Uzziah (also 2 Ki. 15:13, 30: Is. 1:1; 6:1; *etc.*). Of Josiah's sons (v. 15), *Johanan* is not mentioned in Kings and may have died young, and *Shallum*, the throne name of Jehoahaz (2 Ki. 23:31–34 = 2 Ch. 36:2–4; *cf.* Je. 22:11), is described here as the youngest of the four brothers, even though he reigned before *Jehoiakim* (2 Ki. 23:35 – 24:7 = 2 Ch. 36:5–8) and *Zedekiah* (2 Ki. 24:17 – 25:7 = 2 Ch. 36:11–14). The information here cannot be reconciled with what is said about their ages in 2 Kings 23:31, 36; 24:18, and it is easiest to assume some scribal error in connection with the numbers.

The name of *Jehoiachin* (NIV, GNB; 'Jeconiah', MT and other EVV; also v. 16), the penultimate king of Judah whose release from prison raised hopes of a restoration of the Davidic monarchy (*cf.* 2 Ki. 25:27–30), introduces the final stage of the dynasty.

17–24. *Jehoiachin's* description, *the captive* (v. 17; AV, 'Assir'), involves a very minor change in MT. He is mentioned with five of his children (*cf.* vv. 17–18) in Babylonian texts of the exile as receiving regular food rations. An inscription also mentions the name *Shelomith* (v. 19). She was either a high-ranking official in Judah or the wife of such a person, and was quite possibly the same person as in Chronicles' list.[1]

Of the several textual problems in this passage, two are worthy of special mention. *Zerubbabel's* father is called *Pedaiah* here (v. 19) but *Shealtiel* (v. 18) elsewhere (Ezr. 3:2; Hg. 1:1; Mt. 1:12, *etc.*). Pedaiah may have been his real father, with fatherhood perhaps attributed to Shealtiel through a levirate marriage, or perhaps he was really Shealtiel's son but Pedaiah then became the head of the family after the former's early death. The real crux, however, concerns the number of generations underlying verse 21. There are two main possibilities; either the six names from *Pelatiah* to *Shecaniah* are more or less contemporaries, or five successive generations

---

[1] N. Avigad, *Bullae and Seals from a Post-Exilic Judean Archive*, Qedem 4 (Jerusalem: Hebrew University Press, 1976), No. 14; *cf.* H. G. M. Williamson, 'The Governors of Judah under the Persians', *TB* 39, 1988, pp. 59–82, especially pp. 69–77.

are represented by *Jeshiah* to *Shecaniah*. In favour of the former are the references (v. 22) to two sons of Shecaniah, *Shemaiah* (Ne. 3:29) and *Hattush* (Ezr. 8:2) approximately 65 to 75 years after Zerubbabel, who would therefore precede Shecaniah by two generations. Although the names are common and the over-all chronology of Ezra is disputed, this is preferable to regarding Shecaniah as the seventh generation from Zerubbabel. *Elioenai*'s sons (v. 24) are otherwise uunknown and their names seem totally forgettable to most modern readers. But for Chronicles they are the corporate incarnation of a living hope also exemplified in the names of Zerubbabel's sons (v. 20) – *Hashubah* (= 'thought about, considered'), *Ohel* (= '[God's] tent'), *Berekiah* (= Yahweh blesses'), *Hasadiah* (= 'Yahweh is love'), and *Jushab-Hesed* (= 'May love be restored').

g. Further clans of Judah (4:1–23). Several short genealogies are now listed, none of which has any parallel in the rest of the Old Testament. Some clearly supplement the information about the families of *Perez* (vv. 1–8) and *Shelah* (vv. 21–23), while others probably describe some of the smaller clans. Six sections can be discerned, *viz.* the clans of (a) *Hur* (vv. 1–4; *cf.* 2:19–20, 50b–55) and *Ashhur* (vv. 5–8; *cf.* 2:24), who were sons of Caleb and Ephrath and descendants of Perez (v. 1, *cf.* 2:4–5); (b) *Jabez* (vv. 9–10); (c) *Kelub* (vv. 11–12); (d) *Othniel* and *Caleb*, the Kenizzites (vv. 13–16); (e) other lesser-known groups (vv. 17–20); and (f) *Shelah*, son of Judah (vv. 21–23; *cf.* 2:3). By finishing with the first of Judah's sons to produce children, a sense of completeness is given to the list.

Most interest centres on a series of short notes. For example, the formula, 'father of + place name' occurs several times (vv. 3, 4, 5, 11, 12, 14, 17, 18, 19, 21), showing interest in various localities (*cf.* comment on 2:21). Other notes provide important and rare information about pre-exilic craft guilds, such as *linen workers* (v. 21) and *potters* (v. 23; *cf.* also v. 14 and 2:55), and details of another mixed marriage (vv. 17–18; *cf.* 2:3, 17, 34–35). The most fascinating note concerns the otherwise unknown *Jabez* and his effective *prayer* (vv. 9–10; there is no obvious connection with the place name in 2:55). Two of his four requests are about his physical circumstances (for enlarged *territory* and freedom from *pain* – his name sounds like the Heb. for 'pain') and two about his relationship with God (*blessing* and God's protective *hand*). The point is not simply that he prayed, but that *God granted his request*. Chronicles' inclusion of other answered prayers of a similar nature (*e.g.* for increased land, *cf.* 1 Ch. 5:20–22; 2 Ch. 20:6–12; for physical healing, *cf.* 2 Ch. 32:24) is a reminder that God still hears and answers specific prayers.

1. One expects 'Caleb' rather than *Carmi* here (*cf.* 2:9, 19).

3. Scribal error seems to underlie the start of this verse (lit., 'These are the father of Etam'). Since *Etam* is a place (v. 32; near Bethlehem, *cf.* v. 4, and Tekoa, *cf.* v. 5), the most likely solution is to supply before 'father' either 'sons of *Hur*' (GNB, Curtis and Madsen, Michaeli; *cf.* v. 4) or 'sons of *Hareph*' (Noth, Myers, *etc.*), the only son of Hur whose descendants are not listed in 2:50b–55. The usual reading of EVV (*These were the sons of Etam*) is less satisfactory.

13–15. *Othniel* was *Caleb*'s younger brother (Jos. 15:17; Jdg. 1:13), and the Kenizzites to whom they originally belonged were one of several smaller clans gradually incorporated into Judah. The last phrase in verse 15 can be read as either *The son of Elah: Kenaz* (NIV, NEB, *cf.* GNB) or as a summary, 'These are the sons of Kenaz' (Curtis and Madsen, Williamson; *cf.* vv. 4, 6, 11).

22. *Who ruled in Moab* (NIV, RSV) might be translated, 'who went to Moab to take wives' (JB, *cf.* Tg.), or better, 'who worked for Moab', continuing the occupational theme of verses 21–23.[1] 'Lehem' (RSV) is probably a place, possibly Bethlehem (so NEB; *cf.* NIV, *Jashubi Lehem*), corresponding to the places of residence of the workers in verses 21, 23.

iii. The tribe of Simeon (4:24–43)

4:24 – *cf.* Numbers 26:12–13
4:28–33 – *cf.* Joshua 19:2–18

The sections 4:24 – 5:26 and parts of chapter 7 are Chronicles' only detailed treatment of the tribes of the old northern kingdom of Israel. They offer a vignette of Israel's history from conquest (4:38–43; 5:8–10, 16) to exile (5:25–26). The Chronicler's influence is visible in the design of these passages and in the appearance of his favourite themes. The section

---

[1] *Cf.* M. Dijkstra, 'A note on 1 Chr. IV 22–23', *VT* 25, 1975, pp. 671–674; Williamson, p. 61; see also NEB.

5:20–22 in particular betrays the Chronicler's special contribution, emphasizing the value of *trust* and *prayer*, and that *the battle was God's*. He is also responsible for the important paragraph (5:1–2) which explains why Reuben does not head the tribal lists.

The Promised Land receives more emphasis here than anywhere else in chapters 1–9. Prominence is given to the ways in which individual tribes increased their inheritance (4:28–31, 39–43; 5:9–10, 16, 22, 23; *cf.* also 4:10), such as the extension of Israel's traditional northern limit of Dan (1 Ch. 21:2; 2 Ch. 30:5) to *Mount Hermon* (5:23) not far from Damascus. It is also stressed three times, however (5:6, 22, 26), that these tribes went into *exile* because they *were unfaithful* to God (5:25). The nature of their relationship with God was the decisive factor linking Israel's various experiences in the land (5:20–22, 25–26).

A variety of sources are employed, as usual. The beginnings of both the Simeonite and Reubenite lists make use of the two other main Old Testament tribal genealogies (Gn. 46; Nu. 26; *cf.* also Ex. 6:14ff.). It is also quite likely that use has been made both of military census lists (5:18, 24) and of local tribal records dealing with pasture-lands, border conflicts, *etc.* (*e.g.* 4:34–43; 5:7–10, 16).[1] Other sources (*e.g.* 5:4–6, 11–15) remain unidentified.

The tribe of Simeon, whose territory lay on Judah's southern edge, is placed here because of its close association with its larger neighbour. The list of places in verses 28–33 (based on Jos. 19:2–8; *cf.* Jos. 15:28–32) was regarded as Judean from very early times, and by *David's* time the takeover was complete (*cf.* v. 33).[2] Nevertheless, some clans retained a separate identity until at least the late eighth century (*the days of Hezekiah*, v. 41). Chronicles may have preserved this memory of Simeon's independence either because of its example of geographical expansion or because post-exilic Jews still lived in the area (*cf.* Ne. 11:26–29).

---

[1] M. D. Johnson, *The Purpose of the Biblical Genealogies* (Cambridge: Cambridge University Press, 1969), pp. 62–68.

[2] Several place-names show variation as compared with Jos. 19. The most interesting are Shaaraim (v. 31; Sharuhen, Jos. 19:6; *cf.* Shilhim, Jos. 15:32), Etam and Token (v. 32), either of which may be equivalent to Ether (*cf.* Jos. 19:7, 15:42), and Baal (v. 33, RSV, NEB) or Baalath (NIV, GNB, JB), a shortened form of Baalath Beer (Jos. 19:8).

25–27. *Shaul*'s line is the only one continued for several generations. It may have been the largest clan in the tribe or its Canaanite ancestry was perhaps of special interest (*cf.* Gn. 46:10; Ex. 6:15).

34–43. The list of clan leaders (vv. 34–38) relates to the dual expansions to the west (vv. 39–41) and the south-east (vv. 42–43). Westward, their destination was the area of either *Gedor* (v. 39, NIV, RSV, NEB), possibly the same as Geder (Jos. 12:13), or 'Gerar' (GNB, JB, *cf.* LXX), the well-known town midway between Gaza and Beersheba. The description of the *land* uses familiar post-exilic language (*cf.* Ne. 9:25, 35), but it is also reminiscent of the conquest (*cf. e.g.* Ex. 3:8), as in the statement that they *completely destroyed* them (v. 41, NIV; *cf.* JB, 'put them under a ban).' Everything associated with idolatrous worship, including the defeated population, had to be destroyed, but the Israelites would gain nothing for themselves (*cf.* Dt. 7:2; 20:17). The *Hamites* (vv. 40–41),[1] are presumably one of the Philistine or Canaanite peoples of 1:11–16, though such a wide-ranging term is unexpected. The *Meunites* (v. 41), associated in the Old Testament with the Philistines (2 Ch. 26:7) and with Mount Seir (2 Ch. 20:1, 10, 22), may be located in the southern Negev.[2] 'Mount Seir' (v. 43, RSV) could also be in the same area, though its traditional association with Edom would place it somewhere to the south and/or east of the Dead Sea. The *Amalekites* (v. 43) were a nomadic group in the Negev and Sinai area, who were defeated by both Saul (1 Sa. 15:7–8) and David (1 Sa. 30:1–18; 2 Sa. 8:12 = 1 Ch. 18:11).

iv. The Transjordanian tribes (5:1–26)

5:3 – *cf.* Numbers 26:5–6; Exodus 6:14
5:26b – *cf.* 2 Kings 17:6b; 18:11b

a. The tribe of Reuben (5:1–10). The Transjordanian tribes are listed next, *viz.* Reuben (vv. 1–10), Gad (vv. 11–17), and the half tribe of Manasseh (vv. 23–24).

1–2. A special note explains why *Reuben* did not head the list of tribes, although *he was the firstborn* (v. 1; *cf.* Gn. 29:31–32). Inheritance customs in the ancient Near East were strictly observed, and a birthright was forfeited only for serious

[1] Reading 'people [lit. tents] of Ham' (*cf.* NIV, NEB) for MT's 'their tents' (*e.g.* RSV) in v. 41.
[2] *Cf.* Williamson, pp. 293–294.

offences against one's parents. Reuben's crime was certainly serious, since going to bed with his father's concubine (*cf.* Gn. 35:22; 49:3–4) was in effect a claim to his father's property (*cf.* 2 Sa. 16:20–22; 1 Ki. 2:13–25).[1] Personal details are less important, however, than the consequences for the tribes. Chronicles has interpreted Genesis 48:5 in the light of a law giving a double share to the firstborn (Dt. 21:15–17), by assuming that the status of Ephraim and Manasseh as Jacob's full sons was equivalent to their father's double share (*the sons of Joseph*, v. 1). Strictly speaking, this goes beyond Genesis 48, which mentions adoption and the transfer of the firstborn's blessing (*cf.* v. 2, LXX), but it is perfectly reasonable in view of the widespread practice of the firstborn's double share. In this way, Chronicles underlines that the northern tribes had not lost their ancient privileges (*cf.* 2 Ch. 28:5–15; 30:1–12), which is hardly a sign of an anti-Samaritan bias! *Judah* therefore attained a leading position, as the *strongest* tribe from whom was descended a *ruler* (NIV, NEB, GNB) or 'prince' (RSV, JB), *i.e.* David (*cf.* Gn. 49:8–10). This seems to be the reason Judah is placed first in the genealogy.[2] Chronicles' special interest in the demotion of firstborn sons (*cf.* also 1 Ch. 2:3; 26:10) may be intended to emphasize that status before God was a matter of privilege rather than right. The same principle was also applicable to Israel as God's firstborn son (*cf.* Ex. 4:22; Je. 31:9).

3–10. The Reubenites' history is divided into at least three periods (vv. 3–6, 7–9, 10). *Beerah* (v. 6) seems to represent the end of the tribe's existence when they were exiled by Tiglath-pileser III (*Tilgath-pilneser*, here and 2 Ch. 28:20), probably in 733 BC.[3] The whole area of Israelite Transjordan became the Assyrian province of Gal'azu, *i.e.*, Gilead (= 'the land beyond

---

[1] For a fuller discussion and other examples, see M. J. Selman, 'Comparative customs and the patriarchal age', in A. R. Millard and D. J. Wiseman (eds.), *Essays on the Patriarchal Narratives* (Leicester: IVP, 1981), pp. 113–114, 126.

[2] The attempt of REB and NEB, following Rudolph, to attribute the birthright to Judah is seriously flawed. Although it is partly based on LXX, it involves an extremely dubious addition in v. 2 ('his, not') and a (disguised) contradiction at the end of v. 1. Further, the OT nowhere else regards Judah as the possessor of the birthright, especially as he was Israel's fourth son.

[3] *Cf.* H. Donner, in J. H. Hayes and J. M. Miller (eds.), *Israelite and Judean History* (London: SCM Press, 1977), pp. 425–432. This event is generally associated with the Assyrian's Philistine campaign in 734 BC, rather than his campaign against Damascus in 733–732 BC.

the Jordan', Is. 9:1, RSV; see also 2 Ki. 15:29).[1] Verses 7–10 describe Reubenite expansion in earlier times. *Aroer, Nebo, and Baal-meon* (v. 8) were recaptured from Ahab by Mesha king of Moab in the second half of the ninth century BC (*cf.* Nu. 32:3, 38; Jos. 13:16–17). The *Hagrites* (v. 10, *cf.* vv. 19–21), who were defeated in Saul's time in the eleventh century BC, were associated both with the Arabs (*cf.* Hagar) and the Moabites (Ps. 83:6).

b. The tribe of Gad (5:11–22). For the Gadites (vv. 11–17) and the half tribe of Manasseh (vv. 23–24; *cf.* 4:24; 5:3), Chronicles has dispensed with the usual introductory material from Genesis 46 and Numbers 26 and continued with the same sources as for Simeon and Reuben.

11–17. The Gadites' territory (vv. 11, 16) was in *Bashan*, an area renowned for its fertility and whose eastern border extended to *Salecah* (v. 11; *cf.* Dt. 3:10; Jos. 13:11). *Sharon* (v. 16) is not the well-known coastal plain, but a place mentioned on the Moabite Stone (line 13). The chronological data (v. 17) surprisingly include *Jotham king of Judah* as well as *Jeroboam* II of Israel. This could be explained by the compiling of separate records for each kingdom, or by an Israelite event being synchronized with a Davidic king, or it could be derived from 'a synchronistic chronicle written in two columns' (Mettinger).[2]

18–21. These verses are a summary dealing with expansion and conquest by the two-and-a-half tribes. Though no date is given for the number of *trained* soldiers (v. 18), the figures may refer to the conflict with the *Hagrites* (vv. 19–21; *cf.* v. 10). The tribes' opponents were Arab groups (v. 19; *cf.* Gn. 25:15; *Jetur* = Iturea, Lk. 3:1). However, the paragraph's primary concern is to explain why the tribes were successful, underlining the spiritual reasons as much as the military ones. These are summarized in a phrase typical of Chronicles, *the battle was God's* (v. 22, NIV; *cf.* 2 Ch. 20:15, 25:8; 32:8). The three supporting ideas in verse 20 are found throughout Chronicles: (God's) *help* (*cf.* 1 Ch. 12:19; 15:26; 2 Ch. 25:8; 32:8), answered *prayer* in battle (*cf.* 2 Ch. 14:11–15; 20:5–30; 32:20–21) and *trust* in God (*cf.* 2 Ch. 32:10). The causes of the

---

[1] *Cf. ANET*, p. 283.
[2] T. N. D. Mettinger, *Solomonic State Officials* (Lund: Gleerup, 1971), p. 39.

exile, however, were a different matter altogether (*cf.* vv. 6, 25–26).

c. The half tribe of Manasseh (5:23–26). Like the previous section, this paragraph falls into two, part relating to the individual tribe (vv. 23–24, *cf.* vv. 11–17), and part to the two-and-a-half tribes collectively (vv. 25–26, *cf.* vv. 18–22).

23–24. Brief geographical and genealogical details are given for the eastern part of Manasseh. They lived between the boundary with Gad (*Bashan*, *cf.* v. 11) and *Mount Hermon* or *Senir* (*cf.* Dt. 3:9), though LXX (and NEB) extends the northern limit to Lebanon. *Baal Hermon* (only here) may be the site of Caesarea Philippi (so Rudolph). As with the other Transjordanian tribes, the emphasis falls on their extent and large numbers (v, 23, *cf.* 4:38; 5:9, 10, 16).

25–26. The final paragraph provides reasons for the *exile* of the northern tribes in general and the Transjordan tribes in particular. It follows Chronicles' typical practice of quoting earlier biblical material, in this case using 2 Kings 17:7–23 as a general background and selecting specific information from 2 Kings 15:19, 29; 17:6; 18:11. But more importantly, it follows almost exactly the structure of the explanation of Judah's exile in 2 Chronicles 36:14–20, occasionally employing even the same wording. The same four essential elements are found in both passages. (a) Israel and Judah were *unfaithful to God* (*cf.* 2 Ch. 36:14; see note on 1 Ch. 2:7 and *cf.* 9:1); (b) they were especially condemned for their idolatry (*cf.* 2 Ch. 36:14); (c) God sent a foreign army to punish his people (*cf.* 2 Ch. 36:17); and (d) they went into exile (*cf.* 2 Ch. 36:18–20).[1]

The experience of exile was fundamentally the same for both kingdoms in origin, execution, and consequence. *God stirred up the spirit* (NIV, RSV) is a typical post-exilic expression for a new divine initiative in human affairs (*cf.* 2 Ch. 21:16; Ezr. 1:1; Hg. 1:14). *Pul* is another name for Tiglath-pileser III, found in both 2 Kings 15:19 and the Babylonian Chronicle ('Pulu'). *Hara*, which is not in Kings or elsewhere in the Old Testament, may be an error for 'the cities (MT) /mountains (LXX) of the Medes' in 2 Kings 17:6; 18:11 (Curtis and Madsen), or a corruption of 'and the river of' (Rudolph). *To this day*

---

[1] This makes it unlikely that vv. 23–26 are a later addition (*contra* Williamson).

in this case is an addition to Kings, and presumably refers to the Chronicler's own time, but in other places (*e.g.* 4:41, 43) it has been carried over from his sources and relates to a variety of earlier dates.

v. The tribe of Levi (6:1–81)

6:1–4 – *cf.* Exodus 6:16–25
6:16–19 – *cf.* Numbers 3:17–20; 6:16–19
6:54–81 – *cf.* Joshua 21:4–40

Levi stands at the centre of the tribal genealogies. The tribe's importance is indicated by its position and by the amount of space devoted to it – with Judah (2:1 – 4:23) and Benjamin (7:6–12; 8:1–40), it dominates the genealogies. The chapter divides into two: (a) genealogies of the Aaronite priests and other Levites (vv. 1–53); (b) a list of the Levites' settlements (vv. 54–81).

Both sections deal with the priests separately from the rest of the Levites. Two priestly genealogies (vv. 1–15, 49–53) bracket two lists of Levites (vv. 16–30, 31–48), which are then followed by two settlement lists (vv. 54–60 and vv. 61–81). Unusually in Chronicles, the priests seem to have greater priority than the Levites. Only the priestly line is extended as far as the exile (vv. 1–15), and of course only they enjoyed the privilege of entering the *Most Holy Place* (v. 49) to make *atonement* (v. 49, RSV, NIV). In verses 54–81, the material has been rearranged so that the priests are dealt with first (vv. 54–60 = Jos. 21:10–19).

Two notable parallels occur in the lines of Aaron and David (*cf.* 2:10–17; 3:1–16). Only these two families out of all the tribal lists are traced from the patriarchs to the exile (2:10–17; 3:1–24; 6:1–15), indicating that they form the basis of Israel's future survival. Also, both lines follow immediately upon examples of Israelite 'unfaithfulness' which resulted in national disaster (2:7; 5:25; *cf.* 6:15; 9:1). Judah and Levi therefore seem to be the means through which even covenant-breaking sins could be atoned for (6:49; *cf.* 2 Ch. 36:22–23). Chapter 6 underlines the point by repeated reminders of Solomon's temple (vv. 10, 32, 53), which was a visible sign of God's desire to forgive sins (2 Ch. 7:14–16).

a. The Aaronite high priests (6:1–15; MT, 5:27–41).

Although the high-priestly ancestors of *Jehozadak* (vv. 14–15) are traced back to *Levi* himself (v. 1), this is not a complete list of Israel's high priests. Eli and his descendants are not included (*cf.* 1 Sa. 2:27–36; 1 Ki. 2:27), nor are several later high priests (*e.g.* Jehoiada, 2 Ki. 11–12; a third Azariah, *cf.* vv. 9–10 and 2 Ch. 26:20; Uriah, 2 Ki. 16:11ff.; and a fourth Azariah, 2 Ch. 31:10). Although gaps were normally left in ancient genealogies, it has often been suggested that this list is an artificial composition, centred around *Azariah* who *served as priest in the temple Solomon built* (v. 10; this note should probably refer to the Azariah in v. 9, as Zadok was high priest at the start of Solomon's reign, 1 Ki. 1:38; 2:35; *cf.* vv. 8, 53). This view lacks conviction, however, since, even by making Azariah of verse 9 the turning-point, the twelve generations from Aaron to Azariah cannot match the ten from Azariah to Jehozadak. Scholars have tried to supply a further name (*e.g.* Jehoiada (Ackroyd) or Joshua (Michaeli) in an attempt to make a more regular pattern, but there is no unanimity.

The six generations from *Levi* to *Phinehas* (vv. 1–4) are extracted from Exodus 6:16–25 (*cf.* also Gn. 46:11; Nu. 3:17–19; 26:57–61; for *Miriam*, *cf.* Nu. 26:59). They differ in form from the rest of the list in that names of brothers (and one sister!) are given, whereas what follows (vv. 5–14) is a single vertical line of the family of *Zadok* (v. 8; *cf.* Ezk. 40:46; 44:15; 43:19). It is often alleged that Zadok's descent from Aaron is artificial, but in fact, apart from the names of his father Ahitub (2 Sa. 8:17 = 1 Ch. 18:16), his son Ahimaaz (2 Sa. 15:36; 18:19, 27) and his grandson Azariah (*cf.* 1 Ki. 4:2), we know nothing about his family tree apart from the information provided in Chronicles (*cf.* v. 53; 24:3). Repetition of names (*e.g.* 8, 12) is no evidence against authenticity, and is not at all surprising in a family with a strong sense of history and tradition. The real problem is a lack of external verification, so it is arbitrary to conclude that Chronicles is confused. Although the list is incomplete, other evidence suggests that the order here is accurate. Ezra's genealogy, for example, follows the order of Aaron to Meraioth (vv. 3–6) and Azariah to Seraiah (vv. 11–14) exactly (*cf.* also 1 Ch. 9:10–11; Ne. 11:10–11). Several names in the list are known elsewhere in the Old Testament, *viz.* *Azariah* (v. 9; *cf.* 1 Ki. 4:2), *Amariah* (v. 11; *cf.* 2 Ch. 19:11), *Hilkiah* (v. 13, *cf.* 2 Ki. 22:4ff.), *Seraiah* (v. 14; *cf.* 2 Ki. 25:18; Ne. 11:11), and *Jehozadak* (vv. 14–15; *cf.* Hg. 1:1, *etc.*).

b. The Levites' genealogy (6:16–30; MT, 6:1–15). Although this list begins in almost exactly the same way as verses 1–15 ('Gershom', vv. 16, 17, *etc.* [REB, NEB, NRSV, RSV], is Chronicles' usual spelling for the more familiar Gershon, v. 1, Ex. 6:16; Nu. 3:17), it leads into a different subject, *viz.* the three main Levitical divisions of the sons of *Gershon* (vv. 20–21), *Kohath* (vv. 22–28), and *Merari* (vv. 29–30). The beginning (vv. 16–19) is determined by Chronicles' source (Nu. 3:17–20), and is in no sense a duplicate of the previous list. Seven generations are given both for the Gershonites and the Merarites, and all three lines seem to end at the time of David, as indicated by *Samuel*'s sons (v. 28; *cf.* 2 Sa. 8:2) and *Asaiah* (v. 30; *cf.* 15:6).

The Kohathites present more of a problem, however. *Amminadab*, named as Kohath's son (v. 22), is never mentioned elsewhere (*cf.* vv. 2, 18; Ex. 6:18; Nu. 3:19; 1 Ch. 23:12). Since this makes it unlikely that he was a fifth son, four alternatives remain: (i) he was Aaron's father-in-law (*cf.* Ex. 6:23), (ii) he was a grandson or later descendant, (iii) this is another name for Izhar (*cf.* vv. 18, 38), or (iv) another name for Amram (*cf.* v. 18). The main ground for the last view is a hypothesis that each line is represented through firstborn sons, but this is unproven. In fact, comparison with Heman's family suggests he was equivalent to Izhar (*cf.* v. 38).

The Kohathite line is also unusually long and complex. The problem seems to be solved by the assumption of horizontal lines occurring in verses 22–23 (*Assir* to *Ebiasaph*, *cf.* Ex. 6:24), verse 25 (*Ahimoth*, = 'brother of death'!, should be Mahath, *cf.* v. 35), and verse 28 (EVV rightly add *Joel*, *cf.* 2 Sa. 8:2), and by the practice of resuming a vertical line by repeating a name. For example, MT has five Elkanahs (four in EVV), though there are probably only two or three (those in vv. 25–26 could be identical).[1] The main list therefore should probably look like the diagram below.

Interestingly, this also produced seven generations, as with the Gershonites and Merarites.

Samuel's genealogy has been added to this basic tree (vv. 26–28; beginning with *Elkanah his son*), raising the further problem that Samuel's father is also an Ephraimite (1 Sa. 1:1). There are two possible solutions. Either the family has been

---

[1] A. Lefèvre, 'Note d'exégèse sur les généalogies des Qohatites', *Recherches de Sciences Religieuses* 37, 1950, pp. 287–292; *cf.* M. D. Johnson, *The Purpose of the Biblical Genealogies* (Cambridge: Cambridge University Press, 1969), pp. 71–73.

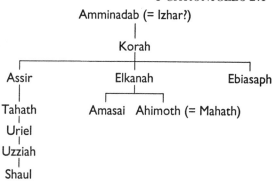

grafted on because Heman (v. 33) was regarded as a Levite, or 'Ephraimite' refers to the locality in which Elkanah lived rather than his family descent. In favour of the latter is the laxity with which Levites were treated in the Judges period, and Samuel's mother's desire to present him to the Lord (*cf.* 1 Sa. 1:22) is less surprising if Samuel had genuine Levite ancestry. Samuel's line has been included because of its intrinsic interest, and particularly as a result of their relationship with Heman, the musician (vv. 33–38).

c. The Levitical musicians' genealogy (6:31–48; MT, 6:16–33). This paragraph summarizes the Levites' functions (*cf.* 1 Ch. 23–26). Basically they were *in charge of the music* (v. 31, *cf.* v. 32; 'singing', JB, or 'the service of song', RSV, is too limited) and with the *duties of the tabernacle* (v. 48). 'After the ark rested' (v. 31, RSV), the musicians were divided between the ark in Jerusalem and the *Tent of Meeting* (v. 32) in Gibeon (*cf.* 16:4–6, 41–42). Their work is characterized as the 'service' (NRSV, RSV; *duties* NIV) *of the house of God* (v. 48; *cf.* 23:28, 32; 25:6; v. 32, *ministered*). No distinction was made between the various forms of service, for each received its value as worship offered to God.

The genealogies are those of the three musical leaders appointed by David, *viz.* *Heman*, a Kohathite (vv. 33–38), *Asaph*, a Gershonite (vv. 39–43), and *Ethan*, a Merarite (vv. 44–47). The arrangement is somewhat different from what we know of post-exilic Israel, where Hemanites do not appear

111

(Ezr. 2:41 = Ne. 7:44; Ne. 11:17), and nothing in these lists requires a date later than David (see comments on vv. 20–30, 50–53, and on 1 Ch. 23–26). The Hemanite genealogy is basically the same as verses 22–28, except that all the names are placed in one vertical line. Throughout Chronicles' genealogies, 'son' can have the sense of 'descendant', but here it must be widened to 'relative'. Attempts have been made to turn the Asaphites into descendants of 'Shimei' (*cf.* v. 17; by reversing *Jahath* (v. 43) and *Shimei* (v. 42), by omitting Jahath, or by adding another Shimei), in order to derive each line from each family's second son by analogy with lines descended from the first son in verses 20–30 (*e.g.* Williamson). But this is too precise and hypothetical from the evidence available.

d. The tasks of the Aaronite high priests (6:49–53; MT, 6:34–38). This paragraph ties in with the high priests' genealogy (vv. 1–15). By ending this shortened version (vv. 50–53) with *Ahimaaz*, a contemporary of Solomon, attention is drawn to the temple (*cf.* 1 Ch. 21–29; 2 Ch. 2–7) as the divinely given means for carrying out the priestly tasks described in verse 49. Two aspects of the priests' sacrificial role are mentioned, *viz.* to be responsible for the *offerings* (RSV, NIV; 'sacrifices', NEB) of the *Most Holy Place* (RSV, NIV, GNB; 'most holy things', JB), and 'to make atonement' (RSV, *cf.* NIV). Although all priests were involved in these activities, Chronicles appears to be thinking especially of the ministry of the high priest on the Day of Atonement (Lv. 16:11–17).

e. The settlements of the Levites (6:54–81; MT, 6:39–66). A rearranged and slightly summarized version of Joshua 21 indicates that, as representatives of all Israel, the Levites were to be settled throughout the Promised Land. If this list represents historical reality, it is most likely to have originated in the Davidic–Solomonic period when many Canaanite towns were first incorporated into Israel, but it is more probable that it paints an idealistic picture which may never have been completed.[1] The main change from Joshua 21 is that the *descendants of Aaron* have been brought forward (vv. 54–60; *cf.* Jos.

---

[1] For a discussion of this issue and a defence of Albright's view that the list is an historical record from David's time, *cf.* C. Hauer, 'David and the Levites', *JSOT* 23, 1982, pp. 33–54.

21:10–19), re-emphasizing the central importance of the priestly line.

The structure is as follows:

vv. 54–60: Aaronites from the *Kohathite* clans;
vv. 61–63: Summary of individual Levite clans
            (*cf.* vv. 66–81);
vv. 64–65: General summary (v. 65 refers to the Aaronites,
            cf. Jos. 21:4, 9);
vv. 66–70: *Rest* of the *Kohathite* clans (*cf.* v. 61);
vv. 71–76: *Gershonites* (*cf.* v. 62);
vv. 77–81: *Merarites* (*cf.* v. 63).

There are some minor variations from Joshua 21, and Chronicles occasionally seems to be using a different text base (*e.g.* vv. 77–78; *cf.* Jos. 21:34–36). Sometimes, Chronicles' reading is superior, as in verse 7 (*Bileam* [MT] or '*Ibleam*' [VSS] for Gath-rimmon, Jos. 21:25, *cf.* v. 24), and possibly in verse 59 (*Ashan* for Ain, Jos. 21:16). Conversely, *Juttah* (v. 59; *cf.* Jos. 21:16), *Gibeon* (v. 60; *cf.* Jos. 21:17), Eltekeh (v. 69; *cf.* Jos. 21:23) and Gibbethon (v. 69; *cf.* Jos. 21:23) have probably been accidentally omitted from MT, while verse 61 should read 'clans of the tribes of Ephraim, Dan, and half Manasseh' instead of the confusion of many EVV (and MT; *cf.* Jos. 21:5). As part of his summarizing technique, the Chronicler has also not identified *Golan* (v. 71), *Kedesh* (v. 76), *Bezer* (v. 78), and *Ramoth* (v. 80) as cities of refuge (*cf.* vv. 57, 67; Jos. 21:13, *etc.*; Nu. 35:9–34; Jos. 20:1–9).

vi. The West Jordan tribes (7:1–40)

7:1 – *cf.* Genesis 46:13; Numbers 26:23–24
7:13 – *cf.* Genesis 46:24–25a; Numbers 26:48–49
7:30–31a – *cf.* Genesis 46:17; Numbers 26:44–46

These six or seven tribes are treated quite briefly in contrast to the treatment given to Levi (ch. 6). All apart from Benjamin belonged to the old northern kingdom. As in chapter 5, attention is drawn to the history and geography of those parts of the Promised Land which in the Chronicler's day were no longer Israelite. Perhaps influenced by prophecies such as Ezekiel 37:15–28, Chronicles retained a sense of all the tribes of Israel united together. Later in the book, united action also appears in the support for David's kingship (1 Ch. 12) and the preparations for Solomon's temple (1 Ch. 27). It appears that the Chronicler's hopes for future unity depended on Israel's

113

accepting God's purposes for David's line and the centrality of temple worship (*cf.* 2 Ch. 30).

The records available in Jerusalem for those tribes in the distant north of the old kingdom of Israel were probably rather sketchy. In some cases (Issachar, Naphtali, Asher), Chronicles' account is clearly based on earlier biblical material in Genesis 46 and Numbers 26, but for other tribes (Benjamin, Dan, Manasseh, Ephraim) even this foundation was not used, and one can only make an informed guess as to the exact sources. Geographical information of the type frequent in chapters 2–6 is provided only for the Joseph tribes (vv. 28–29), and some use has clearly been made of military census material.

a. The tribe of Issachar (7:1–5). The four basic divisions (v. 1) follow Genesis 46:13, Numbers 26:23–24 very closely, but after that only the descendants of *Tola* are given. Some of these names reappear in Judges 10:1, but that verse merely testifies to the continuing popularity of the names of the tribe's ancestors. Verses 2–5 seem to be taken from a military census in *David's* reign (v. 2; *cf.* 4:31), either the ill-fated enterprise of 2 Samuel 24 = 1 Chronicles 21 (*cf.* 1 Ch. 27:23–24) or a count of the soldiers who joined David at Hebron (*cf.* 1 Ch. 12:23–37). Issachar's leader under David, Omri son of Michael (1 Ch. 27:18), could also be related to the *Michael* of verse 3. This reference to David suggests that the tribal lists are intended to point to him as the person who really united Israel. The list is obviously incomplete, since the total in verse 5 is more than the sum of those in verses 2 and 4. The number *five* (v. 3) must include *Izrahiah* as well as his four sons. Their family seems to have been at least one of the largest in Israel (*cf.* the figures in 5:18; 7:2, 7, 9, 11, 40) – hence the note, *they had many wives and children* (v. 4).

b. The tribe of Benjamin (7:6–12a). These Benjaminite names are probably taken from the same military census list as verses 1–5 (*cf.* the repeated numbers of *fighting men*), with only minimal contact with Genesis 46:21; Numbers 26:38–40. If that is so, they are probably of Davidic origin, and are of a different character from the geographical data about Benjamin and the Saulide genealogy in chapter 8. If the census was based on David's Hebron assembly, most Benjaminites were then still loyal to Saul's house (*cf.* 1 Ch. 12:29), so explaining the small number of Benjaminite clans here as compared with the earlier texts. The genealogy is regular in structure, listing the descendants of *Bela* (v. 7), *Beker* (vv. 8–9), and *Jediael* (vv. 10–11, unknown elsewhere) in the order of verse 6. The *Shuppites and Huppites* (v. 12) or 'Shuppim and Huppim' (RSV, *cf.* GNB), unnecessarily omitted by REB, NEB, appear in slightly different forms in Genesis 46:21; Numbers 26:39, and may also be the same as Shephuphan and Huram in 1 Chronicles 8:5.

c. The tribe of Dan (?) (7:12b). Most commentators recognize the existence of a very brief statement about Dan here (REB, NEB, GNB). In favour of this are that Dan follows Benjamin in both Genesis 46 and Numbers 26, that *the descendants of Bilhah* (v. 13) implies another tribe besides Naphtali, and that 'Hushim' (*Hushites*, NIV) is the only son of Dan in Genesis 46:23 (*cf.* Shuham, Nu. 26:42). Corrections to the text to support this, following Klostermann (1898), are neither essential nor convincing, *viz.* changing *the descendants of Ir* (NIV, *cf.* RSV, JB) into 'the sons of Dan' (NEB, *cf.* GNB), and *the descendants of Aher* (NIV, *cf.* RSV) into 'his son, one' (Myers, Rudolph, *cf.* GNB). The omission of Dan (and in 6:61, 69) is more likely to be the result of an accident in transmission than a deliberate snub against this northernmost tribe (*cf.* especially its appearance in 2:2; also 12:35; 27:22).[1]

d. The tribe of Naphtali (7:13). The four main clans of Naphtali appear exactly as in Genesis 46:24; Numbers 46:48–49, with the exception of *Shallum* (NIV fn.) for Shillem. Their neighbour Zebulun is excluded altogether, though on the basis of the order in the earlier texts, it might be expected after Issachar. *Bilhah* was one of Jacob's concubines (*cf.* Gn. 46:25).

e. The half tribe of Manasseh (7:14–19). The genealogy of Manasseh is in some disarray, and can be reconstructed only with the help of Numbers 26:29–33 and Joshua 17:1–2 (see also 2:21–23; 5:23–26). Even then, the relationship between

---

[1] For v. 12b as referring to Benjaminites, *cf.* H. G. M. Williamson, 'A note on 1 Chronicles VII 12', *VT* 23, 1973, pp. 375–379.

Makir the father of Gilead (vv. 14–17) and the other clans remains unclear. *Asriel's* (v. 14) ancestor was apparently one of Gilead's descendants (Nu. 26:31), but the real interest here is in his foreign mother (or wife?). Such mixed marriages (*cf.* 2:3, 35; 3:2) were outlawed by Ezra and Nehemiah. *Maacah* appears to be Makir's wife (v. 16) and sister (v. 15), but 'sister' probably has the sense of relative rather than anything more specific (the same may also be true of *Hammoleketh*, v. 18). *The Huppites and Shuppites* (v. 15, *cf.* v. 12) are more likely to have been Maacah's relatives (NIV) rather than Makir's sons (RSV GNB, JB), since these tribes are not attributed to Manasseh elsewhere. *Zelophehad* (v. 15), a descendant of Hepher (Nu. 26:33; 27:1–11; Jos. 17:3–4), and *Shemida* (v. 19) were further clans within the tribe. *These were the sons of Gilead ...* (v. 17b) looks very much like a concluding sentence. It could refer either to verses 16–17 or to the whole tribe up to that point. In either case, verses 18–19 seem to be a supplement.

f. The tribe of Ephraim (7:20–29). 20–27. This is a genealogy in two parts (20–21a, 25–27), and an historical note (21b–24). The first part of the genealogy has a design unique to Chronicles, in which brothers (*Shuthelah, Bered, Tahath, cf.* Nu. 26:35) are placed in a vertical relationship (*cf.* the Kohathite genealogies in 6:22–28, 33–38). Whether this applies elsewhere in this genealogy, it is now impossible to say. The second part gives the ancestry of *Joshua* (v. 27). Although mentioned only here in Chronicles, his name is consistent with the genealogies' emphasis on the conquest and occupation of the Promised Land (*e.g.* 4:38–43; 5:8–10, 18–22; 6:54–81) and on the subsequent completion of the task by David (*e.g.* 13:5; 17:9–10; 18–20).[1]

The historical note probably also refers to the period of the conquest or to some later incident in the settlement of Canaan. This kind of date is preferable to one in patriarchal times for two reasons: *went down* (v. 21) is inappropriate for a journey from Egypt to Canaan, and the building of the two *Beth Horons* (v. 24) is a natural activity for a clan already resident in the area. *Gath* (v. 21) may be Gittaim rather than the famous Philistine city (*cf.* 2 Sa. 4:3), since the latter was nearer to Beth

---

[1] For further discussion of this genealogy, *cf.* N. Na'aman, 'Sources and redaction in the Chronicler's genealogies of Asher and Ephraim', *JSOT* 49, 1991, pp. 99–111, especially pp. 105–111.

Horon, but an Ephraimite raid on either locality is quite feasible. *Ezer and Elead* (v. 21) are of uncertain relationship with the genealogies, while *Ephraim* (v. 22) on our interpretation must be a later descendant of Joseph's son. *Beriah*'s name (v. 23) is associated with the similarly sounding Heb. word for 'disaster' (NEB), 'trouble' (GNB) or 'misfortune' (NIV, JB).

28–29. The geographical details relate to both Ephraim and Manasseh, as indicated by *the descendants of Joseph*. Although the material is loosely based on parts of Joshua 16–17, the inclusion of former Canaanite cities like *Gezer* and *Megiddo* implies their submission to Israelite sovereignty under David.

g. The tribe of Asher (7:30–40). These names are based on a military census list (*cf*. v. 40), combined with the basic clan names (v. 30) from Genesis 46:17 and Numbers 26:44–46, and, as with Issachar, only one clan (*Beriah*) is followed through. The genealogy has several symmetrical patterns, and is structured around two descendants who each had four descendants, *viz. Heber* (v. 32) and his offspring *Helem* (v. 35). Since Helem is probably identical with *Hotham* (v. 32), and *Shomer* (v. 32) with 'Shemer' (v. 34, RSV), descendants of each of Heber's sons occur in verses 33–35. The first two each had three sons, assuming *Ahi* (v. 34, NIV, NEB) is really 'his brother' (GNB, RSV). Further descendants of Helem occur in verses 36–39, possibly in a regular pattern based on the names in verse 35. *Zophah* clearly recurs in verse 36, and the same may apply to *Imna/Imra* (v. 36), *Shelesh/Shilshah* (v. 37), and *Amal/Ulla* (v. 39). *Ithran* (v. 37) also appears to be the same as *Jether* (v. 38). Some of the names seem to be connected with the southern parts of Mount Ephraim, in the area where Saul's asses went missing (*cf*. 1 Sa. 9:4–5). This may well explain the inclusion of Asher after Ephraim (the order is different in 1 Ch. 2:1–2), but its significance for a tribe that was otherwise located in western Galilee remains unclear.[1]

vii. The tribe of Benjamin (8:1–40)
8:28–38 – *cf*. 1 Chronicles 9:34–44

Benjamin has already been dealt with in 7:6–12a, so why the apparent repetition? In fact, the two lists differ in character

---

[1] See further D. Edelman, 'The Asherite genealogy in 1 Chronicles 7:3–40', *Biblical Research* 33, 1988, pp. 13–23; N. Na'aman, *art. cit.*, pp. 100–105, 109–111.

and purpose, and there is little overlap. The military census which lies behind 7:1–40, for example, is not evident here. One suggestion for allocating extra space to Benjamin is that it was, albeit briefly, a royal tribe,[1] but an interest in tribal geography is more likely to be the key to this chapter's inclusion. It is concerned mainly with Benjaminite settlements, especially Jerusalem (vv. 28, 32), but also Geba (v. 6), Ono and Lod (v. 12), Aijalon (v. 13), Gibeon (v. 29), and even Moab (v. 8). Benjamin's last position in the tribal lists is paralleled by the account of the first tribe, Judah, which also emphasizes tribal geography (*cf.* 2:42–55; 4:1–23). In fact, 'Judah and Benjamin' are frequently mentioned together in Chronicles, and Benjamin very rarely appears on its own, either in Chronicles (*cf. e.g.* 2 Ch. 11:1ff.; 14:8; 15:2ff.; 31:1) or in Ezra–Nehemiah (*cf. e.g.* Ezr. 1:5; 4:1; Ne. 11:4–9). Together they formed first the southern kingdom of Judah and then the post-exilic community. Benjamin's appearance here, therefore, is a sign of its partnership with Judah in preserving Israel's identity and traditions. In particular, the antiquity of Benjamin's claim to its tribal territory must have been a real source of encouragement for Chronicles' readers who lived in the same area (*cf.* 9:2ff.). The land mattered, because it was part of a promise which God had not withdrawn.

But to which period does this list refer? Many of the Benjaminite settlements mentioned here recur in Ezra and Nehemiah (Ezr. 2:26ff. = Ne. 7:30ff.; Ne. 11:7–9 = 1 Ch. 9:7–9; Ne. 11:31–36), suggesting a possible post-exilic origin. Since, however, the places listed in Ezra 2:26ff. are said to be *re*settled, 1 Chronicles 8 might equally refer to the pre-exilic period, either during the United Monarchy or perhaps the expansion under Josiah. There seems little to choose between these various alternatives.

The chapter divides clearly into two parts:

(a) *heads of families* (vv. 6, 10, 13, 28) listed according to their places of settlement (vv. 1–28); and

(b) a genealogy of *Saul's* family (vv. 29–40).

a. Settlement of Benjaminite families (8:1–28). Two strands may be discerned, the families of *Ehud* (vv. 1–7) and of

---

[1] Wilcock, pp. 44–45.

Elpaal (vv. 8–27). The names listed as the descendants of *Benjamin* (vv. 1–2) and of his firstborn son *Bela* (vv. 3–5) seem to lead to *the descendants of Ehud* (v. 6), especially if *Gera the father of Ehud* (v. 3, NIV fn., NEB, JB) is read instead of *Abihud* (NIV, RSV). This seems quite probable in view of Judges 3:15, and Ehud's prominence here is more easily understood if he is identified with the famous judge of the same name (Jdg. 3:12–30). If this is accepted, it is also possible that the following names in verses 4–5, *Abishua, Naaman, Ahoah, Gera*, were either Ehud's sons (*cf.* the first three names in v. 7) or further sons of Gera. The second *Gera* (v. 5; were there really two brothers with the same name?) either belongs to a later generation than the first or is possibly a second reference to the same individual. This reconstruction is not arbitrary, but based on passages such as 6:22–25, 33–38; 7:20, where brothers are given as sons and a name may be resumed by repeating it. *Shephuphan* (= Shephupham, Nu. 26:39, and Shuppim, 1 Ch. 7:12) and *Huram* (= Hupham, Nu. 26:39, and Huppim, 1 Ch. 7:12) in verse 5 may be regarded as either Bela's descendants or having a looser relationship with Benjamin (*cf.* Gn. 46:21; Nu. 26:39). The resulting family tree, centred on Ehud, may have looked something like the diagram below.

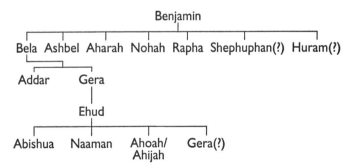

Although this genealogy cannot be harmonized exactly with Genesis 46:21, Numbers 26:38–40, and 1 Chronicles 7:6–12a, this reconstruction does tie in with the position of *Addar* (v. 3; *cf.* Ard, Gn. 46:21; Nu. 26:40) and *Naaman* (vv. 4, 7) in Numbers 26:40 as later descendants of Bela, as well as easing the difficulties over the position of Shephuphan and Huram.

The list also focuses on the location of Ehud's descendants in *Geba* (v. 6). This was a well-known Benjaminite town (*e.g.* 1 Ki. 15:22; 2 Ki. 23:8), but, since its inhabitants preferred to return from Babylon to its northern neighbour Michmash (Ne. 11:31; *cf.* 1 Sa. 14:5; Is. 10:29), the period of residence mentioned here is most likely to refer to pre-exilic times, if not to the days of the judges. The apparent deportations in verses 6–7 are more likely to refer to tribal movements (a third migration to Moab is implied by v. 8), since *Manahath* (v. 6) was in either Edom (1 Ch. 1:40) or Judah (1 Ch. 2:52, 54).

How verses 8–27 relate to the preceding paragraph is not clear. Like Saul's genealogy (vv. 28–40), it is probably an independent list, though there is a possible link through Ehud's Moabite connections (*cf.* v. 8 and Jdg. 3:28–30). The names are those of *heads of families* (vv. 10, 28), descended from an otherwise unknown *Shaharaim* (v. 8) through his wives *Hodesh* (vv. 9–10a) and *Hushim* (v. 11, *cf.* v. 8; 'Mahasham', NEB), and centred on one of his sons *Elpaal* (vv. 11, 12, 18). The basic pattern is quite regular: after tracing Elpaal's parentage (vv. 10–12), the relatives of his sons named in verses 13–14 are listed in verses 15–27, *viz.* Beriah (vv. 13, 15–16), *Shema/Shimei* (vv. 13, 19–21), *Shashak* (vv. 14, 22–25), and *Jeremoth/Jeroham* (vv. 14, 26–27).[1] Although this leaves one group of Elpaal's sons without descendants (v. 12) and another in an unexpected position (vv. 17–18), these exceptions might be explained by the geographical notes embedded in the lists.

These notes offer clear evidence of the Benjaminites' expansion (especially v. 13). Several of the places mentioned were on Benjamin's borders, and the passage invites comparison with the emphasis on tribal advance in *e.g.* 4:24 – 5:22.

---

[1] 'Ahio' (v. 14, NIV, RSV, NEB, GNB) should almost certainly be read as either 'his brother' (JB, with slight vocalic changes) or 'their brothers' (with LXX(L)).

Ono and *Lod* (v. 12) were on the coastal plain near Joppa, while *Aijalon* was strategically located on Judah's border with the Philistines and the northern kingdom. Although Ono and Lod are mentioned in the Old Testament only in post-exilic passages (Ezr. 2:33 = Ne. 7:37; Ne. 6:2; 11:35), they certainly existed from the middle of the second millennium. This kind of expansion might derive from the reigns of David, Rehoboam (*cf.* 2 Ch. 11:10; 28:18), Hezekiah (*cf.* 1 Ch. 4:41) or Josiah. The move to *Moab* (v. 8) seems to be due to the special circumstances of *divorce* (*cf.* v. 8, NIV, GNB), though it could reflect David's conquests in that area (1 Ch. 18:2). Most of these families, however, lived in *Jerusalem* (v. 28). Verse 28 is certainly a conclusion to this section rather than an introduction to the next, even though it is repeated with verses 29–38 in 9:34–44. Its ending, 'they lived in (place name)' is reversed as a deliberate contrast at the start of verse 29, 'In (place name) they/(he?) lived', and Saul's relatives are associated with their own locations (vv. 29, 32).

b. Genealogy of Saul's family (8:29–40).

The final section is centred on *Saul*, the best known of all the Benjaminites in the Old Testament. The genealogy, most of which is repeated in 9:35–44, follows the same pattern as the two preceding it, with the main figure in the centre dividing the rest into two parts: the period up to Saul and his four sons (vv. 29–32), and twelve generations from Saul's son *Jonathan* (vv. 33–40).

Most EVV rightly supply *Jeiel* (NEB, 'Jehiel') in verse 29 (*cf.* 9:35). *Father of Gibeon* (v. 29) is a phrase reminiscent of Judah's genealogy (see comment on 2:21–23). Since individuals normally gave their names to places rather than the reverse, and since the Gibeonites were originally Canaanites incorporated into Israel (Jos. 9), it appears that Saul's ancestry included some Canaanite blood. On the analogy of verses 3–5 (Bela's sons), the names in verses 30–32a may be Jeiel's relatives rather than specifically his sons. At any rate, *Ner* (v. 31, NIV, GNB, JB) should probably be included (with 9:36 and LXX (A) among them, even though it is impossible to reconcile all the details of verses 30, 33 with 1 Samuel 9:1; 14:49–51. Many scholars emend the text of 1 Samuel in the light of this list, making Ner Saul's grandfather (in 1 Sa. 9:1) and Abner his uncle (1 Sa. 14:50), but an equally possible alternative is that Ner was the name of both his uncle (v. 30; 9:36; 1 Sa. 14:50) and his grandfather (v. 33; 9:39). The differences cannot be explained by regarding this list as a post-exilic creation, for the inclusion of 'Baal' names (vv. 30, 33, 34) shows that it originated probably no later than the ninth century BC. *Esh-Baal* (v. 33) is known elsewhere as Ishvi (1 Sa. 14:49) and Ishbosheth (2 Sa. 2:8 – 4:12), while *Merib-Baal* (v. 34) is Mephibosheth (2 Sa. 4:4; 9:6ff.). The names from *Micah* (v. 34) onward are unknown apart from the parallel list in chapter 9, nor is it certain whether they come down to the exile as in the lines of David (3:10–16) and the high priests (6:1–15), especially as the number of generations here is smaller. *Bokeru* (v. 38) might be read as 'his firstborn', and there are a number of minor differences with 9:35–44.

viii. Conclusion to tribal lists (9:1)

This verse is a conclusion to the tribal lists, parallel to 2:1–2, and does not belong with the rest of chapter 9. *All Israel* (*cf.* 2:1) includes all the tribes, not just those who happened to form the Chronicler's own community (those listed in 9:2–34). In fact throughout these lists the Chronicler has shown a healthy discontent with his contemporary situation, pointing instead to God's promises concerning the land (hence the emphasis on Jacob and the continuity from his sons to the exile). However, the mention of exile shows that the current situation was no accident, but the result of *unfaithfulness* (see comment on 2:7; 5:25) towards God. The downfall of Saul's kingdom (10:13) and of the northern (*cf.* 5:25) and southern (2 Ch. 36:14) kingdoms were all traced to the same underlying cause. The inclusivist nature of this verse suggests that 'all Israel' is the subject of *were taken captive*, which would be quite consistent with Chronicles' description of the northern and southern kingdoms.[1] As a result, 'Book/Scroll of the Kings of Israel and Judah' (*cf.* JB and 2 Ch. 27:7; 35:27; 36:8) is preferable to *book of the kings of Israel* (*cf.* 2 Ch. 20:34), despite the Massoretic punctuation.[2] This source refers either to the census list from which parts of the genealogies derived, or to a much longer official source containing Israel's genealogies and history.

---

[1] *Cf.* Williamson, *IBC*, especially pp. 102–109.
[2] This view is independently adopted in W. Johnstone, 'Guilt', p. 138, n. 25. *Cf.* also Braun, p. 130.

C. Repopulating Jerusalem (9:2–34)

1 Chronicles 9 is made up of two lists: verses 2–34, those who resettled Jerusalem; verses 35–44, the genealogy of Saul. The main subject matter is the list of Jerusalem residents, since the latter section really introduces the account of Saul's dynasty (ch. 10). Occupation of Jerusalem is a key feature in the restoration of post-exilic Israel, and is the natural outcome of Chronicles' geographical emphasis in 2:1 – 9:1, especially the sections on Judah and Benjamin. The list is almost certainly intended to be read as a unit, even though its contents are uneven and it shows substantial differences from Nehemiah 11 (see below). More significantly, apart from 3:17–24, it is the only part of Chronicles from approximately the author's own time.

Verses 2–17 have several points of contact with Nehemiah 11:3–19, but the exact nature of the relationship is not immediately obvious. A number of commentators (*e.g.* Curtis and Madsen, Ackroyd) believe that both Chronicles and Nehemiah have used a common original for their own separate purposes, but it is also possible that either Chronicles or Nehemiah is the source for the other. To illustrate the difficulty, Myers has noted that there are about 81 personal names in Nehemiah's list and 71 in Chronicles' version, but only about 35 in each list correspond. In fact, the most probable solution is that Chronicles is the borrower, as shown by four considerations. Firstly, the numbers in Chronicles are consistently higher, though the differences are not enormous. Compare, for example, the 956 Benjaminites (v. 9) as against 928 in Nehemiah 11:8, and the 7 named Levites (vv. 14–16) as against 6 in Nehemiah 11:15–18. Secondly, Nehemiah 11:1–2 describes the beginning of Nehemiah's policy of the resettlement of Jerusalem, and the higher numbers in Chronicles would make sense if they reflected a continuation of that policy. Thirdly, reference to the *temple servants* in verse 2 (Heb. *nᵉṯînîm*) is unique in Chronicles, and is not followed up in the subsequent list, but they do occur frequently in Ezra–Nehemiah (*e.g.* Ezr. 7:7; 8:20; Ne. 10:28; 11:3; 21). Finally, verse 2 (= Ne. 11:3) is already part of the editorial framework in Nehemiah 11 rather than the list itself (so Rudolph, Williamson, *etc.*).

It may be possible to pinpoint the relationship between the

two lists a little more precisely. The fact that the numbers in 1 Chronicles 9 represent only a slight increase over those in Nehemiah 11, while many individuals remain the same, suggests that a new generation has partly replaced the earlier *heads of families* (*cf.* vv. 9, 13, 34), and that 1 Chronicles 9 is perhaps half a generation later than Nehemiah 11:2–17.

This conclusion, however, determines only the nature of the relationship between the two passages, and does not by itself settle the date of 1 Chronicles 9:2–34. For this latter issue, there are two main alternatives. Either 1 Chronicles 9:2–34 derives from about half a generation after the repopulation of Jerusalem (Ne. 11:1–2) which probably took place under Nehemiah or else it belongs after the final compilation of the lists in Nehemiah 11–12. In the latter case, at least three generations after Nehemiah and a musical contemporary of his named Mattaniah must be allowed (Ne. 11:17; 1 Ch. 9:15), because of the mention of the great-grandsons of both Mattaniah (Ne. 11:22) and of Eliashib, high priest under Nehemiah (Ne. 12:11, 22). It is tempting to adopt the former possibility, since this would allow the conclusion that the compiler of 1 Chronicles 9:2–34 was actually describing changes in his own time. Perhaps some of the new names, especially among the gatekeepers where the variations are much more marked, were even of people known to him personally. This view would also be supported by the observation that the compiler exercises here a far greater freedom with earlier biblical material than is evident elsewhere in the genealogies. Certainty is unfortunately not possible, and neither can we know whether the compiler was the Chronicler himself or an earlier scribe whose work the Chronicler has taken over.

Whichever view is preferred, the more important point is that verses 2–34 are a sure sign that the restoration of Israel and Jerusalem was a continuing process. Here at the meeting-point of the genealogies (1 Ch. 1–9) and the narratives (1 Ch. 10 – 2 Ch. 36), post-exilic Israelites are shown to be caught up in God's still-developing purposes for Israel. They are heirs of the generations descended from Adam (ch. 1) and from the twelve tribes (chs. 2–8) – it is surely no mistake that *Ephraim and Manasseh* (v. 3) are added to Nehemiah 11:4, even though there is no up-to-date information about their settlements. Their return to the Promised Land (v. 2), and particularly to *Jerusalem* (vv. 3–34), is a clear and visible sign that Israel has survived the exile (*cf.* v. 1). Divine judgment on Israel's 'unfaithfulness' (v. 1; *cf.* 5:25; 2 Ch. 36:14) had not after all brought Israel's history to a full stop. Rather, genealogies that once seemed dead are now alive again (*cf.* Ezk. 37:1–14), and the Chronicler and his community are living witnesses to a hope rooted in the very creation of humanity.

All this means that Chronicles has taken the history of Israel a stage further than 1 and 2 Kings. Although 2 Kings ends on a note of genuine hope (2 Ki. 25:27–30), it is restrained and Israel is still in exile. But now the winter is over, and these lists are a definite sign that spring has begun to arrive. The Israel of 1 Chronicles 9 was a visible fulfilment of the prophetic hope (*cf.* Ch. 36:22–23). Though these names are now largely unknown, a real sense of excitement emerges of a community seeing history, and divine history at that, unfold before their very eyes. Not that everything was yet complete. The Chronicler must have been painfully aware of that, but his emphasis on temple personnel and activities (vv. 10–34) naturally points forward to his major concern for the temple (1 Ch. 21 – 2 Ch. 7) and his hope that prayer inspired by the temple will bring a fuller healing and restoration for Israel's land (*cf.* 2 Ch. 7:14). The author of Chronicles therefore saw his generation as being far from helpless spectators of the outworking of God's purposes. They had the opportunity to be participants, to exercise faith in those purposes by continuing to repopulate Jerusalem (vv. 3–9) and giving priority to the details of temple worship (vv. 10–34).

i. Resettling the towns (9:2)

9:2 – *cf.* Nehemiah 11:3a

The exact significance of this verse, which stands apart from the rest of the list, depends on the meaning of the Hebrew *hāri'šōnîm*. Older commentators (*e.g.* Zöckler, Curtis and Madsen) thought that it referred to pre-exilic inhabitants on the basis of the context of chapters 1–8, and therefore had the sense of 'former'. Others translate it 'first', with reference to those who returned in 538 BC in direct response to Cyrus' edict (Noth, Myers),[1] or even as 'chief', like the comparable word in Nehemiah 11:3. Most probably, however, it is a

---

[1] Rudolph also changes 'those who settled' (Heb. *hayyôš⁷bîm*) to 'those who returned' (Heb. *haššābîm*), as also apparently does Myers, but this is unsupported in ancient texts.

general statement that those who came back from exile (v. 1) settled *first* in *their ... towns* (*cf*. JB, NIV) before making any significant move to inhabit Jerusalem (vv. 3–34; MT makes a sharp contrast with the beginning of v. 3, 'But in Jerusalem there lived ...').

'Their ancestral land' (NEB; *their own property*, NIV) is a term rarely found in Chronicles (only 1 Ch. 7:28; 2 Ch. 11:14; 31:1). Its occurrence here evokes its frequent use in the time of Moses (*e.g.* Lv. 25:10ff.; Nu. 27:4) and Joshua (*e.g.* Jos. 21:12; 22:4), confirming the links with earlier Israel.[1] 'Israel' (RSV) here represents the 'Israelite laymen' (GNB, *cf*. NEB), as is usual in Ezra–Nehemiah (*e.g.* Ezr. 2:70; 10:5, 25). The *temple servants* is a group mentioned frequently in Ezra–Nehemiah, but who do not appear elsewhere in Chronicles or even in the rest of the Old Testament. Either they stand for the gate-keepers (vv. 17–26), since the temple servants are omitted in the following list and the gatekeepers are omitted in verse 2, or more probably, since they are elsewhere distinguished from the gatekeepers, they are a further group of temple assistants whose presence is recalled on the basis of Nehemiah 11:3.

The rest of this section (vv. 3–34) is concerned with repopulating Jerusalem. This list appears to be contemporary either with the Chronicler himself, or with the time immediately after the implementation of Nehemiah's policy that at least 10% of the population should live in Jerusalem (Ne. 11:1–2; see also above). It is divided by Chronicles as follows:

ii. Laymen in Jerusalem (9:3–9)

9:3–9 – *cf*. Nehemiah 11:4–8

Representatives of four tribes are mentioned (v. 3) as against two in Nehemiah 11:4–9. Although there appears to be no further information about *Ephraim and Manasseh*, they are surely included as representatives of the twelve tribes of chapters 2–8 (*cf*. 5:23–26; 7:14–29) to indicate Israel's increasing expansion and unity (for similar examples involving these two tribes, *cf*. 2 Ch. 30:11, 18; 34:9). The descendants of *Judah* (vv. 4–6) are classified according to the three sons of Judah himself who produced children, Perez (v. 4; *cf*. 2:4–5; 4:1), Shelah

---

[1] The same term (Heb. *'aḥuzzâ*) also appears frequently in Ezk. (*e.g.* 44:28; 45:5ff.).

(v. 5, = *the Shilonites*, NIV, RSV, JB; *cf.* 2:3; 4:21), and Zerah (v. 6; *cf.* 2:4, 6–8). The names are those of *heads of families* (*cf.* vv. 9, 34). *Jeuel* is not mentioned in Nehemiah 11, *Uthai* might be the same as Athaiah (Ne. 11:4), and *Asaiah* is probably identical with Maaseiah (Ne. 11:5).

Although the two versions of the Judahite genealogies show some variation, divergence is much more marked in the case of the *Benjaminites* (vv. 7–9). Nehemiah 11:7–9 seems to list one family head and four other officials, while Chronicles has four (or five?) leaders. Only *Sallu* is clearly common, though *Hodaviah, the son of Hassenuah* (v. 7) may be the same as Judah son of Hassenuah (Ne. 11:9 – the difference in Heb. is minimal). For both Judah and Benjamin, a small increase in numbers since Nehemiah's time seems probable (956 Benjaminites as against 928).

iii. Priests in Jerusalem (9:10–13)

9:10–13 – *cf.* Nehemiah 11:10–14

The names of six *heads of families* (v. 13) are given, *viz. Jedaiah, Jehoiarib, Jakin* (v. 10), *Azariah* (v. 11), *Adaiah* (v. 12), and *Maasai* (v. 12; = Amashsai, Ne. 11:13). The first three are old traditional families (*cf.* 1 Ch. 24:7, 17; Ne. 12:19, 21), and the last two belong to the families of *Pashhur* and *Immer* who, along with Jedaiah, were part of the first group to return from Babylon (Ezr. 2:36–39 = Ne. 7:39–42). Azariah belongs to the Zadokites, the family of high priests, and much the same family tree is given in 1 Chronicles 6:11–14; Ezra 7:1–2 (Azariah is probably not the same as the Seraiah of Ne. 11:11, since 1 Ch. 6:14, Ezr. 7:1 treat them separately). *Official in charge of the house of God* (v. 11) is almost certainly a term for the high priest (*cf.* 2 Ch. 31:10, 13).

The number of priests has increased substantially over Nehemiah 11:12–14 (*1,760* as against 1,192), but they are considerably fewer than the 4,289 who returned initially. As with the rest of the Jews, there seems to have been some reticence among the priests to take up Nehemiah's challenge to repopulate Jerusalem (the family of Harim, Ezr. 2:39 = Ne. 7:42, for example, does not seem to have participated). Malachi's complaint that not all the priests took their duties seriously seems also to be reflected here (*cf.* Mal. 1:6 – 2:9). The significant numerical increase in Chronicles' list may be reflected in the double commendation of these priests as *able*

men (NIV, RSV; 'men of substance', NEB) who were committed to
the 'service' (RSV, NEB) or ministry (*cf.* NIV) of the temple (v. 13;
– note that 'service' is also a key characterization of the priests'
task in 1 Ch. 24:3, 19).

iv. Levites in Jerusalem (9:14–16)

9:14–15 – *cf.* Nehemiah 11:15, 17

Seven names are given as against six in Nehemiah 11:15–18,
and with some variation. They are probably divided into four
leaders, who are given genealogies, *viz. Shemaiah* (v. 14), *Mattaniah* (v. 15b), *Obadiah* and *Berekiah* (v. 16), and three assistants who are without named ancestors (v. 15a). This
separation is supported by the designation of Bakbukia (=
Bakbakkar?) as 'second' (Ne. 11:17). As indicated in Nehemiah
11, these are the musicians, a factor only hinted at here by the
derivation of Mattaniah from *Asaph* and Obadiah from
Jeduthun. Their ancestors were choir leaders in David's day (*cf.*
6:39; 15:17; 25:2–3), and the leaders in this list led Israel's
praise in Nehemiah's time (Ne. 12:8).

16. *Berekiah* who is not mentioned in Nehemiah 11, is probably also a musician. The *Netophathites*, who lived near Bethlehem, included many singers (Ne. 12:28–29), and the
reference to *Elkanah* may link Berekiah with the Hemanites,
whose descendants are not otherwise included among postexilic musicians (*cf.* 1 Ch. 6:33–38). Only the Asaphites seem
to have returned initially from exile (Ezr. 2:41 = Ne. 7:44), so
that the presence of other groups here is a testimony to an
increasing desire to see the musicians fully re-established in
their traditional groups.

v. Gatekeepers in Jerusalem (9:17–32)

9:17, 22 – *cf.* Nehemiah 11:19

This paragraph marks a substantial addition to the brief note
about gatekeepers in Nehemiah 11:19. The Chronicler has
also departed somewhat from his theme of listing Jerusalem's
population, and the question arises as to why the gatekeepers
have been given as much attention as all the other groups in
the list. One not unreasonable possibility is that the gatekeepers exemplified particularly clearly the Chronicler's
desire to see the Levites take a more prominent role.
Although they must have been a fairly small group, many
seem to have responded to the call to live in Jerusalem and its

surrounding villages (vv. 22, 25). They were also a living witness to Chronicles' theme of the Israelites' 'help' for one another (v. 25; *cf.* comment on 1 Ch. 12:1ff.; 23:24–32), and they showed a real willingness to take on extra duties (vv. 26–32). This latter situation would have arisen because of the general shortage of Levites in post-exilic Israel (*cf.* Ezr. 8:15–20; Ne. 13:10–11).

The section deals with three aspects of the gatekeepers' 'service' or ministry (vv. 19, 28), their authority (vv. 17–23), their leadership (vv. 24–27), and their additional work (vv. 28–32). As often in Chronicles, the question of authority is settled by an appeal to tradition, both genealogical and spiritual. The four current families (v. 17; only two occur in Ne. 11:19) trace their ancestry through their 'leader' (v. 17, GNB) *Shallum* back to *Korah* (vv. 19, 31), the original leader of one of the Kohathite (*cf.* v. 32) groups of Levites (*cf.* 6:22, 37).[1] Shallum's leading role is indicated by his being stationed at the *east* gate, which in the post-exilic period was known as the *King's Gate* (v. 18; *cf.* 1 Ch. 26:14). This was an important governmental position, as well as one that involved guarding the very doors of the sanctuary (v. 19).[2]

Their formal institution as gatekeepers was *David's* task (v. 22; *cf.* 1 Ch. 26), when *Zechariah son of Meshelemiah* had been in office (v. 21; 1 Ch. 26:2, 14). But just as important was their spiritual heritage, represented here by *Phinehas* the priest (v. 20), who had dramatically defended the holiness of the sanctuary (Nu. 25:6ff.), and by *Samuel* (v. 22), who had evidently been a gatekeeper in his youth (1 Sa. 3:15). This appeal to the past is also supported by language reminiscent of the Mosaic period. Both 'camp' (vv. 18, RSV; also v. 19) and *Tent* (= Tabernacle, vv. 19, 23) occur twice, and *entrance to the Tent of Meeting* (v. 21) is taken straight from the story of Phinehas (Nu. 25:6).[3] The fact that *the LORD was with him* (= Phinehas, v. 20, RSV, NIV) indicates that the Lord was also with those gatekeepers of the Chronicler's day who followed in the same

[1] Shallum is probably identical with Meshullam in Ne. 12:24, but there is no reason to regard him as the same person as David's contemporary Meshelemiah / Shelemiah (1 Ch. 9:21; 26:1, 14), as some commentators do.

[2] *Cf.* J. W. Wright, 'Guarding the gates: 1 Chronicles 26:1–19 and the roles of gatekeepers in Chronicles', *JSOT* 48, 1990, pp. 69–81, especially pp. 74–76.

[3] The mention of David's contemporary Zechariah (v. 21; *cf.* 1 Ch. 26:2, 14) could in fact mean that the intended 'tent' was either the sanctuary at Gibeon (1 Ch. 16:39) or that in which David initially housed the ark (1 Ch. 16:1).

living tradition of divine service. They had entered into *positions of trust* (v. 22, *cf.* RSV; also vv. 26, 31), which translates a word also meaning 'faithfulness, trustworthiness' (*cf.* JB, NEB, Braun).

The main issue in verses 24–32 is whether some or all of these verses refer only to the gatekeepers or to the Levites as a whole. Many commentators prefer the latter view, dividing the section after verse 23 (Braun), verse 26a (Williamson), or verse 27 (RSV, NIV). The basis for this is the phrase (lit.) 'They were Levites' (v. 26b, *cf.* v. 31), and the extension of duties in verses 26–32. But in fact, the gatekeepers seem to be in the compiler's mind throughout. Of the four additional roles mentioned, that of 'treasurer' (v. 26) was traditionally filled by gatekeepers (1 Ch. 26:15, 17, 20ff.), and that of night-porter (vv. 26–27) is not inappropriate. Certainly, the responsibilities of looking after temple equipment (vv. 28–29a) and preparing the sacrifice (vv. 29b–32) are unexpected, but these jobs too are allocated to gatekeepers and their relatives. *Mattithiah* (v. 31) is the firstborn son of Shallum, the chief gatekeeper (vv. 17, 19), and the *Kohathite brothers* (v. 32) included Shallum's family, the Korahites. The gatekeepers' involvement in other activities, especially financial ones, also occurs in 2 Chronicles 31:14–17; 34:8–13.[1]

The *four principal gatekeepers* (vv. 24–27) are presumably those named in verse 17. The temple doors were closed each night, though a *key* (v. 27) is mentioned nowhere else in the Old Testament. The *morning* (v. 27) was the time for praise (*cf.* 1 Ch. 23:30) and sacrifice (*e.g.* Ex. 29:38–41; Nu. 28:1–8; 2 Ch. 2:4; Ezr. 3:3). Verses 28–29a throughout refer to temple 'vessels' (NEB) or 'equipment' – there is no separate word for 'furniture' (against EVV). Verses 30–32 deal with certain special responsibilities in preparing the sacrifices. *Mixing the spices* (v. 30) remained a priestly prerogative (*cf.* Ex. 30:22–33), but Shallum's son baked the regular 'flat cakes (?)' (v. 31, NRSV) or *offering bread*, and the gatekeepers' closest relatives looked after the showbread (v. 32; *cf.* 23:29; 28:16; 2 Ch. 2:4).

vi. Musicians in Jerusalem (9:33)

It is not clear to whom this verse refers. Either it is the same group as in verses 14–16 but occurring in a different source

---

[1] *Cf.* J. W. Wright, *art. cit.*, *JSOT* 48, 1990, pp. 76–79.

(vv. 17b–33), or these are gatekeepers with musical talents. That some of the musicians in verses 14–16 acted as gate-keepers under Nehemiah perhaps supports the latter inter-pretation, as also does the note about exemption from other duties.

vii. Conclusion (9:34)

This verse is almost identical to 8:28, with only *Levite* added. It forms an inclusion with verse 3 by resuming the theme of *Jerusalem* residence in the earlier part of the list, though the Levites did not appear until verse 14. Its composite character suggests that it has been adapted from chapter 8.

D. Genealogy of Saul's family (9:35–44)

The list is almost identical to 8:29–40, except that 8:39–40 are not repeated. For the details of the list, see comment on chapter 8. The reason for the list's reappearance seems to lie in its different function. Whereas in chapter 8 the emphasis was on the place of residence of three main Benjaminite families, here Saul's genealogy anticipates the account of his kingship in chapter 10. The Chronicler's practice of prefacing narrative passages with appropriate lists throws up a fas-cinating contrast here with the downfall of Saul's dynasty (10:6). Since the genealogy continues for twelve generations after Saul, the fact that his dynasty crashed and his kingship was transferred to David did not remove his family's place in Israelite history. They too had lived in *Jerusalem* (v. 38), and though we do not know whether this continued after the exile, even for them there were signs of hope.

II. THE KINGDOM OF DAVID AND SOLOMON
(1 Ch. 10:1 – 2 Ch. 9:31)

A. Transferring the kingdom to David (10:1 – 12:40)

The Chronicler's portrayal of Saul is quite distinctive. Apart from being the point where many modern readers start to read the books of Chronicles, Saul's appearance at the begin-ning of the narrative section shows the importance of the transition from Saul to David in the Chronicler's version of

Israel's history. This is a very different starting-point from that of the so-called Deuteronomic History (Dt.–Jos. – 2 Ki.), which begins with the events relating to Israel's entry into the Promised Land. For the Chronicler, neither the entry to the Promised Land nor even the return to the land was uppermost in his mind. Nehemiah's generation seems to have been the last for whom this was a central issue. The crucial issue for the Chronicler was how Israel could continue to live in that land, and what their status was to be in the light of an apparently permanent imperial rule. Though the genealogies began to answer the first question, the narrative now provides a fuller response.

That response is about God's kingship in Israel, as if there was an underlying doubt whether God was still in charge of the nation's fortunes (*cf.* Is. 40:27–31). The form of the question seems to be the exact converse of that raised by the people before Saul became king. Then the great issue was whether or not to have a king (1 Sa. 8), but now it is how to preserve any notion of kingship at all in Israel. In reality, however, they are both reflexes of one fundamental issue – what did it mean for God to be king over Israel? The first stage of the answer is found in chapters 10–12, which show how a kingdom was first established in Israel, affirming the importance of the idea of kingdom for post-exilic Israelites, even though there was no prospect of any immediate restoration of the Davidic line.

The brevity of Chronicles' account of Saul has been a long-standing enigma. Practically the entire earlier record of Saul's reign (1 Sa. 8 – 2 Sa. 1) is omitted, with only his final defeat and death being included here. It is apparently assumed that readers will be familiar with the other events of his reign. Similarly, the account of David begins very abruptly with David's inauguration as king over all Israel (11:1–3). The detailed narratives of David's rise to power in 1 Samuel 16 – 2 Samuel 4 are left out, even though 2 Samuel records important events such as David's private anointing by Samuel, his disturbing and extended conflict with Saul, and his seven-and-a-half year reign over Judah (a brief mention of the latter is found in 1 Ch. 3:4; 29:27). Again, however, the reader's knowledge of many of the events in David's earlier life is assumed, as shown by several allusions in 11:10 – 12:37.

By deliberately omitting so much of this material from 1 and 2 Samuel, Chronicles is able to concentrate on two aspects of the kingdom in chapters 10–12. In chapter 10, kingship in Israel is transferred from Saul's house to David's (vv. 13–14), with further references to the importance of this changeover in 11:1–2 and 12:23. The second feature, found in chapters 11–12, traces the gradual expansion of David's kingdom to include 'all Israel' (11:1–3; 12:38–40), repeatedly emphasizing how support was transferred from Saul's former subjects to the new king. In this way, chapters 10–12 serve as an introduction to the United Monarchy under David and Solomon, but also as a challenge to the Chronicler's contemporaries about the true nature of kingship and authority in Israel. The Chronicler gives no direct advice about the practical implications of this material for his own time, and certainly issues no invitation to rebellion against Persian (or Greek) emperors. He is simply content to indicate that the kingdom of Israel transferred from Saul to David was also part of God's own kingdom.[1]

i. The end of Saul's house (10:1–14)

'Therefore the LORD . . . turned the kingdom over to David
the son of Jesse' (10:14, RSV).

10:1–12 – *cf.* 1 Samuel 31:1–13

The key to Chronicles' presentation of *Saul* has usually been viewed in one of two ways. It has been seen either as a mere prelude or foil to the account of David (von Rad, Galling), or more recently as a paradigm of the conditions which ultimately brought about the exile (Mosis, Ackroyd, Williamson).

Chapter 10 itself, however, contains two pointers of its own concerning its meaning. Firstly, the structure emphasizes the unusual significance of the battle of Mount Gilboa. Although the battle itself is summarized in one verse (v. 1), the rest of the chapter is devoted to the effects of Saul's defeat. Details of the king's death (vv. 2–5), the desecration of his corpse (vv. 8–10), and his burial by the loyal inhabitants of Jabesh-Gilead (vv. 11–12) are interspersed with summaries of the military, political (vv. 5–6), and theological consequences (vv. 13–14). The entire account is characterized by key phrases such as the fact that Israel's army *fled* (vv. 1, 7), and especially the *death* of the Saulide *house* (vv. 5, 6, 7, 13, 14).

---

[1] Willi goes beyond Chronicles' evidence in proposing that the main issue in post-exilic Israel was Israel's lost political independence (*CA*, pp. 10–11).

The second pointer is found in the Chronicler's additions to his source (1 Sa. 31). Two changes, in verse 6 and verse 14, are of particular interest. The statement *All his house died together* (v. 6) indicates an unrepeatable crisis. Saul's family actually continued through his crippled grandson Meribbaal/Mephibosheth, as the Chronicler himself recognizes (1 Ch. 8:29–39; 9:35–44). Ishbaal/Ishbosheth, Saul's son, also reigned briefly in northern Israel, as the Chronicler must have known (2 Sa. 2:8 – 4:12). But as far as Israel's leadership was concerned, Saul's 'house' was finished. Israel's God, however, was not defeated. In his hands, the crisis became a turning-point, as 'he transferred the kingdom to David' (v. 14, NEB, REB). Crises of similar magnitude occurred later at the division of the kingdom (*cf.* 2 Ch. 10:15 where the 'turn of events' is from the same Heb. root *sbb* as in v. 14 here) and at the exile, but the changes effected by Saul's death had the greatest impact of all. Repeated references to the changeover are made in Chronicles (1 Ch. 11:1–2; 12:23; 17:13), but they occur supremely in relation to the Davidic covenant (1 Ch. 17:13). No doubt influenced and inspired by God's promise of an everlasting covenant for David in both Psalms (*e.g.* Pss. 89:3–4, 132:11–12) and prophets (Is. 9:7; 55:3; Ezk. 37:24–26), Chronicles underlines the continuing relevance to post-exilic Israel of the Davidic covenant's eternal qualities.

David's kingdom and covenant receive even greater prominence of course in the New Testament. There they are transformed by Jesus, 'great David's greater Son' (J. Montgomery), who is both a turning-point and continuation of the Old Testament's hope. Ultimately, it is Jesus, rather than David, who makes this covenant non-transferable (Lk. 1:32–33; Acts 2:29–36; Phil. 2:5–11). 1 Ch. 10 is therefore neither just a prelude nor a pattern, though it includes elements of both. It highlights a juncture when under the Lord's sovereignty a permanent foundation was laid, which was crucial not only for the rest of Chronicles, but for the whole of biblical history.

a. Saul's death (10:1–5). Saul's final defeat at *Mount Gilboa* took place on the south-east side of the Esdraelon plain at a crossroads linking the southern and northern tribes. The battle strategy is unclear, but there is little doubt that Saul's desperation and fear (1 Sa. 28:4–5) drove him into a disadvantageous position. The Philistines could use their chariots to maximum benefit on the plain, and count on support from the local Canaanite city-states. There is tragic irony in Saul's catastrophe at the hands of an enemy he had been chosen by God and people to overcome (1 Sa. 9:16; 10:1 LXX) and over whom he had already enjoyed partial success (1 Sa. 13–14).

The Amalekite's story of Saul's death in 2 Samuel 1 is ignored, perhaps because its authenticity was doubted in ancient as well as in modern times. The *armour-bearer's* reticence (v. 4) to end Saul's agony was due either to Saul's anointed status (*cf.* 1 Sa. 24:10; 26:11) or to protect himself against blood-revenge. Saul was badly *wounded* (v. 3),[1] but preferred death at his own hand rather than humiliation by the enemy. David's adviser Ahithophel (2 Sa. 17:23), Zimri (king for a week – 1 Ki. 16:18) and Judas Iscariot (Mt. 27:3–10; Acts 1:18–19) are the only other Israelite suicides mentioned in the Bible.

b. The end of Saul's house (10:6–7).

The major alteration from 1 Samuel 31 is in verse 6 (see notes above). 1 Samuel 31:7 suggests that part of the Jordan *valley* as well as Jezreel was lost to the Philistines. The fact that the capital of Ishbaal's short-lived kingdom was at Mahanaim in Transjordan seems to confirm this (2 Sa. 2:8–9). Saul had lost more land to the *Philistines* in the end than he had gained from them, making a mockery of the original hopes for the monarchy (1 Sa. 8:20).

c. Saul's corpse (10:8–10).

The several variations from 1 Samuel 31 in these verses cannot all be easily accounted for, though textual factors may be involved (see Myers, Williamson). Particularly interesting are the specific references to Saul's *head* and *Dagon's* temple (the god's name is not in 1 Sa. 31:10), which have been plausibly explained as a deliberate contrast with Dagon's fall before the ark (1 Sa. 5:1–4) and Goliath's fall before David, underlining the irony as well as the extent of Saul's failure (1 Sa. 17:54). Both, like Saul, lost

---

[1] Possibly 'shook with fear' (*cf.* Tg.), but the present translation fits the context better. Rudolph's suggested revocalization to a Niphal form (as in NEB) is unnecessary, since the MT can probably be read as an apocopated Hophal.

their heads.[1] Dagon was widely worshipped in northern Mesopotamia and Syria–Palestine from the third millennium BC onwards. He may have been a vegetation deity and is associated exclusively with the Philistines in the Old Testament. A minor textual variation ('to carry the good news to their idols', v. 9, RSV, instead of 1 Sa. 31:9's 'to the house of their idols') emphasizes the vast difference between Yahweh and the Philistine gods. While the latter are unaware of the victory which their army has won, Yahweh is in full control of both the Israelites and the Philistines (vv. 13–14).

d. Saul's burial (10:11–12). A simpler version of 1 Sa. 31:11–13. The omission of any reference here to burning Saul's disfigured corpse is probably to avoid associating him with criminal activity (*cf.* Lv. 20:14; 21:9; Jos. 7:25). Together with the burial and seven-day fast (*cf.* 2 Sa. 1:12; Ps. 35:4), this is an important element in modifying the otherwise unfavourable presentation of Saul (further honour was done to both Saul and Jonathan in the sequel of 2 Sa. 21:12–14). The replacement of the rare term 'tamarisk' (1 Sa. 31:13; elsewhere only in 1 Sa. 22:6) by the commoner (generic?) word 'oak' (v. 12, REB, NEB, NRSV, RSV) is a good example of Chronicles' habit of simplifying rare or obscure words.

e. The transfer of Saul's kingdom (10:13–14). A unique theological assessment of Saul. Three reasons are given for Saul's failure: he was *unfaithful* to God, disregarded his *word*, and failed to *seek* (RSV, *etc.*) him properly. The first and third phrases are typical of Chronicles, and are often associated with divine judgment (on unfaithfulness, *cf. e.g.* 1 Ch. 2:7; 9:1; 2 Ch. 12:2; 36:14; on not seeking God, *cf. e.g.* 2 Ch. 12:14; 15:13). The second is more common in Deuteronomy, and occurs elsewhere in Chronicles only in 2 Chronicles 34:21. Together, they form a comprehensive indictment of Saul's attitude to God, and are seen in typical biblical fashion as the real reason lying behind his political and military failures.[2] These theological explanations can be interpreted in two ways. Some have seen them as exhibiting a pattern which

---

[1] Mosis, *UTCG*, pp. 24–26; P. R. Ackroyd, 'The Chronicler as exegete', *JSOT* 2, 1977, p. 6.
[2] For details of these expressions, *cf.* Williamson, pp. 94–95; P. R. Ackroyd, *art. cit.*, *JSOT* 2, 1977, pp. 7–9.

culminated in the judgment of exile, contrasting Saul's reign
with that of David (especially Mosis). Alternatively and more
convincingly, they refer to specific incidents in Saul's life, as
demonstrated by explicit mention of consulting the medium
at Endor (1 Sa. 28). This view is also supported by reference
to specific words from the Lord which Saul rejected, and
which repeatedly mention the transfer of Saul's kingdom to
David (1 Sa. 13:13; 15:22–23, 26; 28:16–19).[1] These phrases
therefore confirm that the main purpose of this chapter is to
show how and why the kingdom was transferred from Saul
to David. Verse 14a does not contradict 1 Samuel 28:6, but
rather illustrates the spiritual truth that God can be sought
either single-heartedly or not at all (*cf.* 1 Ch. 16:11; Ps. 27:4;
Mt. 6:33). Saul's syncretism is a microcosm of Israel's
unfaithfulness in the Old Testament. It is also a contradiction of 'the first and greatest commandment' (Mt. 22:37–38;
Dt. 6:5).

ii. All Israel recognizes David as king (11:1 – 12:40)

'They anointed David King over Israel' (11:3).
'"We are yours, O David! ... For your God helps you"'
(12:18, RSV).

> 11:1–9 – *cf.* 2 Samuel 5:1–3, 6–10
> 11:11–41a – *cf.* 2 Samuel 23:8–39

Chapters 11–12 are a single unit with a clear literary design.
The programmatic theme of David's recognition as king by
the whole of Israel introduces (11:1–3) and concludes
(12:23–40) the whole unit.[2] Significantly, the conclusion to
the whole account of David's reign has an identical emphasis
(1 Ch. 29:25–26), and parallels the opening here.[3] The inter-
vening verses (11:4 – 12:37) develop the basic theme. They
reveal David's widespread support, even from those tribes
most distant geographically from Judah and those who formerly owed allegiance to Saul.

This emphasis on Israel's unity under David must have

---

[1] *Cf.* also S. Zalewski, 'The purpose of the story of the death of Saul in 1
Chronicles X', *VT* 39, 1989, pp. 449–467.

[2] See especially Williamson, pp. 96ff.; *idem*, 'We are yours, O David', *OTS* 21,
1981, pp. 164–176. This commentary makes some modifications to Williamson's structure, particularly in ch. 11.

[3] *Cf.* Rudolph, p. 97. This indicates that David's kingship, rather than the
ark, is the main theme of 1 Ch. 10–29 (*contra* Mosis, *UTCG*, pp. 44ff.).

had considerable implications for post-exilic Israel. Most commentators now accept that the Chronicler was not anti-Samaritan, but that he hoped for the eventual breaking down of the barrier developing between Judah and Samaria. Although Chronicles reports several attempts at reunification during the Divided Monarchy period (*e.g.* 2 Ch. 30:1–12), no other passage expresses so clearly that the open commitment of previously separated groups to God's appointed leader was a vital ingredient in making that unity possible. Though the Chronicler's hope remained unfulfilled in his own day, it did become a real possibility in Christ. Those Jews and Samaritans who first put their faith in Jesus (Jn. 4:4–42; Acts 8:4–25) began a reunifying process which is still moving towards its climax. It was accelerated when 3,000 'Jews from every nation under heaven' (Acts 2:5) were joined by Gentiles from many nations in acknowledging the risen Son of David as God's appointed leader. It remains the church's privilege and task to break down human barriers and to work towards the final gathering of a 'great multitude ... from every nation, tribe, people and language' to Jesus as 'KING OF KINGS AND LORD OF LORDS' (Rev. 7:9; 19:16). Only then will Chronicles' hopes for the Davidic kingship be fully and finally transformed.

a. David anointed king over all Israel at Hebron (11:1–3).

Two features dominate the opening paragraph about David's kingship over *all Israel* – the 'word of the LORD' (RSV) and the sacramental act of anointing (the Old Testament rarely speaks of a king's coronation). They speak of God's purposes for David: the former emphasizing God's call and promise, the latter demonstrating that God equips those whom he calls. Both elements are recognized by all Israel (vv. 1–2) and confirmed by elders from every tribe (v. 3). The ideal unity of God, king, and people is strengthened by a 'covenant' (*compact*, NIV). This covenant would have included the terms of kingship required by David, an oath of loyalty by king and people, and a religious ceremony (for similar, though not identical, covenants between God, king, and people, see 2 Ch. 23:16 = 2 Ki. 11:17; 2 Ch. 34:31–32 = 2 Ki. 23:3). The Chronicler's interest in fulfilled prophecy is reflected in his addition, 'according to the word of the LORD by Samuel' (v. 3, RSV). Neither this nor the divine promise in verse 2b can be traced back to specific occasions, but verse 2b reflects the wording of Nathan's oracle (1 Ch. 17:4–14; esp. vv. 6–7; = 2 Sa. 7:5–16), and verse 3b is probably intended as a summary of Samuel's various pronouncements about David (*cf.* 1 Sa. 13:14; 15:28; 16:1–13). As in 10:13, the concept of 'the word of the Lord' has developed from a single oracle into a collection of a prophet's messages, if not to the entire source used here by Chronicles.

Two metaphors in verse 2b emphasize the special character of Israel's monarchy as conceived and sustained by Yahweh.

(a) The king should be a *shepherd* to Israel. The ideal of a shepherd-king goes back to the third millennium BC in the ancient Near East, though in most cases it proved to be little more than an illusion. The retention of this term (from 2 Sa. 5:2; *cf.* 1 Ch. 17:6 = 2 Sa. 7:7) may reflect a particular interest in God's ideal future shepherd as described by the prophets of the exilic period and later. This figure would be David's descendant, finally replacing those shepherds/kings who had brought Israel to destruction (Je. 3:15; 23:1–4; Ezk. 34:1–24; Zec. 11:4–17). The image of the shepherd, who in ancient times was normally an employee or dependant, also confirms that David as king was answerable to Yahweh for his flock (MT adds a second 'my people' to 2 Sa. 5:2, *cf.* RSV, NRSV, to confirm this).

(b) David was to be a *ruler* (Heb. *nāḡîḏ*; NIV, NRSV, GNB) or 'prince' (RSV, NEB). This term was originally distinct from 'king', Heb. *meleḵ*, but soon became synonymous with the latter, commoner title (*cf. e.g.* Ps. 76:12). *Nāḡîḏ* has two nuances. It describes someone designated for a special task, and often has a military connotation (*cf.* 1 Sa. 9:16; 10:1; 13:14; and Aram. *nᵉḡîḏâ*). The military nature of Israelite kingship appears in verse 2a, *You were the one who led Israel on their military campaigns* (*cf.* NEB, GNB; lit. 'you led out and brought in Israel'), and is reaffirmed in the supporting material of 11:4 – 12:37. By *all Israel* (v. 1, *cf.* vv. 3, 4, 10) is meant all the tribes who chose David and not just the northern tribes formerly ruled by Saul's son Ishbaal (as in 2 Sa. 5:1; note the omission in verse 2a of 'over us' from 2 Sa. 5:2). The Chronicler's emphasis on all Israel (*cf.* 1 Ch. 10:7) reminded his own generation that the people could play a vital role in strengthening God's rule in Israel. *Hebron* (vv. 1, 3) was David's capital during his reign over Judah, and was not replaced as such until Jerusalem had been captured and developed (vv. 4–9).

b. David's capital city (11:4–9). The conquest of the Can-aanite fortress *Jebus* and its subsequent transformation into *Jerusalem*, the *City of David* and *de facto* capital of the Israelite tribes, are presented here as the first major result of David's anointing. Earlier attempts to hold Jerusalem had been only partially successful (*cf.* Jos. 10:1–28; Jdg. 1:8; 19:11–12). *Jebus* was a local name known only from the Old Testament – the name Jerusalem seems to be as old as the nineteenth century BC in the light of its probable mention in the Execration Texts from Egypt. In the post-exilic era, the Chronicler's emphasis on Jerusalem's Davidic origins (absent from Ezr.–Ne.) would have underlined the city's significance for his contemporaries despite repeated hostility against the city (*cf.* Ezr. 4:1 – 5:17; Ne. 4:1–23; 6:1–14). David's success was attributed (with 2 Sa. 5:10) to Yahweh, who, having called David to kingship, did not abandon him to his task but remained *with him* (v. 9).

The details of Jerusalem's capture differ noticeably from 2 Samuel 5:6–10, though the origins of the variations are not always clear. David's personal army is now called *all the Israelites* (v. 4), a change in line with one of Chronicles' favour-ite themes which here is probably based on the varied tribal background of David's supporters (12:1–37; see comment on v. 1). The rather obscure report of the city's capture in 2 Samuel is largely replaced in verses 5–6 by an explanation of Joab's promotion to *commander-in-chief*. Chronicles' interest in *Joab* (his construction activity, v. 8, is unparalleled in 2 Sa.), though often regarded as problematic, is explained by his position as the chief of David's supporters (v. 10). Joab is described as a 'chief' (RSV) just like the 'heads' (EVV 'chiefs', v. 10) of the mighty men, though he is clearly singled out from the others (*e.g.* the Heb. root *r'š*, 'head', occurs four times in v. 6). The note on his military and building achievements (vv. 6, 8) should therefore be understood in the same way as the notes on other leading soldiers in verses 11–25.

8. The word for *supporting terraces* (lit. 'Millo', NIV fn., RSV, NEB, *etc.*, meaning 'fill') may have been as obscure to the Chronicler as it is to modern readers, since only here has he retained the word from his source text (omitting it from 1 Ki. 9:15, 24; 11:27). Although a further reference (not in Ki.) is included at 2 Chronicles 32:5, the wording there seems to be influenced by the present verse. In both verses the Millo is simply a part of the old city of David. Modern archaeological consensus associates it with terracing built by the Jebusites on the steep eastern slope of the south-east hill.[1]

The unusual expression in verse 8b, lit. 'revived, renewed' (*restored*, NIV, GNB; 'reconstructed', NEB) seems to be post-exilic usage, since it reappears in a similar context in Nehemiah 4:2 and is cognate with the term 'reviving' (RSV) in Ezra 9:8–9. It reflects the Chronicler's hope that the post-exilic city, despite disillusionment and deprivation, could be given a new lease of life (for a different interpretation, see Williamson, p. 100).

c. David's mighty men (11:10–47). The lists of David's *mighty men* in 2 Samuel 23:8–39 are expanded (vv. 41b–47) and given a totally new context. They are provided with a significant new introduction (v. 10), which resumes three themes already highlighted in verses 1–3 (David's kingship, all Israel, and the word of God), as well as adding a fourth, that of *strong support* (*cf.* 2 Ch. 16:9, 21:4). The warriors come from various tribal backgrounds. This explains the Chronicler's inclusion of *all Israel* (v. 10), and is a further illustration of his over-all theme of Israel's unity under David. Not all these men necessarily came to Hebron (*cf.* vv. 1–3), since the lists are probably composite. *Asahel*, in fact, died while David was still only king of Judah (v. 26; *cf.* 2 Sa. 2:18–23). The Chronicler's material, like much Old Testament narrative, is often not arranged chronologically, and his persistent attention to detail elsewhere suggests that he was not unaware that the personalities and events in this passage belonged to different periods in David's life. Strengthening David's kingdom was not achieved overnight.

The 'word of the LORD' (v. 10, RSV; *the LORD had promised*, NIV) is to be understood as a summary statement (*cf.* comment on vv. 2–3). The most important of David's soldiers (EVV 'mighty men') are divided into the Three (vv. 18, 20–21, 25) and the Thirty (v. 25), though the distinction between the two

---

[1] K. M. Kenyon, *Jerusalem* (London: Thames & Hudson, 1968), pp. 50–51. The following phrase, $w^{e\epsilon}a\underline{d}hass\bar{a}\underline{b}i\underline{b}$, is suspect, since $s\bar{a}\underline{b}i\underline{b}$ nowhere else occurs as a noun, and its meaning here is uncertain. It seems preferable to regard it as a dittography, and accept the usual correction, 'and as far as the palace', based on 2 Sa. 5:9.

groups is not very clear. The inclusion of these names is primarily to magnify David who, as God's anointed, received loyal service from men of great skill and heroism. Since most of those mentioned in verses 11–31 reappear as commanders of the monthly levies (1 Ch. 27:1–15), it is probable that the whole list contains the names of Israel's recognized leaders. Certainly 'Thirty' is not to be understood in precise numerical terms, as the lists demonstrate, and either is a rather elastic number, or refers to a special kind of military leader. The word 'Thirty' may in fact mean an officer of some kind, either an 'officer of the third rank' or a member of a special three-man squad directly responsible to the king.[1] The group's numbers must have fluctuated, as is sadly indicated by the mention of *Uriah the Hittite* (v. 41; *cf.* 2 Sa. 11:17), though one should recall that numerical titles in military units often do not coincide with actual practice (*e.g.* the Roman centurion hardly ever commanded 100 men, and the Roman legion was usually much smaller than the theoretically standard 600 men). Two leaders of the 'Thirty', not included in chapter 11, are also mentioned in 12:4, 18. Only brief notes on individual names can be given here; for fuller details, see the larger commentaries.

Verses 11–47 can be divided into several groups of names.

(a) *Jashobeam*[2] and *Eleazar* (vv. 11–14), to whom 'Shammah' should almost certainly be added (*cf.* 2 Sa. 23:11–12). Nearly all commentators accept that 2 Samuel 23:9b–11a has been omitted in the middle of verse 13 by a copyist's error, possibly influenced by Shammah's non-appearance in the similar list of army commanders in 1 Chronicles 27 (*cf.* vv. 2, 4). This trio are all characterized by their heroism against the Philistines, through which on at least one occasion *the LORD brought about a great victory* (v. 14; *cf.* 2 Sa. 23:10, 12).

(b) An anonymous group (vv. 15–19), who have been identi-fied with either the preceding (vv. 11–14) or the following

---

[1] *Cf.* N. Na'aman, 'The list of David's officers (*šālišîm*)', *VT* 38, 1988, pp. 71–79; D. G. Schley, 'The *šālišîm* (sic!): officers or special three-man squads', *VT* 40, 1990, pp. 321–326.

[2] Comparison with the list in 2 Sa. 23:8–39 reveals a large number of variants, especially in the spelling of names. The textual differences have arisen in a number of ways, including copying errors, the existence of other possible versions of the same list, and the non-standardization of the spelling of names in ancient times. For a comparative listing of the names, see Myers, *1 Chronicles*, p. 80, and Braun, pp. 161–162.

names (vv. 20–25). The point of David's pouring Bethlehem's precious *water* on the ground is threefold. It highlights a great act of Israelite bravery, it exalts David's ability to inspire extraordinary loyalty, and it was recognized as an act of worship (vv. 18 – not *before the* LORD, as NIV, but 'to the LORD' as NRSV, RSV, REB, NEB, GNB; *cf.* 1 Sa. 7:6).

(c) The third group may also be a trio, including *Asahel* (v. 26) as well as *Abishai* his brother and *Benaiah* (vv. 20–25).[1] Abishai and Benaiah are mentioned for their *great exploits* (v. 22), but neither apparently attained to the Three (vv. 21, 25).[2] The 'ariels' (RSV; lit. 'lions of God') of verse 22 could be either 'lions' (Hertzberg) or 'champions' (REB, NEB; *cf.* 'lionlike men', AV).

(d) *The mighty men* (vv. 26–47). The list is longer than that in 2 Samuel 23 (that list ends at *Uriah the Hittite*, v. 41a here), which is one possible reason for omitting 'The Thirty' from the title (2 Sa. 23:24) and the concluding total (2 Sa. 23:39). It seems to proceed in some sort of geographical order. Most of the first ten names from *Elhanan* to *Heled* (vv. 26–30) originated from Judah, several in verses 31–37 are from northern communities, and men of non-Israelite origin are listed in vv. 38–41a. The addition of verses 41b–47 is couched in a slightly different style from vv. 26–41a, and probably comes from a separate source. These extra names, several of which have Transjordanian connections, are a testimony to fluidity in the size of the group. They might be later replacements, or even assistants to some of those listed earlier (*cf.* the reference to Joab's *armour-bearer*, v. 39).

Chapter 12 continues the theme of all-Israelite support for David's kingship with material that has no parallel in the Old Testament. Two aspects are emphasized: the increasing defections to David during the period of his persecution by Saul (vv. 1–22), and the gathering of the militia from all the tribes at Hebron (vv. 23–40). Chapters 11–12 are arranged in an over-all chiastic structure, *viz.*,

[1] See Rudolph, pp. 99f.; Hertzberg, pp. 406f.; both following K. Elliger. The list of the Thirty in 2 Sa. 23:24–39 contains exactly thirty names without Asahel.

[2] MT is not clear to which group they really belonged, a confusion amply illustrated by NIV's translation in vv. 20, 21 ('Abishai . . . was chief of the Three . . . and became their commander, even though he was not included among them').

    a. All the tribal elders anoint David at Hebron (11:1–3)
      b. Tribal support at Ziklag (12:1–7)
        c. Tribal support at the stronghold (12:8–15)
        c_1. Tribal support at the stronghold (12:16–18)
      b_1. Tribal support at Ziklag (12:19–22)
    a_1. All the tribes anoint David at Hebron (12:23–40).[1]

The whole scheme also shows a clear chronological development, underlining the gathering momentum of David's support from the earliest period at 'the stronghold', then at Ziklag and finally at Hebron. At the very centre stands a prophetic word affirming God's own support for David (12:18). The impetus behind David's increasing support is thus shown to come from God himself.

Two further threads run through the chapter: help for David (vv. 1, 17, 18, 19, 21, 22), and Israel's wholeheartedness (vv. 17, 33, 38). *Help* is one of Chronicles' favourite terms, expressing commitment and co-operation rather than merely assistance. The references in this chapter usually describe military support, but according to verse 18 the really significant reason for this co-operation lies in God's active support. The various uses of 'help' in chapter 12 further confirm the solidarity of God, king, and people in the choice of David as king.[2] This unity is a wholehearted one, as underlined twice in verse 38 (lit. 'whole heart' . . ., 'one heart . . .'; NRSV, RSV, 'with full intent . . . of a single mind'). The initiative comes from David, perhaps developing from a pre-monarchy alliance with those who had not previously committed themselves to him (v. 17, *cf.* NRSV, RSV 'My heart will be knit to you'). The people's response is exemplified by the undivided loyalty of the hardened soldiers from distant Zebulun (v. 33). In sharp contrast with many other generations of Israelites, their faith is here characterized by its God-centredness, resulting in practical

---

[1] See introductory comment on ch. 11.

[2] Ginsberg's proposal to translate 'those who help' (Heb. *'zr*, vv. 1, 18) as 'warriors' ('A Ugaritic parallel to 2 Sam. 1.21', *JBL* 57, 1938, pp. 209–213, *cf.* pp. 210f., n. 4), though often accepted, is probably unnecessary. It is based on a Ugaritic homophone, but the two roots probably belong together since their semantic range overlaps (*cf.* Williamson, p. 106, for references, and *cf.* J. Barr, *Comparative Philology*, Oxford: Clarendon Press, 1968, p. 139, n. 332). Some have also found an Aramaic spelling of the same verb, 'to help', in vv. 33, 38 (*'dr*), but while this could be appropriate in v. 33 (*cf.* LXX, Vulg.), it does not fit in v. 38 (against Rudolph). Possible translations that suit both verses are 'bold' (NEB) or 'congregate' (Bertheau, p. 209).

obedience, fresh hope (v. 18), and joyful generosity (vv. 39–40). It sets a pattern for New Testament faith, which, when centred on Jesus, Son of David and Son of God, joyfully unites believers within God's great purposes for all people (*cf.* Eph. 2:1 – 4:16).

d. Tribal support at Ziklag: the Benjaminites (12:1–7).[1]

David's stay in *Ziklag*, to which verses 19–22 also relate, belongs to his sixteen-month period with the Philistines (see 1 Sa. 27 – 2 Sa. 1). David's retinue is swelled by twenty-three experienced and well-armed soldiers from Saul's own tribe, the *Benjaminites* (*cf.* also vv. 16, 29), though others from the same tribe remained loyal to Saul's house even after Saul's death (v. 29 and 2 Sa. 2:15, 25). *Ishmaiah*'s admission to the Thirty (see ch. 11 for comment) is an indication of David's trust in a former opponent (v. 4). The identifiable place-names are Benjaminite: Gadera (v. 4), Haruph (v. 5), Korah (v. 6), and *Gedor* (v. 7) remain uncertain, though Judean locations have been proposed.

e. Tribal support at the stronghold: the Gadites (12:8–15).

With verses 16–18, this section refers to David's earlier period of persecution by Saul. The *stronghold* could be either Adullam (1 Sa. 22:1) or Engedi (1 Sa. 23:29; 24:1), though David used a number of similar places (1 Sa. 23:14). David is here joined by eleven officers (vv. 9–14a) from Gad, a Transjordanian tribe in Southern Gilead, who are characterized by strength and bravery (vv. 8, 15). Verse 14 is probably a reference to their leadership qualities (as NRSV and the VSS, especially Vulg., LXX)[2] though it is more often understood as a further indication of their courage (NIV, REB, NEB, *etc.*). *They put to flight everyone living in the valleys* (v. 15, *cf.* NRSV, RSV) is better translated, 'they barred all the valleys' (*e.g.* Rudolph).

f. Tribal support at the stronghold: the Benjaminites and Judahites (12:16–18).

Like verses 8–15, this section is associated with the *stronghold*, but it deals poignantly with the uncertain loyalty of some men from *Judah* and Benjamin (v. 17)

---

[1] MT v. 5 begins with 'Jeremiah' of v. 4 in EVV; as a result, Heb. verse numbers are one higher than in English translations for the rest of the ch.

[2] Tg. is more equivocal here than is sometimes supposed, *cf. TC*, 1, p. 69.

rather than with their tribal origins. Internal division bedevilled Israel throughout their entire existence as a nation. The problem continued under David, especially through Absalom's rebellion, and was finally institutionalized in the division of the monarchy, when the slogan of the northern tribes (2 Ch. 10:16) was a direct contrast to Amasai's unifying prophecy (*cf.* Ackroyd, Williamson). Here, however, the people are so attuned to God that even a soldier speaks prophetically (v. 18). *Amasai* might be identified with Amasa, Absalom's army commander (2 Sa. 17:25) who was later reinstated by David (2 Sa. 19:13), or less probably with Abishai (*cf.* 1 Ch. 11:20–21). The prophecy confirms God's declared purposes for David; the *spirit* (Heb. is indefinite, *cf.* NRSV, REB, NEB) can be understood as being sent by God or might possibly be identified with God (*i.e. Spirit*, RSV, NIV). 'A spirit clothed Amasai' is a literal but striking translation of the Hebrew, and the phrase recurs in the Old Testament only in Judges 6:34 and 2 Chronicles 34:20. However, it has a strong echo in Jesus' promise that the early Christians would be 'clothed with power from on high' (Lk. 24:49). The message of 'peace' (or *success*, NIV, GNB) and *help* is placed at the fulcrum of the chapter, and puts in a nutshell the hopes not only of these soldiers, but of all the tribes.[1]

g. Tribal support at Ziklag: the Manassites (12:19–22).

Seven leading Manassites defected to David shortly before Saul's final defeat. Chronicles assumes the reader knows about the Philistines rejecting David's assistance before the battle (v. 19; *cf.* 1 Sa. 29) and about David's subsequent victory over the Amalekite *raiding bands* (vv. 20–21; *cf.* 1 Sa. 30, especially verses 8, 15, where the word 'band' – RSV; *'raiding party'*, NIV – reappears. The theme of *help*, following verse 18, is especially prominent (vv. 19, 21, 22). In this context, David's withdrawal from the Philistine army must be understood as divine providence. Verse 22 probably summarizes the whole of verses 1–21, though it also supplies a link to verses 23–27. According to 1 Samuel 27:2, David's personal army numbered 600 before he moved to Ziklag; eight years later at Hebron, it must have

---

[1] Verse 18 is the only poetic piece in Chronicles not directly paralleled in Samuel–Kings or Psalms. This may well indicate that this verse too was borrowed, but from a source otherwise unknown (G. E. Schafer, 'The significance of seeking God', Louisville Th.D., 1972, p. 22).

swelled considerably and seemed like *great army* (NIV, NRSV, RSV; *cf.* GNB, REB, NEB), especially as Saul's standing army was very small. The final phrase in Hebrew is literally 'like the camp/army of God', perhaps hinting at unseen divine support, as in the only other occurence of this phrase (Gn. 32:2, MT, v. 3).

h. Tribal support at Hebron (12:23–37). This passage lists the numbers of soldiers from each tribe who gathered at Hebron, complementing the lists of leading individuals in 11:10–47. The reference to transferring Saul's kingdom to David (v. 23) confirms 10:14 (*turn over to* is the same Heb. verb as 'transfer' in 10:14), and understands these tribal movements as a response to God's declared purpose ('according to the word of the LORD', v. 23, NRSV, RSV). The list's authenticity is indicated by some unexpected elements: the meagreness of Judah's contingent (v. 24) and the mention of thirteen tribes, including the Levites (v. 26) and both Joseph tribes (vv. 30, 31, 37). The numbers curiously contrast substantial contributions from the tribes of the north (vv. 29–37) with the low figures for Judah (v. 24) and Levi (vv. 26–28). Both these latter tribes are of special interest for Chronicles. Perhaps the list excludes those whose allegiance to David had already been publicly declared, such as at his earlier anointing as king over Judah (2 Sa. 2:1–4), since even Judah only gradually committed itself to David (vv. 16–18). The northern tribes would generally have been allied to Saul's house up to this point, as suggested by several annotations (vv. 29, 31, 33), so that the list's main purpose may be to confirm the extent of support transferred to David during the indecisive period following Saul's death. Some of the notes, particularly verses 27–28, 29, 31, 33, betray the Chronicler's own contribution.

26–28. The Levites were never prohibited from engaging in military activity, despite their religious duties. *Jehoiada* is the father of Benaiah (1 Ch. 11:22–25; 1 Ki. 1:8ff.) on the basis of 1 Chronicles 27:5 where he is apparently called high priest (*cf.* REB, NEB), though his relationship with David's priest Abiathar (1 Sa. 20:20–23; 1 Ch. 15:11; 27:34; *etc.*) is unclear. *Zadok*, here a young man, eventually replaced Abiathar after the latter's involvement in the Adonijah conspiracy (1 Ki. 1:7ff.) and became Solomon's high priest (1 Ki. 1:8ff.).

32. The note about *Issachar* is tantalizingly vague, though no

147

evidence connects this tribe with astrology (against Williamson, Rudolph, *etc.*). In this context, the note refers to their discernment of God's will for their own day.[1]

i. Celebration of David as King at Hebron (12:38–40). The conclusion to chapters 11–12, and closely associated with 11:1–3. It amplifies the contribution made by the people (*all Israel*, v. 38), especially the soldiers (*cf.* vv. 23–27) and *all the rest of the Israelites* (v. 38). The latter phrase (Heb. *šĕrît*, 'rest'), possibly referring to the former adherents of Saul's kingdom, may also contain an allusion to the remnant, and so point to the potential for unity in the post-exilic community (*cf.* also 1 Ch. 13:2; 2 Ch. 30:6). The paragraph as a whole, however, shows that the people of God are the real heroes of the chapter. These Israelites exemplify the principle that when God's people become committed to one another (*cf.* the use of *help* throughout the chapter) in obedient service to God's chosen king, they find both unity and joy (*cf.* Jn. 15:9–11).

The unparalleled three-day festival (vv. 39–40) is the climax of the covenant (11:3). Covenants of all kinds were often celebrated by a special meal (*e.g.* Gn. 31:54; Ex. 24:11), including the Lord's Supper as the celebration meal of the new covenant. This feast of David's kingship is marked by plenty and joy, exemplifying the people's practical concern for one another as well as for their king. It portrays with graphic simplicity, as perhaps nowhere else in the Old Testament, the potential for real unity between God, king, and people.

B. David brings the ark to Jerusalem (13:1 – 16:43)

Chapters 13–16 describe how the ark of the covenant was brought to a permanent site in Jerusalem. It is clearly assumed that readers are aware of the earlier history of the ark (see 1 Sa. 4:1 – 7:2), when it had been totally neglected in the Judean

---

[1] This is indirectly confirmed by J. P. Weinberg ('Der Mensch im Weltbild des Chronisten, seine psyche', *VT* 33, 1983, pp. 295–316, especially pp. 307, 311), who concludes that the Chronicler's main view of human intellectual ability is a consistently practical one, often applied to political decisions and activity. Although he regards the 'knowing' of 12:32 as the sole exception, it is in fact no exception and forms a good example of the Chronicler's practical approach to knowledge and wisdom (MT *yôḏᵉʿê bînâ*, lit. 'those who know understanding').

village of Kiriath-jearim (*cf.* 13:3) during most of Samuel's leadership and Saul's entire reign.[1] Now, however, David's 'seeking' God (13:3) by means of the ark is a crucial event for all Israel. It is given greater significance than David's achievements in building, family life, and military endeavour (ch. 14), a point that is underlined by the repositioning of 2 Samuel 5:11–25 (now = 1 Ch. 14:1–16) after chapter 13. In fact, the new arrangement is part of a wider pattern employed by Chronicles in the account of kings such as Abijah (2 Ch. 13), Jehoshaphat (2 Ch. 17–20), and Hezekiah (2 Ch. 29–32). According to this pattern, a king's military victories and his sovereignty over other peoples are understood as consequences that result from seeking the Lord.[2] David's seeking is not only in sharp contrast with his predecessor Saul(1 Ch. 10), but leads directly to God's renewing of the covenant (1 Ch. 17) and the preparations for the temple (1 Ch. 22–29).

The ark itself was a wooden box covered with gold and containing the two stones inscribed with the Ten Commandments. In chapters 13–16 it is known primarily as either *the ark of God* (*e.g.* 13:5) or *the ark of the covenant* (*e.g.* 15:25ff.), symbolizing the active presence of God and the Mosaic covenant. David's care for the ark therefore represents his obedience to the Mosaic/Sinaitic covenant, and leads naturally into the formation of the Davidic covenant in chapter 17. A third feature of the ark's symbolism, that it represents Yahweh's throne or footstool, appears in 1 Chronicles 13:6; 28:2 (*cf.* Pss. 99:5; 132:7).

Although the ark probably perished in Nebuchadnezzar's destruction of Jerusalem (*cf.* Je. 3:16), the Chronicler gives greater emphasis to it than the compiler of 2 Samuel. This is presumably because he wanted his own generation to give priority to their own symbols of God's covenant and presence, especially the temple. The same concern is reflected in the special interest attached to the temple articles brought back from exile (*e.g.* Ezr. 1:7ff.; 5:14f.; 7:19). The ark is now long gone, of course, but the New Testament understands the ark's

---

[1] The one possible exception to this neglect is 1 Sa. 14:18. Though the LXX reading 'ephod' is usually preferred to MT's 'ark' (*e.g.* R. W. Klein, *1 Samuel*, WBC, Waco: Word Books, 1983, p. 132), the issue remains open (*cf.* H. W. Hertzberg, pp. 113–114; P. R. Davies, 'Ark or ephod in 1 Sam. XIV 18?', *JTS* 26, 1975, pp. 82–87).

[2] *Cf.* Mosis, *UTCG*, pp. 44–81.

significance as still continued in Jesus. In his own person, he had instituted a better covenant and made God's presence directly accessible to every believer (Heb. 9:1–12, especially vv. 4–5; *cf.* Rev. 11:19 for the ark's symbolic presence in heaven). David's concern for the ark, therefore, is an encouragement to Christian believers to seek God's way of obedience, confident that his presence, once made known through the ark, is now available through Jesus and the new covenant.

i. The ark begins its journey (13:1–14)

'Let us bring the ark of our God back to us' (13:3).

13:5–14 – *cf.* 2 Samuel 6:1–11

Chapter 13 clearly commends the priority David gives to the ark, but it also contains a warning that it was much more than a symbol of the divine presence. The enthusiasm of verse 3 (*Let us bring the ark of our God back to us*) gives way swiftly to David's despair, *How can I ever bring the ark of God to me?* (v. 12). Even David could not take the reality of God's presence for granted. If Chronicles' readers wanted Israel's former glories restored, they too must reckon with a God whose dynamic holiness could not be contained within human limitations. The chapter is also notable for recording one of David's two failures in the Chronicler's account (for the other, see 1 Ch. 21). David makes the fundamental error of failing to recognize God's true nature, and as a result, both here and in chapter 21, some Israelites have to pay the ultimate price. While it is true that the Chronicler omits several details from earlier accounts of David's private life, including the Bathsheba incident (2 Sa. 11–12), he certainly does not whitewash David's reputation, as some have alleged.

a. The decision to move the ark (13:1–4).

This introduction, identifiable by characteristic vocabulary and themes, has been added by the Chronicler to 2 Samuel 6. Three themes, none of them found in 2 Samuel 6, dominate these verses. The first, continued from chapters 11–12, is 'all Israel' (v. 5, RSV, *etc.*), described in verses 2, 4 as *the whole assembly*. In the light of the tribes' commitment to David at Hebron (11:1–3; 12:38–40), bringing back the ark is no longer just a military initiative undertaken by David's men (*cf.* 2 Sa. 6:1), but a religious enterprise of the whole people. The *assembly* in this context must refer to representatives from most if not all the tribes.[1] The unity theme is amplified twice, by references to *priests and Levites*, who will play a key role in the ark's transportation (chapters 15–16), and to *the rest of our brothers throughout the territories of Israel* (*cf.* 12:38). The latter contrasts Israel's disintegration after Saul's final defeat (*cf.* 10:7), and offers new encouragement after David's victory over the Philistines (14:8–17) to those too hesitant to attend the anointing at Hebron (11:1–3).

The second theme is that of consultation, a special interest of Chronicles rarely found in Samuel or Kings. Kings such as Solomon (2 Ch. 1:2), Jehoshaphat (2 Ch. 20:21), and Hezekiah (2 Ch. 30:2; 32:3) are commended for this,[2] in stark contrast with the failure of Rehoboam (2 Ch. 10:6–14) and Amaziah (2 Ch. 25:16–17) to follow good advice. David's consultation here allows the Israelite people to take a corporate decision on the central issue of the ark's future (v. 4). In so doing, Chronicles presents a leadership ideal for the people of God very different from authoritarian patterns well known in ancient and modern times. It is notable that in Chronicles, the kings who consult their people are also those who seek Yahweh (*cf.* v. 3; 2 Ch. 1:5, Solomon; 2 Ch. 20:3–4, Jehoshaphat; 2 Ch. 30:18; 31:21, Hezekiah).

'Seeking' God is the third theme in this paragraph (v. 3), and sets a pattern for the whole of David's reign.[3] It forms a further step away from absolutism as Chronicles' model for kingship, for 'seeking' Yahweh requires constant dependence on him.

In verse 2, the verb that lies behind *let us send . . . far and wide* (*cf.* NRSV, RSV) is important in chapters 13–15, but is of uncertain meaning here (Heb. *prṣ*, 'to break out'; see comment on vv. 9–12). Most likely it has the sense of NIV, NRSV, RSV, though it could be treated as part of the conditional clause and read as

---

[1] Heb. *qāhāl* ('assembly'), occurring in vv. 2, 4, for the first time in Ch. (with a verbal form in v. 5) and over 30 times in all in the two books, is used in a representative sense in Ch. (*cf.* L. Coenen, *NIDNTT*, I, p. 293).
[2] The Hebrew word *wayyiwwā'aṣ* (v. 1) occurs in identical form in the passages about Jehoshaphat and Hezekiah, and has become part of the Chronicler's technical vocabulary of kingship.
[3] C. Begg, '"Seeking Yahweh" and the purpose of Chronicles', *Louvain Studies* 9, 1982, pp. 132–134.

a slightly different word, as in LXX ('and if it is the will of the
LORD our God', GNB, *cf.* JB).[1]

b. The action of moving the ark (13:5–8). 2 Samuel 6:2–11
is retained with a few changes in verses 6–14, and the beginning of the account in 2 Samuel 6:1 is also preserved in
skeleton form in verse 5. The 'all Israel' theme of verses 1–4 is
continued, but now in verses 5–6 it is applied explicitly to the
moving of the ark. Thus, 'all the chosen men of Israel' (2 Sa.
6:1) and 'all the people who were with David' (2 Sa. 6:2) have
now become simply 'all Israel' (vv. 5, 6, RSV, *etc.*). This inclu-
siveness is further underlined by the extremely wide description of Israel's boundaries. Instead of the usual 'Dan to
Beersheba' (*e.g.* 1 Sa. 3:20; 2 Sa. 3:10),[2] Israel extends from
the *Shihor* river, probably the easternmost branch of the Nile,[3]
to Labo of Hamath (Lebo Hamath, NIV, REB, NEB, NRSV; 'the
entrance of Hamath', RSV), probably modern Lebweh at the
watershed of the Beqaʿ valley. This extended Israel is based on
Joshua's vision of the Promised Land, and David here is the
one who turned hope into reality (*cf.* Jos. 13:2–5).[4] *Baalah*, on
the Judean-Philistine border, where the ark had been abandoned (= Baale-Judah, 2 Sa. 6:2), seems to be understood as
an alternative name for *Kiriath Jearim*, on the basis of Joshua
15:9 (*cf.* Jos. 15:60; 18:14).

Two contrasting attitudes to the ark are revealed. On the
one hand, it represents Yahweh's majestic presence, as in the
rare formula 'enthroned above the cherubim' (v. 6, RSV; *cf.* 1
Sa. 4:4; 2 Sa. 6:2; = 1 Ch. 13:6; 2 Ki. 19:15 = Is. 37:16; Pss.
80:1; 99:1), and the abbreviated expression *called by the Name*
(*cf.* 2 Sa. 6:2). The former phrase indicates that the ark may
have been regarded as Yahweh's empty throne, and the latter
that the ark, like the temple, belonged to God as his earthly

---

[1] Though L. C. Allen regards LXX only as a paraphrase of MT (*SVT* 25, I,
1974, p. 128. REB, NEB's 'if the LORD our God opens a way' is an attempt to
retain the usual sense of the Heb. in the conditional clause.

[2] In the only two references in Ch. (the only post-exilic work where the
phrase occurs), the author perhaps reveals his southern orientation by
uniquely placing the southern boundary first, as here ('Beersheba to Dan', 1
Ch. 21:2; 2 Ch. 30:5; *cf.* also 2 Ch. 19:4).

[3] K. A. Kitchen, *IBD*, pp. 430–431; or the Wadi el-Arish (M. Noth, *etc.*).

[4] For the historical issues involved, see *e.g.* J. Bright, *History of Israel*, rev. ed.
(London: SCM Press, 1972), pp. 200f.; J. H. Hayes and J. M. Miller (eds.),
Israelite and Judean History (London: SCM Press, 1977), pp. 349–352.

residence (*cf.* Dt. 12:11; 1 Ki. 8:29; 2 Ch. 7:16). Such majesty was acknowledged and celebrated with all Israel's might and music (v. 8). On the other hand, the awareness of divine majesty was diminished by the ark's being separated from the Tent (still at nearby Gibeon – 1 Ch. 16:39ff.; 21:29–30; 2 Ch. 1:3, 13), and by its transportation on a *new cart* (v. 7). The use of such inadequate transport showed David unthinkingly continuing a Philistine superstition (1 Sa. 6:7), and failing to 'seek' God (1 Ch. 15:12–15, especially v. 13). In other words, Israel got into difficulties because they failed to recognize that worship of the true God meant they could no longer simply follow contemporary pagan practices.

c. God's deadly holiness (13:9–12). That *Uzzah*'s practical concern for the ark was punished with apparently unjustified severity has often puzzled modern western readers, but the incident is intelligible if read on its own terms. In the Old Testament, God's holiness possessed genuine power and could have striking physical and spiritual effects (*cf.* Lv. 10:1ff.; Is. 6:1ff.). It was often associated with cultic objects such as the ark, in a way that is no longer familiar to most readers and which has now been superseded by the work of Christ (Heb. 9:1–12). Further, David's contemporaries would not have been entirely unaware of similar tragedies which had recently struck both the Philistines (1 Sa. 5) and Israelites from Beth-Shemesh (1 Sa. 6:19–20). Their experiences might have given a warning that to be in possession of the ark was no unqualified guarantee of divine blessing. Uzzah *died*, therefore, because neither he nor those responsible for the transportation arrangements (including David) recognized the real nature of the relationship between the ark and its God, the Holy One of Israel. Chronicles confirms that this dynamic holiness was personal and divine rather than magical by simplifying 'before the ark of God' (2 Sa. 6:7) to *before God* (v. 10).[1]

Two results followed from the disaster of Uzzah's death. David turned from great joy to being *angry* (v. 11) and *afraid*

[1] On the textual issues in this section, see the larger commentaries. Although the MT of ch. 13 is generally accepted as superior to its equivalent in 2 Sa. (especially in vv. 8, 10), it is not clear exactly what happened to the oxen when the ark fell, or why the name of the threshing-floor is so different from that in the earlier text (v. 9).

(v. 12), demonstrating at a vital moment his inability to maintain the high expectations associated with him. The incident was primarily remembered, however, as the occasion of God's 'breakout' (Perez Uzzah = breaking out against Uzzah; the Heb. word for 'breakout' is a key word, appearing three times in v. 11, and also in 13:2; 14:11; 15:13). The God of the ark was a sovereign Lord who could not be confined, either by human fallibility or by good intentions. A similar incident in the New Testament concerns Ananias and Sapphira, when the Holy Spirit broke out unexpectedly in judgment upon a growing spiritual movement (Acts 5:1–11). That God is a 'consuming fire' (Dt. 4:24; 9:3) is a New Testament truth (Heb. 12:29) as well as an Old Testament one.

d. God's unconditional blessing (13:13–14). God's breakout continues in unexpected and unrestrained blessing upon *Obed-Edom*. Though some have equated him with the Levite(s) of the same name in chapter 15 (see 15:18, 21, 24; also 16:5, 38; 26:4ff.), the non-Israelite form of the name and the epithet *Gittite* (= inhabitant of Gath) make it more likely that he was a Philistine.[1] David apparently thought that since the ark might bring further trouble to Israel, Philistines ought first to be exposed to the risk, especially as God had not hesitated previously to show his displeasure with the Philistines over the ark (*cf.* 1 Sa. 5). The result, however, is as unexpected as the preceding tragedy, and David is as unaware of the nature of Yahweh's mercy as he was of his holiness. David may have already conquered Gath (*cf.* 18:1), but it is Yahweh rather than David who brings blessing to its inhabitants, extending his bounty to Obed-Edom's whole household (emphasized by the triple use of Heb. *bayit* in v. 14 for *family/house/household*), even to future generations (26:5). The theme of Yahweh's peaceful intentions for David's international neighbours continues in chapter 14.

ii. God's blessings on David's kingdom (14:1–17)
'And David knew that the LORD had established him as king

[1] Alternatively, 'Gittite' has been thought to refer to the Levite village of Gath-rimmon near Shechem (Jos. 21:25, 1 Ch. 6:69), but sheer distance from Kiriath-Jearim makes this location less likely than Philistine Gath (*cf.* R. K. Harrison, *Introduction to the Old Testament*, London: Tyndale Press, 1969, p. 1166).

over Israel and that his kingdom had been highly exalted for the sake of his people Israel' (14:2).

14:1–16 – *cf.* 2 Samuel 5:11–25

The position of chapter 14 is unexpected. This is partly because it has been removed from its original position in 2 Samuel following David's anointing and the capture of Jerusalem (= 1 Ch. 11:1–9), and partly because the Philistine wars (vv. 8–16) remain separate from David's other military exploits, which include further conflicts with the Philistines (1 Ch. 11:11–25 and especially chs. 18–20). The most likely explanation for the current arrangement is to treat chapter 14 as the sequel to chapter 13, for the following reasons.

(a) The 'seeking' theme of chapter 13 continues to play a prominent role in this account of the Philistine wars (vv. 10, 14). It is related to a wider pattern by which military victory and international recognition are regarded as benefits received as a result of seeking God (*cf.* comment on ch. 13).

(b) David's kingship over *all Israel*, continued from chapters 12–13, is now confirmed (vv. 2, 8).

(c) The constant focus on Jerusalem throughout chapter 14 as not only David's conquered city (11:4–9), but also where David receives God's varied blessings, marks it out as a city prepared for the ark.[1]

(d) God's 'breakout' in judgment (13:9–12) now becomes a 'breakout' in blessing for Israel as well as for Obed-Edom's household (v. 11; *Baal Perazim* means 'lord who breaks out/through'). The ark can finally proceed to Jerusalem because God's mercy and blessing have now removed and overwhelmed the consequences of his anger (*cf.* Jn. 3:16–17).

Two other factors further clarify the purpose of chapter 14. In verse 17, the Chronicler's main addition to his source, the whole chapter gives evidence of international acknowledgment of David's kingdom and God's sovereignty. Secondly, comparison with chapter 10 shows that Saul's defeat by the Philistines has now been completely reversed. This is made explicit at several points:

(a) David's house is fertile (14:3–7), but Saul's was finished (10:6).

(b) the Philistines' raiding activity (14:9, 13) and their

---

[1] See also P. Welten in A. H. J. Gunneweg and O. Kaiser (eds.), *Textgemäss* (Göttingen: Vandenhoeck & Ruprecht, 1979), pp. 174f.

stripping the dead (10:8, 9), both expressed by the same Hebrew verb (*pāšaṭ*), can be resisted only by David.

(c) David enquires of God (14:10, 14), Saul did not (10:13–14).

(d) David captures and burns the Philistine gods (14:12), before whom Saul's head and armour were presented as trophies of war (10:9–10).

(e) Saul's kingdom was transferred (10:14), but David's is confirmed (14:2, 17).

In the light of all these factors, it is clear from chapter 14 that for the first time a kingdom was established in Israel under God's blessing, as a result of which *Jerusalem* is established at the centre of the kingdom. Into this secure setting the ark of God's might can now come to its resting place (*cf.* 2 Ch. 6:41), so reversing the catastrophic defeat by the Philistines at Aphek when the ark was first captured (1 Sa. 4).

All this would have reminded the Chronicler's own generation that in spite of the exile, God was still willing to pour out the blessings of his kingdom on those who would seek him for direction. The aim of the chapter is therefore much wider than glorifying David (Michaeli) or even underlining David's saviour role (Williamson). A similar pattern emerges in the New Testament, though it is greatly enlarged and transformed. As God's kingdom was finally established by Christ's resurrection and ascension, God poured out many gifts in blessing (Eph. 4:7–13). A crucial difference, however, is that the Old Testament's typically this-worldly blessings are overtaken, though by no means obliterated (*cf.* Mt. 6:31–32), by the New Testament's infinitely vaster promise of 'every spiritual blessing in Christ' (Eph. 1:3; *cf.* Mt. 6:33).

a. David's palace (14:1–2). *Hiram* I of Tyre (Chronicles usually has Huram, though the name is possibly short for Ahiram) had much more to do with Solomon than with David (*e.g.* 2 Ch. 2:11–16; 9:21). He is usually thought to belong to the second half of David's reign (*c.* 1000–960 BC), and the date of Hiram's reign is often based on Albright's figures of 969–936 BC, but other proposals vary from 980–947 BC (Peñuela, Cross) or even earlier (Green) to as late as 962–929 BC (Lipinski).[1] His

[1] *Cf.* A. R. Green, 'David's relations with Hiram', in C. L. Meyers and M. O'Connor (eds.), *The Word of the Lord Shall Go Forth* (Winona Lake: Eisenbrauns, 1983), pp. 373–397.

recognition of David, whether for trade (GNB), tribute (Ackroyd), or for other purposes, demonstrated Yahweh's renewed blessing for David's 'house' (v. 1, NRSV, RSV, REB, NEB; *palace*, GNB, NIV) and *kingdom* (v. 2), in anticipation of the covenant blessings of 17:10bff.

b. David's sons (14:3–7). The list of thirteen names, repeated in 1 Chronicles 3:5–8, is included as a continuation of the house theme of verse 1, in a further foreshadowing of the house/dynasty of chapter 17. It is assumed that God is the source of this fertility, though not necessarily approving of David's polygamy. The *more wives* and *more sons and daughters* (v. 3) assume the reader's knowledge of the earlier list at Hebron (2 Sa. 3:2–5). If, as is likely, the names are given in order of birth, Solomon was actually tenth in the line. The original form of *Beeliada* (v. 7), with its unique first syllable, was probably Baaliada, the present text being influenced by the alternative form Eliada (2 Sa. 5:16; 1 Ch. 3:8).[1]

c. David's Philistine wars (14:8–16). David had been no great threat to the Philistines while Israel and Judah remained divided, but an all-Israelite kingdom (v. 8) was a different matter. So the Philistines gathered in *Rephaim* valley, probably located south west of Jerusalem near Bethlehem (the incident of 11:15–20 is linked here). The first attack certainly took place before the ark's entry into Jerusalem, although its precise timing and military significance remain uncertain. The probability is that it followed David's anointing ceremony quite quickly (v. 8), since David's headquarters at this time were at Adullam (1 Ch. 11:15ff. = 2 Sa. 23:13ff.; *cf.* the statement that 'he went down to the stronghold' (2 Sa. 5:17) which cannot refer to the hill on which Jerusalem stands). It seems therefore to precede 11:4–6 and chapter 13 chronologically, though others have placed this battle in the three-month period of the ark's residence with Obed-Edom (*cf.* 13:14), or even after Jerusalem's capture.[2]

Whether the second battle (vv. 13–16) occurred at the same

---

[1] Barthélemy, *CTAT*, pp. 240f.
[2] It is quite possible that this first conflict was a fairly minor border raid, *cf.* N. L. Tidwell, 'The Philistine incursions into the Valley of Rephaim', in J. A. Emerton (ed.), *Studies in the Historical Books of the Old Testament*, SVT 30, 1979, pp. 190–212.

place and time is much less clear. Because a place-name is omitted in verse 13, and *Gibeon* (2 Sa. 5:25 'Geba') is mentioned in verse 16, many commentators (*e.g.* Hertzberg, Michaeli) have concluded that the second conflict was an attempt to recapture the city from David and took place in the Gibeon area north west of Jerusalem (*cf.* Is. 28:21, where Mount Perazim and Gibeon are linked in an apparent reference to this battle). On the other hand, Rephaim appears in 2 Samuel 5:22 and is perhaps assumed in verse 13 here (so LXX, P), suggesting a similar location to the first battle. However, the extensive pursuit towards *Gezer* (v. 16) on the edge of the coastal plain is a hint that the fighting covered a much wider area than any single battlefield.

Of greater importance to the Chronicler, however, is the repeated emphasis that in these battles David sought God's direction (vv. 10–14), and that God was the chief agent of victory (*God has broken out*, v. 11; *God has gone out in front of you*, v. 15). The Chronicler uses the phrase *enquired of God* in a typical fashion, as he did for Saul (1 Ch. 10:13–14), illustrating this as a feature of David's whole life orientation (the same verb *šā'al* is used of David in 1 Sa. 23:2, 4; 30:8; 2 Sa. 2:1). The initial victory is understood as a divine breakthrough comparable with an irresistible onrush of water (v. 11), perhaps having in mind heavy rainfall in hilly country (Hertzberg) or 'the breaking of a clay vessel full of water' (Tg.). After the first battle, the captured *gods* were burned (v. 12), hinting at David's faithfulness in the covenant (*cf.* Dt. 7:5, 25).[1] The precise species of the *balsam* trees (vv. 14–15) is uncertain. Other possibilities include the pear-tree (LXX), mulberry (AV), or aspen (REB, NEB). Interestingly, Tg. foreshadows modern translation practice in preferring the generic term 'trees' for an unidentifiable technical word.

d. David's fame (14:17). Though the different elements in chapter 14 come from various periods in David's reign and are not listed chronologically, international recognition of David's *fame* (lit. name) and Yahweh's *fear* are seen as exemplifying David's blessing under the covenants. A great name for the Davidic dynasty is a covenant blessing foreshadowed here

---

[1] 2 Sa. 5:21 has 'David and his men carried them off'. For a detailed discussion of the issues, including the possibility that the Chronicler was using a different text, *cf.* Williamson, p. 118.

(*cf.* 1 Ch. 17:8) and also later enjoyed by Uzziah (2 Ch. 26:8, 15). Similarly, Yahweh's awe-inspiring activity was acknowledged by other nations through Asa (2 Ch. 14:13) and Jehoshaphat (2 Ch. 17:10; 20:29; *cf.* 19:7). The promises contained in the Mosaic covenant (Dt. 2:25; 11:25) were therefore already being fulfilled through David and his dynasty.

iii. The ark completes its journey (15:1–29)
'So all Israel brought up the ark of the covenant of the LORD'
(15:28).
15:25–29 – *cf.* 2 Samuel 6:12b–16

The ark's final journey to Jerusalem is completed in chapters 15–16, though the chapter division does mark a useful distinction between the last stage of the journey (ch. 15) and the celebrations surrounding the ark's arrival (ch. 16).

The major subject of chapter 15 is easily discerned from the repeated phrase *to bring up* (Heb. *l^eha^{ʿa}lôt*) *the ark of the LORD* (vv. 3, 12, 14, 25, 28), which finds an echo in the fact that the Levites *carry* (Heb. *nāśā'*) *the ark* (vv. 2, 15, 26, 27). The journey from *the house of Obed-Edom* (v. 25; *cf.* 13:13–14) until the ark *came to the city of David* (v. 29, NRSV, RSV) is described in two phases: verses 1–15, preparing the people and the place for the ark; verses 16–29, celebrating the journey with joyful worship.

This basically simple structure is consistent with the Chronicler's aims and methods, though this may not be immediately apparent. A major problem for many readers is the way the narrative (vv. 1–3, 11–15, 25–29) is interrupted by repetitious lists (vv. 4–10, 16–24). For example, just at the moment when the ark is raised on to the Levites' shoulders (v. 15), apparently unrelated lists of musicians and gatekeepers occur. As a result, commentators have often alleged that verses 4–10 and 16–24 are secondary additions and that the Chronicler himself contributed only the narrative portions (*e.g.* Noth, Rudolph, Myers).

The problem may be solved by firstly recognizing that this account, like others in Chronicles, is not arranged chronologically. Secondly, the lists actually have an important function in anticipating the next section of narrative. The Levites who sanctified themselves (vv. 11–15) are shown to have had a valid ancestry (vv. 4–10; this was a live issue in post-exilic

Israel, *cf.* Ezr. 2:59–63 = Ne. 7:61–65), while the presence and qualifications of the musicians in verses 27–28 is explained by their selection in verses 16–24.[1] Thirdly, the unusual six-fold organization of the Levites (vv. 4–10) and the non-consecutive relationship between verse 15 and verse 25 are indications that the Chronicler himself was largely responsible for the present position of the disputed passages (Williamson).

The Chronicler seems to have been particularly inspired by the report of the second stage of the ark's journey into Jerusalem in 2 Samuel 6:12–19. In fact, four quite separate themes have been developed from the earlier account. Firstly, God's very evident blessing on Obed-Edom's household, which was the original reason for resuming the ark's journey (2 Sa. 6:12), has been developed into a description of blessing throughout David's kingdom (ch. 14). Secondly, the original comment about the ark's safe arrival (2 Sa. 6:17 = 1 Ch. 16:1) has been amplified by a further statement about David's preparation of a special tent for the ark (1 Ch. 15:1). Thirdly, the joyful worship of 2 Samuel 6:14–16 has been extended into a full paragraph (15:16–29). All these changes draw attention to the special nature of the occasion as one of supreme importance and happiness for Israel.

But the chief development from 2 Samuel concerns the place of the Levites. A passing reference to 'those who were carrying the ark' in 2 Samuel 6:13 has become a detailed account of the Levites as carriers of the ark and leaders of worship (vv. 2–3, 11–15, 25–29), with the Levitical lists included as well. Although one cannot always be certain which parts of the material about the Levites derive from sources of the Davidic era and which parts reflect the probably varied interests of the post-exilic period, the following points can be made at this juncture. (a) Very little is known about the history of the Levites, especially in the pre-exilic period (Nu. 3–4, 8, 18 deal with a short transitional period, describing ideals to be attained rather than a record of events). (b) A consistent post-exilic tradition persists, with which verse 16 is in complete harmony, that David instructed the Levites about

[1] It is notable that the two main groups of lists and genealogies in Ch., *viz.* 1 Ch. 1–9 and 23–27, also have an anticipatory function, so that the use of vv. 4–10, 16–24 in this chapter appears to be part of a wider method consistently used by the Chronicler.

leading music and praise (*e.g.* Ne. 12:24, 36, 46); (c) A fundamental change in the Levites' role was necessitated by the existence of the temple. Once the ark was deposited in Jerusalem, the Levites were required only twice more to act as carriers (2 Sa. 15:24; 1 Ki. 8:1–9 = 2 Ch. 5:2–10; *cf.* Nu. 4:1–33),[1] and it is this change to which attention is directed here.

It is a moot point how far the Chronicler was attempting to ensure that the singers and gatekeepers of his own day were fully regarded as Levites, though this is often assumed by commentators. In fact, the main source for Levitical history, Nehemiah 9–13, is ambivalent. Sometimes in the post-exilic period, these and other groups were treated separately (*cf.* Ne. 7:39–45 = Ezr. 2:36–42; 10:28, 39; 12:28–29, 45–47), but on occasion the musicians at least seem to be merged with the Levites (Ne. 11:15–17; 12:24, 27).[2]

However, the main aim of chapter 15 is not to describe the Levites' history and organization. The two central themes seem to be David's role *vis-à-vis* the Levites and the priority of worship in Israel. David is the person chiefly responsible for the Levites' transformed role (vv. 3, 11, 16). This is not meant to eulogize David's kingship, but to emphasize his stature as a second Moses, adapting Moses' original instructions (*e.g.* Nu. 3:5–9) to new circumstances. This theme, however, is subsidiary to the primary aim of giving specific encouragement about the activities and personnel of Israel's worship. Israel had neglected the Levites in the days of Nehemiah (Ne. 13:10), which effectively meant that God himself was being neglected. It is therefore probable that Chronicles was stimulating both all Israel (vv. 3, 28) and the Levites (vv. 4–15) to ensure that proper preparations were made for the nation's worship. If they adopted David's priorities, Chronicles' readers could see God's glory (1 Ch. 16:24; *cf.* Ezk. 44:4) and salvation (1 Ch. 16:35) restored again to his people.

The coming of God in Christ is the New Testament's development of God's coming to his people in the symbolism

---

[1] Instructions to the Levites in Nu. (especially 4:1–33) emphasize their carrying role. This emphasis is quite different from the Chronicler's interest in their role in worship, and would be simply irrelevant in the post-exilic period.

[2] For the possible pre-exilic non-priestly role of the Levites, see *e.g.* M. Haran, *Temples and Temple Service* (Oxford: Clarendon Press, 1978), pp. 92–99; R. Abba, *IBD*, pp. 876–889; D. A. Hubbard, *IBD*, pp. 1266–1271.

of the ark. If repentance was the proper preparation to be made for God's advent under the old covenant, the New Testament insists on no less a requirement. 'Prepare the way for the Lord' (Mk. 1:3) was John the Baptist's call inaugurating Christ's earthly ministry, and the same appeal is given in relation to the presence of the risen Christ in the early church. The letter to the Hebrews especially encourages believers to put aside their sins (Heb. 12:1) and offer him a continual sacrifice of praise (Heb. 13:15), in order to draw near to God in the Most Holy Place (Heb. 10:19–25).

a. Preparing a place for the ark (15:1–3). The *Levites* (v. 2) are introduced quite suddenly, without any explanation as to how David realized that their absence had been a serious contributory factor to the disaster of chapter 13. However, their participation in this second stage of the ark's journey is already implied by the reference to the 'carriers' of the ark in 2 Samuel 6:13 (previously it had been 'driven', 2 Sa. 6:3). The Levites' major roles in Chronicles are combined succinctly in verse 2: *to carry the ark* and 'to serve' (REB, NEB, GNB; *to minister to*, NRSV, RSV, NIV) *the* LORD – the transition of emphasis from one to the other is developed later in the chapter. Serving included a variety of practical duties, out of which Chronicles emphasizes their musical leadership (1 Ch. 6:32; 16:4; 2 Ch. 29:11). By carrying out these roles and by recognizing that *the* LORD *chose them* (v. 2; 2 Ch. 29:11), the Mosaic law about the Levites, especially in its Deuteronomic form, was being fulfilled under David's rule (Dt. 10:8; 18:5).

The *tent* (v. 1; *cf.* 16:1), also mentioned briefly in 2 Samuel (6:17; 7:2), is not to be confused with that at Gibeon (16:39; 21:29). Attention is drawn to it probably to demonstrate the completeness of David's preparations as evidence of repentance for his earlier negligence.

b. Preparing the people to carry the ark (15:4–10). The family affiliations and total number of participants in the ark's transportation are listed under the leaders of the non-priestly *Levites* (v. 11). The first three represent the major Levitical divisions (vv. 5–7), the latter three are groupings within the Kohathites (vv. 8–10; *cf.* Ex. 6:18, 22; Nu. 3:19, 30; 1 Ch. 6:18). The real interest is in these smaller groups, since the Kohathites were to be responsible for the care (Nu. 3:31) and transportation (Nu. 4:4–6, 15; 7:9) of the ark. In selecting the correct group of Levites, David's faithfulness to the old law is again underlined.

c. Preparing the leaders (15:11–15). The second stage of the Levites' preparation was to 'sanctify' themselves (vv. 12, 14, NRSV, RSV; lit. 'make yourselves holy'). This was an important activity in getting ready for the service of God, and was also undertaken by priests and Levites during the reigns of Solomon (2 Ch. 5:11), Hezekiah (2 Ch. 29:5, 15, 34; 30:15, 24; 31:18), and Josiah (2 Ch. 35:6). In every instance, God's favour subsequently rested upon Israel.[1] Sanctification required separation from every form of 'uncleanness' (Lv. 16:19; 2 Sa. 11:4), and in the Old Testament might include temporary abstinence from sexual intercourse (Ex. 19:15), dirty clothing (Ex. 19:14), or contact with corpses (Lv. 21:1–4), or more permanently for the priests, not marrying a divorcee, prostitute, or even a widow (Lv. 21:13–15).

This need for personal holiness was an essential part of the arrangements for transporting the ark in the *prescribed way* (v. 13), and, in contrast to *the first time* (vv. 13–15), David now recognized God's will in this matter. Though Chronicles' explanation is unparalleled in Samuel, there is nothing inherently improbable in David submitting to the scriptural authority of *Moses* (v. 15; *cf.* v. 13) in place of his previous inclination towards pagan superstition (v. 13; *cf.* 13:7–11). The fact that the ark was permanently fitted with rings and poles (Ex. 25:12–15; 37:3–5) should in any case have made it fairly obvious how it was intended to be carried. The importance of the word of God is reflected in a variety of contrasting scriptural allusions. God had shown his displeasure previously when he broke out against Uzzah (v. 13; *cf.* 13:11), and because Israel did *not enquire of* God (v. 13; *cf.* 'not sought his guidance', REB, NEB; 'not worshipping', GNB). The latter phrase also recalls the conditions of Saul's reign (*cf.* 13:3; the Heb. verb 'seek', is the same in both verses). Now,

---

[1] A command to the people occurs by contrast only once in Ch., and then only in a negative sense (2 Ch. 30:17). In the rest of the OT, the national dimension of sanctification was of greater importance (*e.g.* Jos. 3:5; 7:13; 1 Sa. 16:5; *cf.* Ex. 19:10, 14; Ezk. 44:19), which suggests that for Ch. the leaders had a special responsibility in the resurgence of national life.

however,[1] David involved *priests and Levites* (v. 14) as required
by Numbers 4:4–20, and the Levites *carried* the ark on their
shoulders (v. 15), in accordance with Numbers 7:9; Deuteronomy 10:8. Obedience to *the word of the LORD* (v. 15)
therefore removed God's anger and became the basis of
renewed blessing.

d. Preparing for a joyful celebration (15:16–24). A series of
brief lists of appointments, giving background information
about several features in verses 25–29. For example, verse 16
shows that the purpose of these appointments was to 'raise
sounds of joy' (RSV), so explaining the rejoicing of verse 25
(the word 'joy' (EVV 'joyful', 'rejoicing') is in an emphatic position in vv. 16, 25, and is one of Chronicles' main themes, *cf.*
e.g. 1 Ch. 12:40, 2 Ch. 7:10; 20:27; 30:21–25). The Levites'
role as 'musicians' (*cf.* REB, NEB; this translation of *mᵉšōrᵉrîm*, vv.
16, 19, 27 is preferable to the more usual 'singers', *cf.* NRSV,
RSV, in view of the activities listed in vv. 19–22) is highlighted
in anticipation of verse 27.

The main appointments are given in verses 17–18, and
divided in verses 19–21 into a Levitical orchestra of three
sections comprising *cymbals, harps,* and *lyres* (the identification
of the last two instruments is not exact), anticipating verse 28.[2]
The three leaders include *Ethan* (vv. 17, 19; *cf.* 6:44), a wise
man who is usually identified elsewhere with Jeduthun (*e.g.*
1 Ch. 16:41–42; 25:1, 6). Whether these are alternative names
for the same person or different people remains unknown.
Kenaniah's role (vv. 22, 27) is obscured by two translation
difficulties. The rendering 'instructor'[3] (*cf.* AV) is preferable to
in charge (NIV, REB, NEB, GNB), which is the reading of the vss
and a few Hebrew MSS, and the context suggests 'music' (REB,
NEB, NRSV, RSV) rather than 'transport' (Michaeli, *cf.* Tg.) or
'oracle' (Vulg.) as Kenaniah's sphere of responsibility. The

---

[1] Though 'seek' might have 'the ark' rather than 'God' as an alternative
direct object (also in 13:3; as NRSV, RSV in both instances), the use of 'seek'
throughout Ch. is against this interpretation. The Heb. expression in v. 13a,
translated 'because you were not present' in REB, NEB (*cf.* GNB), is rather abrupt
and a verb has to be supplied in English. REB, NEB's rendering is the commonest solution, but the meaning could equally be 'because you did not carry
it' (NRSV, RSV; *cf.* RV, NIV) or even 'because you did not sanctify yourselves'.
[2] For the musical terms in vv. 20, 21, see the larger commentaries on the Pss.
and Ch.
[3] See KB; also Rudolph, Keil.

number and identity of the *gatekeepers* or *doorkeepers* (vv. 18, 23, 24) is also problematical. Some of them seem to have doubled up as musicians (*cf.* 9:33; 16:37–38). All thirteen names in verse 18 might be counted as gatekeepers (restricting the latter to the last two names, as NRSV, RSV, REB, NEB, GNB, is an interpretation based partly on v. 24), though the relationship of the four named gatekeepers in verses 23–24 to those in verse 18 is also unclear. *Obed-Edom* (vv. 18, 21, 24) is a further complication. He is probably but not necessarily identical with Obed-Edom the Gittite (v. 25; *cf.* 13:13–14; 26:4–8). If the identification is accepted, it seems that the term 'Levite' could have a functional as well as a genealogical sense, at least during the monarchy. Such a liberal attitude was less popular in post-exilic times. The acts of *sacrifice* performed on the journey (v. 26; *cf.* 16:1–2) and the blowing of *trumpets* (v. 28; *cf.* 2 Sa. 6:15), instruments traditionally played by the priests, are sufficient to explain the occasional references in the lists to the priests (vv. 4, 11, 24).[1]

e. The people's joyful celebration (15:25–29). Though based on 2 Samuel 6:12–16, this paragraph has reinterpreted the earlier text extensively. The primary change is that the homecoming of the ark (described here repeatedly as *the ark of the covenant*, vv. 25, 26, 28, 29) has become a corporate act by *all Israel* (v. 28; *cf.* v. 3) rather than an expression of David's personal faith. David, mentioned alone in 2 Samuel 6:12, is now joined by Israel's *elders* and *commanders* (v. 25) as well as by the Levites (v. 26), and David's personal sacrifice is replaced by those of the people's representatives. Similarly, God's help (v. 26) a theme applied to David in 1 Chronicles 12:18, is now a collective experience of the Levites. Even the mention of David's linen ephod, which could be understood as either the smock-like priestly garment of post-exilic times or the scantier pre-exilic version (2 Sa. 6:14, 20, 22), is less important than the fact that David and the Levites were all dressed in *fine linen* (v. 27).

The reference to *Michal* (v. 29), much briefer than in 2 Samuel 6:16, 20–23, should therefore also be understood corporately. Not only did she despise David, but also, uniquely

---

[1] For the suggestion that vv. 17–24 reflect temporary arrangements for the procession of a Levitical choir led by Kenaniah which accompanied the ark to Jerusalem, *cf.* Kleinig, *Song*, pp. 47–51.

in Israel, she was out of sympathy with the great joy and concern over the ark. 'Typical of unfaith' (Ackroyd), the isolation of Saul's daughter was a further demonstration of the unfitness of Saul's house to lead the people of God.

iv. Blessing, worship and praise (16:1–43)
'Let them say among the nations, "The LORD reigns!"' (16:31).

> 16:1–3, 43 – *cf.* 2 Samuel 6:17–20
> 16:8–22 – *cf.* Psalm 105:1–15
> 16:23–33 – *cf.* Psalm 96:1–13
> 16:34–36 – *cf.* Psalm 106:1, 47–48

The primary objective of chapters 13–15 is fulfilled by the ark's arrival in Jerusalem (v. 1). With the symbol of God's presence restored to the centre of his people's life, Israel is about to receive renewed blessing (vv. 2, 43), and a transformation of their entire pattern of worship.

The chapter is arranged chiastically, with a psalm celebrating Yahweh's kingship over the nations as the central feature:

a. 16:1–3, God's blessing for every Israelite
  b. 16:4–7, Levites appointed for worship at Jerusalem
    c. 16:8–36, Psalm of praise
  b₁. 16:37–42, Levites and priests appointed for worship at Gibeon
a₁. 16:43, Blessing for David's household.

The outer sections of this chiasm (a, a₁) are taken over from the much briefer account in 2 Samuel 6. The two Levitical lists (b, b₁) surrounding the psalm (c) are the only parts of chapter 16 not deriving from a readily identifiable source, but are presumably taken from official temple records.

a. Blessing for every Israelite (16:1–3). The ark's arrival results in renewed sacrificial worship, and blessings and food given to the people (on *the tent*, see comment on 15:1). The various *offerings* (vv. 1–2) are brought by the people, rather than just by David as in 2 Samuel 6:17, consistent with the corporate emphasis of 15:25–29. Blessing the people (v. 2; *cf.* v. 43) was an activity usually carried out by priests (*cf.* Dt. 10:8; 1 Ch. 23:13), but also occasionally by other leaders, notably Moses (Ex. 39:43). Apart from David, Solomon was the only other Israelite king known to have exercised this privilege (1 Ki. 8:14, 55; *cf.* 2 Ch. 6:3). David therefore appears in a semi-priestly role, mediating temporal (v. 3) as well as spiritual blessings. The second item of food (known only here and in 2 Sa. 6:19) was either a *cake of dates* or a 'portion of meat' (REB, NEB, NSRV, RSV; *cf.* GNB, AV) – if the latter is correct, it was an especially generous act since meat rarely appeared on domestic menus in ancient Israel.

b. Levites appointed at Jerusalem (16:4–7). The two lists of Levitical appointments (here and vv. 37–42) relate to more permanent arrangements for worship required by the ark's presence in Jerusalem (note the word *regularly*, NIV, NSRV; 'continually', RSV, in vv. 6, 37, 40). These verses describe a transitional stage before the temple was completed. For the time being, Israel's worship activities and personnel were to be divided between the ark at Jerusalem (vv. 4–7, 37–38) and the tented altar at Gibeon (vv. 39–42). It has been suggested that this separation authenticated synagogue worship (Rothstein, Myers, *etc.*), but the whole tenor of chapters 13–16 towards centralization rather than dispersal of worship makes this hypothesis unlikely. In fact, it is more probable that Chronicles is underlining the value of the use of Scripture in the sacrifice of praise alongside the required rituals (*cf.* vv. 8–36).

The named *Levites* (v. 4) under *Asaph* are taken from those listed in 15:17–21; those in that list not named here were allocated to Gibeon (v. 41, *the rest of those chosen and designated by name*). The Levites' task was to *minister* (v. 4; 'serve', REB, NEB; *cf.* v. 37 and 15:2) before the ark, and to lead in praise especially with music (v. 4, *cf.* ch. 25). The three phrases 'to invoke', 'to thank', and 'to praise' (v. 4, NRSV, RSV) should be understood as a collective reference to the activities of worship, according to the Hebrew custom of expressing the comprehensiveness of an idea by a series of near synonyms (*cf.* Pr. 1:2–6 on wisdom, Ps. 119 on law) rather than as separate liturgical activities (Michaeli, Curtis and Madsen) or types of psalm (Ackroyd). The suggestion that the first verb (Heb. *hazkîr*, possibly 'proclaim') alludes to the priests' blowing of trumpets (*cf.* Nu. 10:9–10) is also improbable, since David is expressly appointing the Levites to new tasks.[1] The *priests* are dealt with separately (v. 6), since the instruction that they should *blow the trumpets* (*cf.* 15:24) had long been established

---

[1] *Cf.* Kleinig, *Song*, pp. 35–37.

(Nu. 10:2; 8–10). Their role at Jerusalem was primarily to call the people to worship, especially at festivals (*cf.* Ezr. 3:10; Ps. 98:6), though they would also have accompanied the sacrifices mentioned in verse 1 (*cf.* also vv. 39–40). Trumpets certainly have a dual function in the New Testament in announcing the final resurrection (1 Cor. 15:52), and playing a part in heavenly worship (Rev. 11:15; note the reference to the heavenly ark in Rev. 11:19).

c. The Lord is king (16:8–36). The psalm inserted here celebrates in faith that as the ark comes to the centre of Israel's life, so Yahweh *comes* (v. 33; or possibly 'has come') to his people. A belief in God's coming to his people is reaffirmed throughout the Old Testament (*e.g.* Ex. 19:9; 24:11; Is. 6:1; 59:20). God's coming to earth in the person of Christ was therefore not totally unexpected, even though it was much opposed. Here God comes as King (v. 31) and Judge (v. 33). He is praised for his demonstrable faithfulness to his covenant people in the past (vv. 8–22), which gives the psalmist fresh confidence to ask God to *deliver us from the nations* (v. 35).

The MT's introduction to the psalm emphasizes that it was David who 'first appointed' (NRSV, RSV) 'ordained' (REB, NEB) the Levites to sing God's praise, rather than that this psalm was actually sung on the occasion of the ark's arrival, despite REB, NEB's colon at the end of verse 7 (NIV's *this psalm* is not in the Heb. and is even more misleading). The form of the psalm is almost certainly the Chronicler's own compilation, as suggested by his habit of adapting material from the psalms for his own purposes (*e.g.* 1 Ch. 29:10–18; 2 Ch. 6:41–42; 20:21) and the presence of many of Chronicles' characteristic themes.[1] It is of course closely based on parts of three Psalms, *viz.* 105, 96, and 106, but a number of small variations make it almost certain that earlier Scripture has been reinterpreted and applied to the circumstances of the Chronicler's time. It is therefore mistaken to try to 'correct' the text in the light of that found in the Psalter, as for instance in the RSV.

The psalm's structure is based on its three constituent parts. The original pieces, however, have been welded together into an organic whole to form a new hymn of praise, as is evident

[1] *Cf.* T. C. Butler, 'A forgotten passage from a forgotten era (1 Chr. XVI. 8–36)', *VT* 28, 1978, pp. 142–150, especially pp. 146ff.

from at least two factors. Regular introductions are provided for each section by repeating imperatives such as *Give thanks!* (vv. 8, 34) and *Sing!* (v. 23, *cf*. v. 9), while natural bonds are formed between the three sections by words such as God's *name* (vv. 8, 10, 29, 35), God's *holiness* (vv. 10, 29, 35), and *the nations* (vv. 20, 24, 31, 35).[1]

i. Covenant promises fulfilled (16:8–22). The opening section (vv. 8–13) is a series of invitations to Israel to *praise* God. It contains a triple reference to *seek* God (vv. 10b–11), an important theme in Chronicles (*e.g.* 1 Ch. 10:13–14; 13:3; 2 Ch. 7:14), which refers to a dependent and expectant attitude in worship rather than simply looking for direction in life. The thematic statement of Psalm 105 concerning the *covenant* occurs here in verses 14–18, special attention being given to God's promise of *land*. That promise is seen to be finally fulfilled by the ark's arrival (v. 18), as a sign of God's permanent residence with Israel in the Promised Land. So Israel must *remember* that covenant (v. 15 – GNB, NRSV rightly retain MT's imperative, but NIV, REB, NEB, RSV unnecessarily 'standardize' to Ps. 105:8's 'he remembers'). Remembering in the Old Testament includes acting upon that which is recalled, and is much more than a purely intellectual exercise. The change from 'Abraham' (Ps. 105:6) to *Israel* (v. 13) is consistent with Chronicles' preference for this patriarch rather than Abraham and for this name rather than Jacob. The portrayal of the patriarchs as *few in number* and vulnerable to foreign powers (vv. 19–20) would have been especially evocative for post-exilic Israel, but God's presence and protection comprise another covenant promise which does not fail (vv. 21–22). *My anointed ones* and *my prophets* (v. 22) are heightened descriptions of the patriarchs, based on their election through covenant and on Abraham's status as a prophet (Gn. 20:7).

ii. God is king over all the earth (16:23–33). Mention of divine protection leads naturally into a song about God's universal kingship (v. 31). Like the preceding section, it begins with invitations to worship, but the greatness of the theme demands the widest possible extension. Praise is offered by *the heavens* (v. 31) and *all the earth* (v. 23), including *the sea, the*

---

[1] *Cf*. A. E. Hill, 'Patchwork poetry or reasoned verse? Connective structure in 1 Chronicles XVI', *VT* 33, 1983, pp. 97–101.

fields, and *the trees* (vv. 32–33) as well as the *families of nations* (v. 28). God's kingship is demonstrated in his acts of *salvation* (v. 23), creation (v. 26), and judgment (v. 33), and is particularly relevant to contemporary Israel in his supremacy over *all the gods of the nations* (v. 26). Since in the ancient world the fortunes of nations were identified with the fortunes of their chief deities, this passage is a direct challenge to Israel's sense of futility under imperial rule. It encourages them to renewed faith and hope by magnifying the greatness of the God who is now present at the centre of national life.[1]

Several significant textual differences occur in this section. The most substantial is the changed order of several phrases in verses 30–31 (*cf.* Ps. 96:10–11), though this has little effect on the meaning and may simply be a textual variant. Of more interest is the replacement of 'his sanctuary' (Ps. 96:6) and 'into his courts' (Ps. 96:8) by *his dwelling-place* (v. 27) and *before him* (v. 29). These changes have often been explained as attempts to avoid anachronisms prior to the construction of the temple, but it may well be that they simply reflect the language of the context. The ark's 'place' has already been prepared (15:1, 3; *cf.* 16:1), while the repeated phrase 'before God/the LORD/him' (vv. 1, 27, 33) is closely associated with the worship that took place 'before the ark' (vv. 4, 6, 37). As the Chronicler led his readers in praise, the place where the ark stood was less important than the one whose presence it represented.[2]

iii. Prayer for deliverance (16:34–36). This brief final section contains an intercessory element which affects the interpretation of the entire psalm. Two key Hebrew words in verse 35 have been added to the original psalm, *viz. yišʿēnû* (= 'of our

---

[1] It has been proposed that the structure of vv. 23–26 is reflected in Rev. 14:3, 6–7, and that various elements in the vocabulary (LXX) of the entire psalm are emphasized in Rev. 14:7 (W. Altink, '1 Chronicles 16:8–36 as Literary Source for Revelation 14:6–7', *Andrews University Seminary Studies* 22, 1984, pp. 187–196). Even if such dependence were to be confirmed, however, the NT passage has been extensively transformed through being combined with material from other OT sources.

[2] NEB's 'he has fixed' (v. 30) on the basis of LXX(L), is an unnecessary divergence from MT's 'stands firm' (RSV, *etc.*). The phrase, which also occurs in Pss. 93:1; 96:10, is treated quite inconsistently in the LXX, both as regards the Heb. root (sometimes *tkn* for MT's *kûn*) and the mood of the verb (*cf.* Barthélemy, *CTAT*, p. 456).

salvation', NRSV, RSV, JB; *our Saviour*, NIV, REB, NEB, GNB) and *haṣṣîlēnû* (= 'save us', NRSV, RSV, REB, NEB; 'rescue us', GNB, JB; *deliver us*, NIV). When these are combined with the imperatives taken over from Psalm 106:47, *Save us* (NIV, GNB, JB; 'Deliver us', RSV, REB, NEB) and *gather us*, it can be seen that verse 35 has become an augmented plea for deliverance or salvation (Heb. does not distinguish between these two English words).

The reasons which have led the Chronicler to make this repeated request lie in verses 8–33 and in the events of chapters 13–15. He has firstly been encouraged by praising God for his *wonderful acts* (v. 9, *cf.* vv. 8–12), which in this context must refer to the great work of bringing the ark into Jerusalem (chs. 13–15). This is not seen primarily as David's achievement, but as *what he [i.e.* God] *has done* (v. 8) A second reason for the prayer is the psalm's emphasis on God's supremacy over *the nations* (vv. 24, 26, 28, 33), expressed through his *judgments* (vv. 12, 14; *cf.* v. 33) or victories on Israel's behalf. In the context, this must refer primarily to the final defeat of the Philistines (14:8–17). Chronicles, therefore, understands by faith that the events of the ark's arrival (chs. 13, 15) and Israel's victories (ch. 14) are evidence of God's *salvation* (v. 23).

These wonderful works of God's past salvation form the basis for making Israel's present known to God. The request is for two things. Firstly, the Chronicler asks God to *save/deliver* his people again and to *gather* them *from the nations* (v. 35; *cf.* Dt. 30:3). What exactly the Chronicler has in mind remains unspecified. It is sometimes proposed that frankness was politically inadvisable, but more probably the real thrust of the prayer is that Israel might regain its lost identity. The Chronicler's readers were very aware of being subject to a pagan imperial power, and they needed above all to be reidentified as the people of the God who reigns over the nations (v. 31). Whether this involved a gathering from Babylonia (*cf.* Ezr. 1–2, 7–8) or from the scattered villages of Judah (*cf.* 1 Ch. 9:2–34; Ne. 7:4–5; 11:1–36) cannot be decided. What matters is that Israel should have a new understanding of its status as God's covenant people (*cf.* vv. 14–18).

The second request is that Israel may have a new understanding of God: *that we may glory in your praise* (v. 35). Deliverance could happen only by God's intervention. Again, details are not given, but the Chronicler pleads with God to show himself unmistakeably as the supreme Deliverer/ Saviour, and to act in such a way that praise and glory could be given only to him.

The whole psalm, therefore, is much more than an illustration of the post-exilic liturgical cultus (Michaeli, Myers) or an establishing of the identity of Jerusalem's cultus.[1] It is an impassioned plea for God to restore his own and his people's identity in the Chronicler's own generation by performing fresh acts of salvation.

The psalm's contemporary relevance is underlined for the Chronicler's readers in two further ways. One is the use of Psalm 106:1, 47–48 (= vv. 34–36 here) as a prayer for God to keep his promise given in Jeremiah 33:11 that the land of Israel will be filled with praise after the exile.[2] Secondly, there are hints in verses 35–36 that the Chronicler's psalm was actually being used in contemporary post-exilic worship. Instead of the jussive ('let all the people say'), and imperative ('praise') of Psalm 106:48, there is a new imperative, 'Say also' (v. 35; NRSV, RSV; *cf.* JB, GNB; *Cry out*, NIV; *cf.* REB, NEB) followed by the statement (v. 36), *all the people said* and 'praised' (GNB, NRSV). It seems therefore that the people had actually responded and made the Chronicler's prayer their own. Furthermore, the Levites appear to have provided the leadership in this matter. The words *give thanks* (vv. 34, 35) and 'praised' (v. 36, NRSV. RSV) are a deliberate echo of verse 4 and are a practical demonstration of the Levitical functions described there. If, as seems likely, the Chronicler is the actual compiler of the psalm, then it is probable that he too should be counted among the Levites.

Finally, the psalm provides a firm foundation for the following chapters. By affirming that God has kept his covenant promises to Abraham and Jacob (*cf.* vv. 15–22), it prepares the way for the Davidic covenant of chapter 17. By linking these promises with the ark, the Chronicler shows that this God is near to his people, not far away from them. Above all, the ark's association with God's presence gives confidence that God's presence will also be found in the temple where the ark will be located (*cf.* 1 Ch. 21 – 2 Ch. 7). Israel can therefore be

[1] T. C. Butler, 'A forgotten passage from a forgotten era (1 Chr. XVI 8–36)', *VT* 28, 1978, p. 149.
[2] W. Beyerlin, 'Der Nervus rerum in Psalm 106', *ZAW* 86, 1974, pp. 56–64. Note the close correspondence between Je. 33:11 and v. 34 here (= Ps. 106:1).

confident about God's promises and may bring prayer and joyful praise to the place of God's earthly presence. In the New Testament, it is the Holy Spirit who brings the sense of God's presence and gives access to the Father in the heavenly temple (Eph. 2:18). Christians too should be encouraged to offer praise and prayer through Jesus, their own High Priest (*cf.* 1 Cor. 12:3; Eph. 5:18–20; Heb. 4:14–16).

d. Levites appointed at Jerusalem (16:37–38).

A concluding summary about the arrangements for regular worship at Jerusalem, confirming verses 4–7. Verse 38 emphasizes *Obed-Edom*'s role, which is best understood as a dual one of musician and gatekeeper (*cf.* 15:18, 21, 24), though MT is awkward and uncertain. It reads literally, 'and Obed–Edom and their brothers' – possibly Jehiah (*cf.* 15:24) or Hosah has dropped out after Obed–Edom, or alternatively 'their' could refer to Asaph's brothers in verse 37.

e. Levites appointed at Gibeon (16:39–42).

A note concerning David's arrangements for regular sacrifice at Gibeon (see also comment on vv. 4–7). The reference to Gibeon is unexpected, because only Solomon is associated with worship there in pre-exilic texts (1 Ki. 3:5; 9:2; *cf.* 2 Ch. 1:3). However, sacrifice was offered to Yahweh on various altars during the United Monarchy and later, most interestingly at Nob which was within a few miles of Gibeon and known as 'the town of the priests' (1 Sa. 22:19; *cf.* 1 Sa. 21:1f.; 1 Ki. 1:39; 2:28). For a fuller discussion, see Williamson, pp. 130–132. The history of the Tent (or tabernacle) is also obscure, since the Old Testament locates it after the Mosaic period only at Shiloh (Jos. 18:1; Ps. 78:60; *cf.* Je. 7:12) and probably also at Nob (1 Sa. 21). Chronicles, however, emphasizes the continuity between Moses' Tent and this one (1 Ch. 21:29; 2 Ch. 1:3), which is achieved here through David's faithfulness to the written law (*cf.* v. 40).

Several translation problems obscure the details, notably the lack of any main verb after *left* in verse 37 and some repetition in verses 41–42, but it is clear that the passage deals with the appointment of priests (vv. 39–40), musicians (vv. 41–42a) and gatekeepers (v. 42b; for Levitical equivalents at Jerusalem, see vv. 4–7, 37–38). *The priest* (v. 39) is the usual pre-exilic term for the later 'high priest' (*cf.* 1 Sa. 14:19, 36; 2 Ki.

11:9ff.). *Zadok*, one of David's loyal supporters (2 Sa. 15:24ff.; 1 Ki. 1:8ff.; 1 Ch. 12:29; 29:22), is often partnered by Abiathar (*e.g.* 2 Sa. 15:35–36; 1 Ch. 15:11), and may have been so here.

This apparently mundane list of duties is given a vital theological ingredient: *his love endures for ever* (v. 41). This phrase, which occurs also in the psalm (v. 34), is a frequent refrain in Chronicles (*e.g.* 2 Ch. 5:13; 7:3; 20:21) showing that the central theme of Old Testament praise is the love of God. The Chronicler does not portray God as a rigid and demanding ritualist, but as one whose unending love undergirds the whole of national life. He would certainly have agreed with Paul's dictum, 'Love never ends' (1 Cor. 13:8).

f. Blessing for David's household (16:43). A brief sentence from 2 Samuel 6:19b–20a which probably functions as a conclusion to the whole ark narrative of chapters 13–16. The entire enterprise has ended in blessing for every Israelite home (*cf.* v. 3). The unsavoury episode of Michal, David's wife (2 Sa. 6:20b–23), is simply no longer relevant, since the dishonour of Saul's house needs no further proof (10:13–14; 13:3; 15:29). God's kingdom is now firmly in David's hands, and is ready to be confirmed for ever (ch. 17).

C. God's covenant with David (17:1–27)

This chapter lies at the heart of the Chronicler's presentation of history. 1 Chronicles 17:3–15 together with 2 Chronicles 7:11–22 are the two 'words of God' around which his entire work is constructed. Here David receives a divine promise about God's 'house', which is really two houses in one. The first is a dynasty which God will build for David (vv. 10b, 14), and the second is a temple which David's son is to build for God (v. 12). The oracle's significance depends on the various meanings of the Hebrew *bayit*, 'house', which can mean 'dynasty', 'temple', and even 'household' (16:43).

God's promise arises out of his refusal to allow David to build a temple (v. 4). This rejection cannot be because the temple is unimportant, since preparation for its construction is the dominant theme in the remaining account of David's reign (chs. 21–29). Nor is it a preference for David's son as a 'man of peace and rest' over against David as a 'man of war'

(22:8–9; 28:3). The matter is rather one of priorities, for the man-made temple must be subordinate to a divinely built house which man had not even envisaged. Both houses must also have their foundations in God's promises rather than David's high-minded but more limited intentions. In other words, the Chronicler's interest in the temple is not an end in itself, but an expression of something much more enduring. The Chronicler is no mere ritualist, but a genuine theologian of the word of God.

God's promise here, sometimes called the Dynastic Oracle, forms the cornerstone of what is known as the Davidic covenant. Covenants in the ancient Near East were solemn, binding agreements expressing mutual trust and commitment, and were used in relationships as varied as a marriage bond (Je. 31:31–32) and an international treaty (I Ki. 20:34). Any covenant in which God was involved, however, invariably became grounded in God's initiating will and actions. In the case of those made with Abraham and David, the element of divine promise is so striking that they are often known as promissory covenants. Though the term 'covenant' is not actually found in either 2 Samuel 7 or 1 Chronicles 17, it does occur in several psalms (*e.g.* 89:3, 28) and prophetic passages (*e.g.* Is. 55:3) based on this oracle. 2 Samuel 7:11b–16 (= vv. 10b–14 here) has in fact given rise to a whole series of passages which expound a hope not just about an everlasting kingdom descended from David but of a universal divine rule of peace and righteousness (*e.g.* Is. 9:6–7; Je. 23:5–6; Ezk. 37:24–25; Pss. 2:6–7; 45:6; 132:11–12). This is the milieu of the Old Testament's messianic hope, though in Chronicles openness to future messianic developments is implicit rather than explicit.

Two aspects of covenant interpretation are especially significant here. Firstly, the Davidic covenant has much greater prominence in Chronicles than in Samuel or Kings, as indicated by its expansion in passages such as 1 Chronicles 22:6–13; 28:2–10; 2 Chronicles 6:4–11, 14–17; 7:17–18; 13:5, 8; 21:7; 23:3, most of which are unparalleled in the earlier books. Secondly, by a series of small changes from 2 Samuel 7, specific individual and corporate implications are highlighted. In the short term, there is a much sharper focus on Solomon as the individual Davidic descendant who is to be the temple builder (vv. 12, 14; he is explicitly named in 22:9; 28:5). In post-exilic times, this hope was briefly rekindled in Zerubbabel, a Davidic descendant (1 Ch. 3:19) who built the Second Temple (Ezr. 3:8; 5:2; *cf.* Hg 1:12 – 2:9; Zc. 4:6–10). But the Chronicler is also interested in the corporate dimensions of this covenant. Quietly but unhesitatingly, he affirms that the kingdom of God on earth was established through this covenant (v. 14), and as far as the Chronicler was concerned, that divine kingdom was still effective despite the deprivations of the exile and the foreign imperial rule of his own day (*cf.* 1 Ch. 28:5; 29:11, 23; 2 Ch. 9:8). Perhaps the most important feature of this chapter, however, is not the existence but the combination of these individual and corporate applications. For the Chronicler, a proper understanding of the covenant involved recognizing the presence of the kingdom of God as well as God's activity in and through an individual descendant of David who would build God's house/temple. In spite of Solomon's weaknesses, therefore, and the fact that conditions in post-exilic Israel made a mockery of any real hope of restoring David's monarchy, the Chronicler's belief in the ongoing relevance of the Davidic promise surely meant that the contemporary shadow of a theocracy had not exhausted the vitality of God's covenant promise. Chronicles clearly points both to the special significance of Solomon and to a longing for another son of David who would finally rebuild God's house and establish God's kingdom *for ever* (this phrase occurs eight times in 1 Ch. 17).

It comes as no surprise that New Testament writers saw the Davidic covenant in general and 2 Samuel 7:14 = 1 Chronicles 17:13 in particular as fulfilled and transformed by Jesus. In him, they saw the coalescing of the kingdom of God and the kingdom of David, from Jesus' birth (Lk. 1:32) to the final establishment of the kingdom in Jesus' resurrection (Acts 2:30), ascension and exaltation (Heb. 1:5, quoting 2 Sa. 7:14 = 1 Ch. 17:13). Jesus was not just David's heir, however. David was, like Moses, only a servant in God's house (Heb. 3:1–5; Mt. 22:41–46), but Jesus is the faithful son in charge of the whole house (Heb. 3:6) and the builder of God's new temple (Jn. 2:20; Eph. 2:19–22). Biblical thought, therefore, points to the continuity of the two houses of 2 Samuel 7 = 1 Chronicles 17, not in their original form but in the resurrected person of Jesus Christ. The kingdom of God in Christ today still faces the Chronicler's problem that God's people have to submit to political rulers who do not acknowledge Jesus as Lord. Faith, however, is not dependent on political power or favour, or even on religious institutions. It stands on the everlasting reality of God's promise to David, now received in and through Christ. God is still building his house (Mt. 16:18; Eph. 2:19–22; 1 Pet. 2:4–10)!

i. David's good intentions (17:1–2)
17:1–2 – *cf.* 2 Samuel 7:1–3

David's desire to build a temple (vv. 1, 4) is typical of many ancient kings who sought an appropriate expression for their piety and at the same time a public testimony to their achievements.[1] It was natural to enlist the support of *Nathan*, David's chief religious adviser, but even the combined will of king and prophet fell far short of God's own plans (v. 4). Nathan's initial response (v. 2) is a fascinating reminder that even courageous prophets (*cf.* 2 Sa. 12:1–14), like godly kings, are not always infallible interpreters of God's will.

The 'rest' clause is notably omitted in comparison with 2 Samuel 7:1 (*cf.* a similar change in v. 10 from 2 Sa. 7:11). Three main reasons have been proposed for this: (i) to stress the close connection between the ark's arrival (chs. 13–16) and the temple; (ii) to avoid a possible chronological problem in the reference to David's further wars in verse 10 and chapters 18–20; and (iii) to avoid unnecessary conflict with Chronicles' assessment of David as a man of war and Solomon as the 'man of peace and rest' (22:9) *par excellence*. Though all these arguments have some validity, the last is the most persuasive in reflecting Chronicles' own positive presentation of David. David's 'rest' was real enough (*cf.* v. 8), but it was only partial at best.

---

[1] See *e.g.* S. Lackenbacher, *Le roi bâtisseur* (Paris: Éditions Recherche sur les civilisations, 1982); A. R. Grayson, *Assyrian Royal Inscriptions*, 2 (Wiesbaden: Harrassowitz, 1976), ## 54–58, 139, 163, 437, *etc.* Though it was usual to seek divine approval for such building projects, and examples do exist where such permission was not granted, 'the biblical accounts are unique in being the only ones which venture to explain why the deity responded negatively to the request of a king who is otherwise viewed in a positive light' (V. Hurowitz, *I Have Built You an Exalted House*, JSOTS 115 (Sheffield: Sheffield Academic Press, 1992), p. 165.

ii. The promise of the Davidic covenant (17:3–15)
'The LORD will build a house for you' (17:10)
17:3–15 – *cf.* 2 Samuel 7:4–17

a. Introduction (17:3–4a). Apart from this introduction and the conclusion (v. 15), which each identify Nathan's words as a God-given prophecy, the oracle falls naturally into two pre-paratory sections (vv. 4b–6, 7–10a) before reaching its climax in verses 10b–14.

b. David is not to build a temple (17:4b–6). The opening statement, *You are not the one to build me a house* (*cf.* GNB, REB, NEB), sets the scene for the first two paragraphs and forms an effective foil for the initial phrase of the third paragraph ('the LORD will build you a house', v. 10b, NRSV, RSV). Chronicles' more direct form of this prohibition (*cf* 2 Sa. 7:5) shows divine approval for a temple but not for David as its builder. Three reasons in all are given for this. The first is that throughout Israel's existence, from the exodus to the judges,[1] no such place of worship was required. The LORD was a travelling deity, content with a tent-shrine,[2] whose chief distinctiveness was his presence with his people (*cf.* Ex. 33:15–16). Even the structure at Shiloh, though it had doors and doorposts (1 Sa. 1:9; 3:15) and was called a temple (1 Sa. 1:9; 3:3), was evidently far less pretentious than the 'cedar-house' David had in mind (vv. 1, 6).

c. God has kept his earlier promises (17:7–10a). A second reason for delaying the temple was to remind David that his own role as Israel's *ruler* (v. 7; *cf.* 11:2) was bound up with God's purposes, not his own. A succession of first-person verbs in the past (vv. 7–8a, *I have . . .*) and in the future tense (vv. 8b–10a, *I will . . .*) confirm that David's past achievements

---

[1] 'Leaders' (v. 6; lit. 'judges') is superior to 'tribes' (2 Sa. 7:7), with LXX and most commentators. For a defence of the different MT readings in each verse, see Barthélemy, *CTAT*, pp. 245–246.

[2] The MT at the end of v. 5 is a little confused, though the over-all sense is clear. The most preferable solution, which goes back at least to the medieval commentator Saadya, is that the full meaning is implied rather than written, *viz.* 'I was travelling from tent to tent and from dwelling to dwelling' (*cf.* D. K. Reid, 'The fragments of the commentary on Isaiah by Saadya Gaon', unpubl. Ph.D. thesis, University of Wales, 1990, p. 188; *cf.* also Tg.). This is easier than making additions to MT (*e.g.* Rudolph, Dillard).

and his future prosperity are part of an undreamed-of extension of God's past dealings with Israel. Two promises in particular are reaffirmed to David – Abraham's great *name* (v. 8; *cf.* Gn. 12:2; 1 Ch. 14:17) and *a place* for the descendants of Abraham and Moses (v. 9; *cf.* Gn. 13:14–17; 15:18–21; Ex. 3:8; 6:8; Dt. 11:24–25), called here *my people Israel* (vv. 7, 9, 10). In other words, the Davidic covenant represents a new stage in the fulfilment of the Abrahamic and Mosaic covenants.

d. God will build a house for David (17:10b–14). The third and final reason for amending David's proposal is that for the present, God has given a higher priority to his promise of a dynasty than to the construction of a physical temple (v. 10b).[1] This dynasty has five main features:

(a) God will *establish* a *kingdom* and a *throne* for David's *offspring* (vv. 11, 12, 14). This is the major promise of the covenant. The ambiguity inherent in the Hebrew word *zera'* (v. 11), like its English equivalents 'seed' (AV)/*offspring* (NIV, NRSV, RSV), means it can apply both to the dynasty as a whole and to individual members of it (*cf.* the use of the same word in Gn. 3:15; 12:7; 17:7, 16).

(b) One of David's descendants will build the desired temple which will be a sign that David's throne or kingdom has been divinely established (v. 12). Like circumcision in the case of the Abrahamic covenant (Gn. 17), building the temple is the act of human obedience by which God's covenant promise is accepted and confirmed. So the temple will glorify not David's name but God's.

(c) David's heirs will enjoy the privileged status of God's adopted sons, with Yahweh himself as their adoptive Father (v. 13). This promise which was given originally to Israel (Ex. 4:22; *cf.* Is. 55:3) is now concentrated in the Davidic line (*cf.* Pss. 2:7; 89:27). Ultimately it leads to Jesus, in whom this promise is finally and perfectly fulfilled. In the light of Jesus' resurrection and ascension, the early church constantly saw this as the supreme Old Testament promise concerning Jesus

---

[1] The change in v. 10b, 'I declare', from 'Yahweh declares' in 2 Sa. 7:11, is probably best explained as a smoother continuation of the first-person verbs in vv. 7–10 and 11–14 (*cf.* Mosis, *UTCG*, p. 82). NEB's 'I will make you great' follows LXX in combining two words in MT, but is to be rejected as an ineffective echo of v. 8b (*cf.* Rudolph).

as the Son of God, frequently referring to this and similar passages (*e.g.* Acts 2:30; 13:22–23, 33–34; Rom. 1:3–4; Heb. 1:5, 8–9; 5:5). Through Jesus too, it has amazingly been extended by adoption to every believer, so that Jesus is 'the firstborn among many brothers' (Rom. 8:29; *cf.* vv. 15–17).

(d) David's house will be everlasting, ultimately secured in God's love. The future of David's kingdom would be wholly different from the uncertainty and disaster that befell Saul's reign (v. 13). It is initially surprising that the clause in 2 Samuel 7:14b about human sinfulness and divine discipline has been discarded. The reason, however, is not an unawareness of the extent of human failure in the Davidic line or because royal obedience was no longer a priority. David and Solomon were still required to obey God's instructions (1 Ch. 22:12–13; 28:8–9), and the Chronicler does not hide their failures (see 1 Ch. 13:11–12; 15:13; 21:1, 7–8, 17 for David; 2 Ch. 9:29; 10:4, 10–11, 14 for Solomon), any more than he does those of their successors on the throne. Rather, repeated failure by David's line to meet the conditions of the covenant serves only to highlight God's unconditional commitment to David's house. This in fact is the focus of the Chronicler's attention, confirming that even human sin cannot ultimately undermine or divert God's declared purposes.

(e) The most striking development of the Davidic covenant in Chronicles is its explicit association with the kingdom of God (v. 14). Evidence for this at first sight seems quite slender, involving changes of a single Hebrew consonant in each of two words in 2 Samuel 7:16 – *my house and my kingdom* for 'your house and your kingdom'. Though this might be explained as a textual variant in the Chronicler's source, such a solution is unsatisfactory in the light of other adjustments in this verse and of other passages in Chronicles where the same idea is clearly present (especially 1 Ch. 28:5; 29:23; 2 Ch. 13:8; *cf.* 1 Ch. 10:14; 29:11; 2 Ch. 9:8). Although the Old Testament often refers to Yahweh as king (*e.g.* Ex. 15:18; Is. 6:5; Pss. 47:3; 99:2), only rarely, and almost entirely in Psalms, Chronicles and Daniel, does it specifically mention Yahweh's kingdom (*e.g.* Pss. 45:6; 103:19; 145:11–13; *cf.* Dn. 4:3; Ob. 21). It is only Chronicles, however (and possibly Ps. 45:6), which sees the kingdom of God expressed directly in the Davidic kingdom. This is a significant contribution to the development of the idea of the kingdom of God, especially in the light of the

Gospels' understanding of the revelation of the kingdom in the person of David's son Jesus (*e.g.* Mt. 12:28; Lk. 12:32; 17:20–21).[1]

These various elements all concern the covenant's long-term implications. In verse 14, however, a covenant promise is applied directly to an individual, again on the basis of small changes from 2 Samuel 7:16, 'I will confirm him … his throne' (NRSV, RSV) for 'your house will be made sure' and 'your throne' (*cf. he … will build*, v. 12 and 2 Sa. 7:13). On the other hand, the individual emphasis in the EVV of verse 11, *one of your own sons* (NIV, REB, NEB, NRSV; *cf.* GNB; lit. 'one who will come from your sons'), is probably not justified (see Williamson, p. 135). Although the messianic element is not entirely absent (see above), it is quite restrained (against *e.g.* Keil, von Rad, Curtis and Madsen). The oracle looks primarily to Solomon as the individual through whom the covenant is to be established, and it is for this too that David prays (vv. 23–24).

e. Conclusion (17:15). See on 17:3–4a.

iii. David's prayer (17:16–27)
'"And now, LORD, let the promise you have made … be
established for ever"' (17:23)
17:16–27 – *cf.* 2 Samuel 7:18–29

David's response illustrates two central aspects of the Chronicler's view of prayer. Firstly, God's unconditional promises are not to be received casually, as though their advantages were automatic, but with submissive faith and thanksgiving. Secondly, for the Chronicler, faith is often expressed through prayer, notably in the examples of David (also 29:10–19), Solomon (2 Ch. 1:8–10; 6:14–42), Jehoshaphat (2 Ch. 20:6–12), and Hezekiah (2 Ch. 30:18–20; 32:20, 24). Prayers are often strategic in Chronicles, especially those which introduce and conclude the temple-building narratives in the reigns of David and Solomon. Chronicles makes a closer connection between prayer and the building of the temple than Samuel or Kings (1 Ch. 29:10–19 has no parallel), and seems to have specifically encouraged the thought in the post-exilic

[1] *Cf.* M. J. Selman, 'The Kingdom of God in the Old Testament', *TB* 40.2, 1989, pp. 161–183.

period of the temple as a 'house of prayer' (*cf.* Is. 56:7). As in the prayer-psalm in chapter 16 and the Lord's Prayer itself, the requests come towards the end of the prayer (vv. 23–27; *cf.* Mt. 6:11–13). Precedence is given to praise for God's amazing and undeserved generosity.

a. Praise for God's uniqueness (17:16–22). Three rhetorical questions, *Who am I?* (v. 16), 'What is my house?' (v. 16, NRSV, RSV, *etc.*), and *Who is like your people Israel?* (v. 21), and a statement of faith, *There is no-one like you, O LORD, and there is no God but you* (v. 20), form the backbone to the first part of this prayer. The prayer is not just a conventional religious response to good news, for God's word has brought about a marked change in David's perspective. He has a new perception of his dependence (*cf.* v. 1), and the similar questions in the prayer of 29:14 show that this was not a passing phase. Even more importantly, an awareness has emerged of God as not only unique but without any rival (v. 20). Both statements in verse 20 recur elsewhere – *There is no-one like you, O LORD* in the prayers of Asa (2 Chr. 14:11, EVV; v. 10, MT), Jehoshaphat (2 Ch. 20:6) and Jeremiah (Je. 10:6–7); *there is no God but you* in both prayer (Ps. 18:32; Is. 64:4) and divine speech (Is. 45:5l, 21; Ho. 13:4). The development towards monotheism in the Old Testament is quite uneven, but, in the light of these references, the Davidic covenant is to be placed on a par with God's mighty acts of salvation in the exodus (Ho. 13:4) and the return from exile (Is. 45:5, 21) as major evidence for Yahweh's incomparability (*cf.* v. 24).

The prayer confirms that the new covenant promises are also a continuation of God's eternal promises for his people in the Mosaic covenant (vv. 21–22; *cf.* vv. 7–8). By echoing the covenant formula, *You made your people Israel your very own for ever, and you, O LORD, have become their God* (v. 22), the past is resumed (Ex. 6:7; Lv. 26:12), the judgment of exile forgiven (Ho. 1:8–9; Je. 31:33), and the future in Christ anticipated (Rom. 9:25–26; Rev. 21:3). Difficulties of translation occur at several points in these verses, as comparison of the EVV of verses 17, 19, 21 clearly demonstrates. The position is not improved by similar problems in the corresponding verses of 2 Samuel 7, and no consensus has emerged concerning a solution, though the over-all sense is only marginally affected.

For a discussion of these difficulties, see Rudolph, Curtis and Madsen, Michaeli.[1]

b. Request for God to confirm his promises (17:23–27). Two requests emerge in the latter part of the prayer. The first is that God's 'word' (NRSV, RSV) *promise* (NIV, GNB) should *be established for ever* (v. 23). David recognizes that the giving of the promise and its future depend on God, though from now on its success or otherwise will be bound up with the faith and obedience shown by David's descendants. The Davidic covenant is usually described in this chapter as the *word/promise* (vv. 3, 23; *cf.* v. 6), but it is also called *this great thing* (v. 19), 'this good thing' (v. 26, NRSV, RSV), and what God has *revealed* (v. 25; *cf.* v. 15). Verse 23 contains a good example of prayer not always changing the circumstances but the attitude of the person who prays – 'Do what you said' (GNB) or *Do as you promised* (NIV) is in direct opposition to Nathan's original advice to the king (Do *whatever you have in mind*, v. 2).

The second request is that God's *name* ('fame', GNB, REB, NEB) *will be magnified for ever* (v. 24, NRSV, RSV). David has shown understandable human interest in the implications of the divine word for himself and his *house* (vv. 16–19, 23), but the prayer concludes, as the next will begin (29:10–13), with a concern for God's honour. The greatness of God's *name* through both 'houses' is in the end more important to David than the promise of a great name for himself (*cf.* v. 8).

Finally, these requests are based on the confidence that God has already begun to answer David's prayer. God's covenant promise is twice seen as evidence of God's blessing, and this is the real ground of hope that the blessing will not be lost in the future (*You have been pleased to bless . . ., you . . . have blessed*, v. 27 – the note of past blessing is much stronger than in 2 Sa. 7:29). The last phrase of verse 27, which now refers to Yahweh rather than to David's house, should probably be translated, 'For you, O Yahweh, have blessed and you

---

[1] The frequent suggestion in v. 19 of reading 'your servant, your dog' for 'your servant, and according to your will' (*e.g.* Myers, Rudolph, Braun; *cf.* O. Margalith, '*Keleb*: homonym or metaphor?' *VT* 33, 1983, pp. 491–495) cannot be supported. Though the idiom is established in Canaanite and non-biblical Heb. as well as in the OT (*e.g.* 2 Sa. 9:8; 2 Ki. 8:13), it would make no sense if applied to the source in 2 Sa. 7:21.

are blessed for ever', against EVV. Ultimately God alone is to be praised.

D. David's empire (18:1 – 20:8)

Chapters 18–20 contain an outline of David's creation of an Israelite empire. This achievement was mainly the result of external expansion through military victories, though one short passage (18:14–17) shows that internal reorganization also played a part. The material is clearly selective, with few details and little analysis of the causes and progress of individual conflicts. The summary in 18:11 is based on different information from the main narrative, mentioning the Amalekites for the first time (but *cf*. 1 Sa. 30), but excluding the Arameans who otherwise dominate the account (*cf*. 18:3–8; 19:6–9). Other groups subject to David are omitted entirely, especially the Jebusites (11:4–6; *cf*. 2 Sa. 5:6–8) and the Canaanites whom David incorporated into Israel (*cf*. 2 Ch. 8:7–8). Chronicles' version combines accounts of David's victories scattered throughout 2 Samuel 8–23, as the following comparison shows:[1]

	2 Samuel	*1 Chronicles*
ch. 8	David's victories over the nations	= ch. 18
ch. 9	David's kindness to Saul's grandson Mephibosheth	
ch. 10:1 – 11:1	Ammonite war	= ch. 19:1 – 20:1
ch. 11:2 – 12:25	Bathsheba affair	
ch. 12:26–31	End of Ammonite war	= ch. 20:1–3
ch. 13–14	Amnon and Absalom	
ch. 15–20	Rebellions of Absalom and Sheba	
ch. 21:1–14	Death of Saul's descendants	
ch. 21:15–22	Heroism of David's men against four Philistines	= ch. 20:4–8 (against three Philistines)
ch. 22:1 – 23:7	David's words of thanks and last words	
ch. 23:8–39	David's mighty men	(= ch. 11:10–47)

[1] Based on Michaeli, p. 107.

At first glance, this is a somewhat artificial record of David's military successes, which has been produced by leaving out the more interesting narratives and those less favourable to David. This view is rather inaccurate, however, since positive elements such as the birth of Solomon, David's magnanimity to Saul's family, and David's psalms are also omitted. Also, a victory previously subsumed under David's achievements is now credited to one of his generals (18:12–13; *cf.* 2 Sa. 8:13–14). The reason is that Chronicles has chosen to focus on the relationship of David's wars (chs. 18–20) with the Davidic covenant (ch. 17) and the temple preparations (chs. 21–29). Personal considerations such as the adulation of David or mere nationalistic gloating over defeated neighbours are ruled out, and neither is 2 Samuel's objectivity abandoned.

Two major dimensions of David's wars emerge from their present context. Firstly, the Davidic covenant (ch. 17) is already being partially fulfilled:

(a) David's enemies are *subdued/defeated* (the same Heb. verb *hiknîaʿ* is used in 17:10; 18:1, 20:4; *cf.* also 18:2, 3, 5, 9, 10, 12; 19:16, 19; 20:1, 4, 5, 7, 8);

(b) David's *name/fame* (17:8; *cf.* 14:17) reaches to the nations, whose kings must make *peace* (19:19; *greet*, 18:10, is from the same Heb. root) and *congratulate* him (18:10);

(c) by the defeat of Israel's various neighbours, especially their traditional enemies the *Philistines*, the land becomes undisturbed (17:9; 18:1; 20:4–8; *cf.* 11:12–19; 14:8–16).

As a result, the preparations for the temple (ch. 21–29) take on a new meaning:

(a) David's wars are the penultimate stage by which his throne and kingdom are established (*cf.* 17:11, 12, 14), the process being completed by the building of Solomon's temple (17:11–12; 22:6–10);

(b) the 'rest' or peace which was a precondition for building the temple (22:8–9; see also comment on 17:1) is eventually achieved;

(c) it is explained why David as a 'man of war' is personally unable to build the temple (22:8–9; 28:3). David is not thereby guilty (against Rudolph, p. 139). Indeed, the temple will be held back until David has established peace through victories which were seen as God's own work (18:6, 13);

(d) an additional clause in 18:8, *which Solomon used to make the bronze Sea, the pillars and various bronze articles,* underlines

David's dedication of the spoils of war for the temple (18:11 = 2 Sa. 8:11–12 *cf.* 1 Ch. 26:26–28; 2 Ch. 5:1). A comparison between David and Joshua is probably also intended (Jos. 6:24; see also introductory comments).

i. David's victories over the nations (18:1–17)

'The LORD gave David victory everywhere he went' (18:6, 13).

18:1–17 – *cf.* 2 Samuel 8:1–18

Israel achieved the status of empire for the first and only time, through David's victories (vv. 1–13) and Israel's internal re-organization (vv. 14–17). The repeated phrase, retained from 2 Samuel, *the LORD gave David victory* (Heb. *wayyôša'*, lit. 'he saved') *everywhere he went* (vv. 6, 13) provides the over-all theme. Similar references to God's saving activity and victory for Israel are added in 1 Chronicles 16:35; 2 Chronicles 20:9, 17; 32:22 (*cf.* 1 Ch. 11:14; 16:23; 2 Ch. 6:41 where the same thought is already present in the earlier material). The truth that God continues to save and deliver his people in accordance with his promise (*cf.* 17:8–10) is clearly important in Chronicles. The Chronicler's additions in 1 Chronicles 16:35 have already underlined his prayer for his own time that God would deliver his people from the rule of foreign empires. David's victories are therefore one aspect of God's answer to that prayer, as are similar instances in the reigns of Jehoshaphat (2 Ch. 20:9, 17) and Hezekiah (2 Ch. 32:22). In each case, God's victory is sustained by the 'rest' which the temple permanently symbolized (2 Ch. 20:30; 32:22, LXX, Vulg., see NRSV, RSV, *cf.* REB, NEB, GNB, JB).

In a New Testament context, where God's victory and deliverance are demilitarized and denationalized, it is none-theless expected to be part of the believer's experience (*cf.* 2 Cor. 1:10; 2 Tim. 4:17–18). As with David, however, it is not an automatic right, but a free gift dependent on God's promise and sovereign action (2 Cor. 2:14), to be received through faith (1 Jn. 5:14) and prayer (2 Cor. 10:3–5; Eph. 6:10–20).

Israel's extent and influence under David were unsurpassed at any other point in their history. David's control extended beyond the traditional northern boundary of Dan (*e.g.* 2 Sa. 3:10) or Lebo Hamath (1 Ch. 13:5) to Hamath itself (vv. 9–10) and even the river Euphrates (v. 3; *cf.* 19:16). This linked David directly with the promises given to Abraham (Gn.

15:18) and Moses (Ex. 23:31; Dt. 1:7; 11:24; *cf.* Jos. 1:3–4; 1 Ch. 13:5).[1] The whole area, however, was not under Israelite occupation. In many areas, especially in the north, David had to be content to receive tribute (vv. 2, 6) or to make friendship treaties (v. 10; *cf.* 1 Ki. 5:1). Nevertheless, victories in the south (Philistines, Edom, Amalek), east (Moab, Ammon), as well as the north (Aramean states) ensured that David came nearer than any other Israelite leader to completing the task first given to Moses and Joshua. Of David's successors, only Solomon exercised influence in the Euphrates area (1 Ki. 4:21, 24), and then only with partial success (1 Ki. 11:23–25). After the exile, interest in the Davidic–Solomonic empire was maintained by the prophets, who spoke of a future kingdom stretching from 'the River to the ends of the earth' (Zc. 9:10, based on Ps. 72:8).

Chapter 18 appears to have originated from official lists, probably from the court rather than the temple. Verses 1–13 may be a summary of originally longer narratives of the kind now preserved in 19:1 – 20:13. Apart from variants concerning several proper names, the main changes from 2 Samuel are in verses 2, 8 and 17.

a. Victories over the Philistines (18:1). Evidence for David's conquest of *Gath and its surrounding villages* is found in the presence of 600 Gittites in David's entourage (2 Sa. 15:18), even though the corresponding place in 2 Samuel 8:1 is an otherwise unknown Metheg-ammah.

b. Victories over the Moabites (18:2). David's excessive treatment of the *Moabites* in 2 Samuel 8:2, as of the Edomites (1 Ki. 11:16), is omitted, though for what reason is unknown. The native rulers of Gath (*cf.* 1 Ki. 2:39–40) and Moab were not removed, though the Moabites, like the Arameans (v. 6), paid *tribute*.

c. Victories over Hadadezer of Zobah (18:3–10). The main part of the chapter reports David's victory over *Hadadezer* (AV,

---

[1] 1 Ch. 5:9 reports that the Reubenites occupied land in the Euphrates area, but it is unknown at what period and for how long this occurred. Unless it was associated with the reigns of David and/or Solomon, it played no part in establishing the people or kingdom of Israel.

Hadarezer) of *Zobah* (vv. 3–10; *cf.* 19:16–19). Having amalgamated his native Beth-Rehob (2 Sa. 8:3) in south Lebanon with Zobah, a territory north of Damascus, Hadadezer himself ruled an empire of small Syrian states which may have extended beyond the Euphrates (*cf.* 19:16 and inscriptions of the Assyrian kings Shalmaneser III and Ashurdan II).[1] He had clashed with David twice before (19:1–15, 16–19), but this confrontation between the two most powerful kings in Syria–Palestine was his final defeat. It is not clear whether it was David or Hadadezer who set up the victory stela (v. 3, *cf.* NRSV, RSV, REB, NEB; lit. 'hand'; *control*, GNB, NIV) which triggered the decisive battle. David received as spoil the cities of *Damascus* (vv. 5–6), 'Tibhath' (v. 8, REB, NEB, NRSV, RSV; *Tebah*, NIV; also possibly Tubihi), and the otherwise unknown *Cun* (v. 8) and Berothai (2 Sa. 8:8). He retained a few *chariot horses* (v. 4), either as a royal status symbol or to supplement the first small cavalry detachment in an Israelite army,[2] but found greater value in the *bronze* (*cf.* 2 Ch. 3:17 – 4:18).[3] The word translated *shields* (v. 7, NIV, NRSV, REB) is actually an Aramaic loan-word meaning 'quivers' (NEB).[4] *Tou* (spelled Toi in 2 Sa.) of Hamath (modern Hamah – on the Orontes about 120 miles north of Damascus) seems to have made a peace treaty, though his request for peace (EVV 'greet') and congratulations suggest the action of an inferior party (v. 9; *cf.* the parity treaty between David and Hiram of Tyre, 14:1–2).[5] Tou's son was probably called *Hadoram* (v. 10) rather than 'Joram' (2 Sa. 8:10), since the latter's Yahwistic form is unlikely in a

---

[1] See A. Malamat, in D. J. Wiseman (ed.), *Peoples of Old Testament Times* (Oxford: Clarendon Press, 1973), pp. 141–143; *idem*, in T. Ishida (ed.), *Studies in the Period of David and Solomon* (Tokyo: Yamakawa-Shuppansha, 1982), p. 196. On the basis of Jos. 11:6–9, it has also been proposed that hamstringing (v. 4) was an accepted punishment for horses captured from mercenary forces (McCarter, p. 249).

[2] Y. Yadin, *The Art of Warfare in Biblical Lands* (London: Wiedenfeld & Nicolson, 1963), p. 285; Y. Ikeda, in T. Ishida (ed.), *Studies in the Period of David and Solomon* (Tokyo: Yamakawa-Shuppansha, 1982), pp. 215–238.

[3] On the basis of 'these also' (NRSV, RSV) in v. 11 and 2 Sa. 8:11, Rudolph argues that the additional final phrase of v. 8 was in the source used by 2 Sa. 8.

[4] See R. Borger, 'Die Waffenträger des Königs Darius', *VT* 22, 1972, pp. 385–398. Although the word can also mean 'bow-case', this usage is found in Mesopotamian contexts rather than Syro-Palestinian ones.

[5] D. J. Wiseman ('"Is it peace?" – covenant and diplomacy', *VT* 32, 1982, pp. 311–326, *cf.* p. 319) has proposed that Toi's mission was only a preliminary diplomatic move towards an agreed vassal covenant status.

non-Israelite state (*cf.* an eighth-century BC successor named Yaubidi who certainly had no Israelite associations, *ANET*, p. 285).

d. David's gifts (18:11). An important verse summarizing David's victories and indicating that *David dedicated* the spoils of war to the LORD, that is, to the temple project. Additions in v. 8 (*which Solomon used to make the bronze Sea, the pillars and various bronze articles*; *cf.* 2 Sa. 8:8) and in 1 Ch. 26:26–27 (*cf.* also 2 Ch. 5:1) give further details about what eventually happened to this booty. In this way, the Chronicler underlines David's involvement in the temple project in the context of existing statements about the temple as the ultimate beneficiary of David's military activities (2 Sa. 8:11–12; 1 Ki. 7:51). Although the majority of nations from whom this wealth has been taken are included in chapters 18–20, some of the data suggests this list comes from a longer but still incomplete narrative of David's wars. *Amalek* is mentioned only in 1 Samuel 30, while there is no room here for either the Jebusites (1 Ch. 11:4–9) or the Ammonites (1 Ch. 18:3–8; 19:6–19; 20:1–3).

e. Victories over the Edomites (18:12–13). A brief report of David's Edomite war concludes the section. *Edom* (vv. 11–12) is a preferable reading to 'Aram' (2 Sa. 8:12–13), since the setting in verse 12 is clearly Edomite (*cf.* 2 Ki. 14:7), though the difference between the two Hebrew words is minimal. *Abishai*'s role in Edom is attributed previously to David (2 Sa. 8:13) and to Abishai's brother Joab (1 Ki. 11:15–16; Ps. 60: title). However, all three would have had differing responsibilities in the over-all chain of command, with Joab, as army commander (v. 15; 19:8–10; 20:1) and Abishai, chief of the Three (11:20–21; *cf.* 19:11–15; 2 Sa. 20:6–7), enjoying leading military roles. David and Joab were also involved together in the Edomite campaign (1 Ki. 11:15). Edom became a province of the empire, like Damascus (v. 6), and was more strictly controlled than Moab or Zobah (*cf.* vv. 2, 6), though whether by means of *garrisons* (NIV, NRSV, RSV) or 'governors' (JB) remains uncertain (v. 13 – the word is rightly restored in v. 6).

f. David's cabinet (18:14–17). 14. David's control of *all Israel* (*cf.* 11:3; 12:38; 13:2; 15:28) was the foundation of his empire, which was administered by the first 'cabinet' or 'executive' in Israelite history (vv. 14–17). The list is based on 2 Samuel 8:15–18 (*cf.* 2 Sa. 20:23–26), though some overlap with the list of secular officials in 1 Chronicles 26:25–34 also occurs. David's doing what was *just and right* (Heb. *mišpāṭ ûṣᵉdāqâ; cf.* 2 Ch. 9:8) reflects the ancient Near Eastern tradition where rulers took responsibility for their judicial system (*cf.* Absalom's attempt to gain power by usurping David's legal authority, 2 Sa. 15:1–6). The terms 'justice' (Heb. *mišpāṭ*) and 'righteousness' (Heb. *ṣedeq, ṣᵉdāqâ*) also express David's faithfulness to Israelite covenant law. They were God's own principles (Ps. 89:14; Is. 33:5), which became the hallmark of ideal government in the prophetic hope (Is. 11:1–5).

15–17. The 'cabinet' had three 'departments', with two military officers, two in charge of administration, and four priests. The pattern of administration sketched here is usually thought to be modelled on Egyptian practice, the *recorder* (NIV, NRSV, RSV; 'secretary of state', REB, NEB) acting either as 'spokesman, herald' or in charge of protocol, and the *secretary* (NIV, NRSV, RSV, JB; 'adjutant-general', REB, NEB) responsible for official correspondence. Others have sought Canaanite analogies, but native Israelite developments should not be discounted.[1] In the military section, *Joab*, successor to Abner (*cf.* 2 Sa. 3:6–39) and briefly displaced by Amasa (2 Sa. 19:13 – 20:13), was David's chief general, and *Benaiah* was over the royal bodyguard of Cherethite (= Cretan) and Pelethite (= Philistine) mercenaries.

The information about the *priests* is less straightforward, since *Zadok* and Abiathar are the more familiar names of David's priests (*e.g.* 2 Sa. 15:24ff.; 1 Ch. 15:11). The EVV correctly have *Ahimelech* for MT's 'Abimelech' with 2 Samuel 8:17, but the common adoption of Wellhausen's proposal (as in REB, NEB) to remove Zadok's father's name and change the second priest's name to 'Abiathar son of Ahimelech son of Ahitub' (*cf.* 1 Sa. 22:20) does not do justice to a complex problem. Chronicles at least has a tradition that one *Ahitub* was Zadok's father (1 Ch. 6:8, 53; *cf.* 2 Sa. 8:17), which was strong enough to influence the names of later pre-exilic generations

[1] See further J. Begrich, 'Sōphēr und Mazkīr. Ein Beitrag zur inneren Geschichte des davidisch-salomonischen Grossreiches und des Königsreiches Juda', *ZAW* 58, 1940–41, pp. 1–29; G. W. Ahlström, *Royal Administration and National Religion in Ancient Palestine* (Leiden: Brill, 1982), pp. 27–31.

(1 Ch. 6:12; *cf.* 9:11; Ezr. 7:2; Ne. 11:11). A possible analogy for Abiathar and Ahimelech (father or son?) carrying out joint priestly duties is the combined activity of Aaron and his sons (Lv. 8–10). A further problem concerns *David's sons* (v. 17). According to 2 Samuel 8:18 they were 'priests', but here they are only David's *chief officials* (NIV, NRSV, RSV; 'eldest sons', REB, NEB). They were probably either the king's personal priests, *i.e.* a kind of royal chaplain, or high-ranking officials whose priestly function was separate from that of the levitical priests (*cf.* 2 Sa. 20:26; 1 Ki. 4:5).[1]

ii. David's victories over the Ammonites (19:1 – 20:3)

'Be strong and let us fight bravely for our people and the cities of our God' (19:13)

19:1–19 – *cf.* 2 Samuel 10:1–19
20:1 – *cf.* 2 Samuel 11:1; 12:26
20:2–3 – *cf.* 2 Samuel 12:30–31

David extends his conquests to include the Ammonites (*cf.* 18:11) and the Arameans (*cf.* 18:3–8), and the account concludes with the Ammonites' final demise in 20:1–3. Chapter 19 follows 2 Samuel 10 quite closely, though the Chronicler shows a marked tendency to simplify in 19:7, 9, 15–16 (*cf.* 2 Sa. 10:6, 8, 14:16). It is also the only extended narrative Chronicles has taken from the so-called 'Succession Narrative' (2 Sa. 9–20 + 1 Ki. 1–2), whose distinctive historical and theological style is reflected here in its implicit view of God's providence. Even in Israel's double victory, God is mentioned only once (v. 13; contrast 18:6, 13, and the Chronicler's own theologizing in 1 Chronicles 10:13–14).

Chapter 19 seems to cover much the same ground as 18:3–8, except in more detail. However, the four battles described in 18:3–8 and 19:1 – 20:3 are not identical, and they are probably not in exact chronological order. For example, the implied confrontation in the Euphrates area (18:3–4) and the intervention of Damascus (18:5–6) cannot be easily harmonized with the geographical data of chapter 19. Equally, it does not seem likely that David would have been able to march into Syria if he had not first removed the Ammonite threat to his rear. 19:1–15 therefore, seems to precede 18:3–8. As for

[1] For the appointment of a man's son and a Levite as joint personal priests, *cf.* Jdg. 17:5–13. See also G. J. Wenham, 'Were David's sons priests?', *ZAW* 87, 1975, pp. 79–82.

the conflict in 19:16–19 and its apparent climax in 20:1–3, its location too is different from that of 18:3–8 (*cf.* 19:17), and it seems to precede 18:3–8, since the effects of the latter battle appear final. The most likely order of the Ammonite war is therefore 19:1–15; 19:16–19; 20:1–3 and 18:3–8.

The Chronicler probably included this material on the Ammonite war for two reasons. As a major element in the record of David's wars in 2 Samuel, it has obvious relevance for the over-all theme of 1 Chronicles 18–20. Its climax is David's coronation as king of the Ammonites (20:2), the highest honour accorded to David outside Israel. Secondly, 2 Samuel 10 contains two examples of one of the Chronicler's favourite terms, *viz.* 'strength, be strong' (Heb. *ḥzq*) in a verse (2 Sa. 10:12 = v. 13 here) which holds the key to the chapter's theological significance: *Be strong and let us fight bravely* (*cf.* REB, NEB; 'Be of good courage, let us play the man', RSV). Chronicles uses this root in an almost technical sense to refer both to political and military strength (*e.g.* 2 Ch. 1:1; 12:13; 26:8, 15, 16) and to committed obedience to God's law (*e.g.* 1 Ch. 28:7; 2 Ch. 15:8; 31:4). The military element is present here, of course, but verse 13 has other nuances. (a) It is a clear echo of the command 'Be strong and of good courage', invariably associated with the Conquest (Dt. 31:7, 23; Jos. 1:6, 7, 9, all directed to Joshua; *cf.* Dt. 31:6; Jos. 10:25, both plural; for other links between David and Joshua as conquerors of the Promised Land, see introduction to chapters 18–20 above). (b) As a command, it is often accompanied by a promise of divine help, as here (v. 13; *cf.* Dt. 31:7–8; Jos. 1:9; 10:25; 2 Ch. 19:11; 32:7–8). (c) The idea of mutual support here and in 2 Chronicles 29:34 may be intended as the Chronicler's encouragement for greater co-operation in his own day. (d) Victory is gained through united strength – *rescue* (v. 12, twice, NIV; 'help', NRSV, RSV) is from the same Hebrew root as 'gave victory' in 18:6, 13, with which verse 12 is surely to be associated, even though the meaning is slightly different in the two passages. The whole incident therefore shows 'all Israel' co-operating under David and establishing the required 'rest' for building the temple.

This sense of co-operative fellowship is an important aspect of the New Testament concept of the church. The church can grow only 'as each part does its work' (Eph. 4:16), and its gifts used for the 'common good' (1 Cor. 12:7; *cf.* 14:12) rather than for sectional interests. A prime example of the value of corporate Christianity occurs in the context of spiritual warfare in Ephesians 6:10–20. In that context, the plural imperatives, 'Be strong (*cf.* v. 13 here) . . ., put on . . .', are addressed to Christians as a body so that the powers of evil may be successfully resisted (for other applications, see Gal. 6:1–3 on corporate burden-bearing and Phil. 4:14–19 on co-operative financial support).

a. First victory under Joab (19:1–15)

i. *Ammonite insults (19:1–5).* The friendship between David and *Nahash*, the Ammonite king, is probably best explained by their common hostility toward Saul (*cf.* 1 Sa. 11; 14:47). The existence of an Ammonite–Israelite treaty may be implied by *kindness* (v. 2, Heb. *ḥeseḏ*), but the reference is to reciprocal action rather than a state of formal relations (1 Ki. 5:1 suggests Israel and Tyre had a more permanent treaty relationship). *Hanun*'s insults have sometimes been placed in David's early years before David was fully secure, but there is evidence that the fears of the 'Ammonite leaders' (v. 3, GNB, JB) may have been fuelled by more than just contempt for an upstart. Location of the subsequent battle at Medeba (v. 7), south of the Ammonite capital Rabbah, could suggest that David had already subdued Edom and Moab, perhaps even that the Israelite army was returning from victory there (*cf.* 18:2, 12–13). No doubt too, David's embassy to Ammon's old enemy Jabesh-gilead (1 Sa. 11) for their 'kindness' to Saul's family (2 Sa. 2:5–6) was interpreted in some Ammonite quarters as an unfriendly act. Either action could have aroused suspicion that David's real motive was to *overthrow* their land (v. 3).[1] Some have alleged that Chronicles has accentuated the Israelites' humiliation (v. 5) by completely removing their beards and all their body hair down to the waist (Rudolph, Botterweck). More probably, however, the simple *shaved them* (v. 4) is one of the many examples of the Chronicler's preference for abbreviation (2 Sa. 10:5, 'he

---

[1] Although the order of the three infinitives in v. 3 ('to search and to overthrow and to spy out' (NRSV, RSV) is strictly illogical, MT can be accepted by regarding the last as resuming an intention expressed in the first two (the conjunction with 'to overthrow' may be emphatic, *cf.* GK ##114p, 154a[1]). There seems to be no need for Michaeli's 'make a tour' or for Rudolph's emendation 'to search' (*wᵉlaḥpōr* for *wᵉlaḥᵃpōḵ*).

shaved half their beards'). In any case, half a beard was worse than none!

ii. Preparations for war (19:6–9). The remaining paragraphs of the chapter are all introduced by a phrase such as 'When X saw that . . .' (vv. 6, 10, 16, 19), indicating clearly the progressive stages of the narrative. The Ammonites realized they had literally 'made themselves stink' (v. 6), a word used for decaying animal or vegetable matter (*e.g.* Ex. 7:18, 8:10; 16:20; Is. 50:2) and applied metaphorically where relationships had totally collapsed (*e.g.* Gn. 34:30; 1 Sa. 27:12; 25 Sa. 16:21). They therefore formed a temporary coalition with various Aramean states, most, if not all, subject to Hadadezer of Zobah (*cf.* 18:3–6), and *hired* Aramean troops. The price, *a thousand talents of silver* (v. 6), was substantial, and, though not in the MT of 2 Samuel 10:6, is well supported in an early MS of Samuel (4QSam^a).[1] Chronicles has simplified the names of the four Aramean states involved (*cf.* 2 Sa. 10:8). Only *Maacah* (vv. 6–7), on Israel's north-east boundary (Dt. 3:14; Jos. 12:5; 13:11) and *Zobah* (v. 6; *cf.* 18:3–6), reappear from Samuel with 'Beth Rehob' and 'Tob' replaced by the vaguer *Aram Naharaim* (v. 6, NIV, REB, NEB; 'Mesopotamia', NRSV, RSV). Both Israelite (v. 8) and Ammonite/Aramean forces (vv. 7, 9) gathered at *Medeba*, a city mentioned on the ninth century Moabite Stone. Being some distance south-west of Ammon on the King's Highway, it has sometimes been considered an error for 'waters of Rabbah' (Rothstein, Rudolph, Williamson), but Medeba may be connected with a struggle for control of the King's Highway[2] or with Joab's Edomite and Moabite campaigns (18:2, 12–13). The Aramean *kings* were in the *open country* (v. 9) indicating the forefront of the battle, while the Ammonite troops in the rear guarded the *city*, either Medeba or the Ammonite capital Rabbah.

iii. Victory under Joab (19:10–15). Finding himself sandwiched between the opposing forces, *Joab* divided his army, with *some of the best troops in Israel* under his own command

---

[1] E. C. Ulrich, *The Qumran Text of Samuel and Josephus* (Missoula: Scholars Press, 1978), pp. 152–156.

[2] B. Mazar, 'The kingdom of David and Solomon in its contact with Egypt and Aram Naharaim', *BA* 25, 1962, pp. 96–102, especially p. 102.

facing the stronger Arameans (v. 10) and his brother Abishai deputed to contain the Ammonites (v. 11). Joab's two-part instructions are the key to the battle's outcome (vv. 12–13). Each Israelite division was firstly encouraged to give mutual support, *for our people and the cities of our God* (v. 13).[1] The latter phrase is unique in the Old Testament, perhaps suggesting a Davidic origin for the similar, but more familiar, epithet of Jerusalem, 'city of (our) God' (Pss. 46:4; 48:1, 8; 87:3; *cf.* 'city of Yahweh', Ps. 101:8; Is. 60:14; also Ps. 48:9). On the central importance of the command, *Be strong and let us fight bravely* (v. 13), see earlier comment. Secondly, Joab motivated his troops with either a promise (*the LORD will do what is good in his sight, cf.* NRSV, RSV) or a prayer ('the LORD's will be done', GNB, REB, NEB) for divine help – for similar encouragements, see 2 Chronicles 19:11; 32:7–8. The answer to the prayer was immediate. The Arameans (v. 14) and Ammonites (v. 15) both *fled*, apparently without a fight, as soon as the Israelite army took the offensive. The author may intend this as an illustrative echo of the promise given to Jehoshaphat, 'The battle is not yours, but God's' (2 Ch. 20:15; *cf.* Ex. 14:14). *His brother Abishai* (v. 15, NIV, REB, NEB) is rather distant from its antecedent – the original may have read 'Abishai, Joab's brother', as NRSV, RSV.[2]

b. Second victory under David (19:16–19). Joab's success was not conclusive. A second battle was required to end the coalition (v. 19). Even after that, there was further conflict before both the Arameans (18:3–8) and the Ammonites (20:1–3) finally capitulated. Aramean reinforcements were sent from 'beyond the Euphrates' (v. 16, NRSV, RSV)[3] to restore Hadadezer's dented pride, but the earlier result was confirmed as the Arameans again *fled* (v. 18; *cf.* vv. 14–15).[4] This battle may have been located at 'Helam' (2 Sa. 10:16–17), a

---

[1] The proposed alternatives to 'cities', *viz.* 'ark' (Curtis and Madsen, following Smend) and 'altars' (REB, NEB mg.), lack adequate textual support.

[2] *Cf.* L. C. Allen, *The Greek Chronicles* II, *SVT* 27 (Leiden: Brill, 1974), p. 142; Rudolph, p. 138.

[3] Or 'from the area of the Euphrates' (*cf.* REB, NEB, 'from the Great Bend of the Euphrates'). For *b°ēber, mē°ēber*, 'the area/region of, beside', see J. P. U. Lilley, 'By the river-side', *VT* 28, 1978, pp. 165–171.

[4] The impersonal verbs, 'they sent . . . they brought out . . .' (v. 16, NRSV) may be better rendered as passives, as in Aramaic usage, *cf.* 2 Sa. 10:16, 'Hadadezer sent and brought out . . .'.

name possibly concealed in the phrase 'came to them' (v. 17, NRSV, RSV; *advanced against them*, NIV; Heb. *ḥl'mh* for *'lhm*), though neither reading is beyond dispute.[1] Shophach, the general of Hadadezer's army (vv. 16, 18; 'Shobach', 2 Sa. 10:16, 18) is not known elsewhere.

Final victory over the Arameans is attributed to *David* (vv. 17–19; *cf.* 20:2–3), here leading *all Israel* (v. 17), a favourite combination in Chronicles (*cf.* 11:3; 12:38; 15:28; 18:14), but already present in Samuel in this instance.

18. Casualty numbers here are an intractable problem (also in 18:4; 19:7), and Keil's argument for textual corruption in both accounts is still the most likely explanation. *Foot soldiers* is preferable to the 'charioteers' of 2 Samuel 10:18, with the reverse more likely in verse 7 (*cf.* the numbers of foot soldiers in 18:4 and 2 Sa. 8:4), but commentators are divided whether the *charioteers* ('chariot teams', JB) numbered 700 (2 Sa. 10:18) or 7,000 (a similar discrepancy occurs in 18:4 and 2 Sa. 8:4).

19. *Peace* was agreed on terms set by *David* ('Israel', 2 Sa. 10:19), though apparently without payment of tribute (*cf.* 18:2, 6). *Not willing* is more emphatic than Samuel. The Arameans' will to *help* the Ammonites had been broken as a direct consequence of the Israelites' 'help' (v. 12, twice, NRSV, RSV, GNB; *rescue*, NIV – all three occurrences are from the same Heb. root) for each other. Equally important, however, was that Israel's troops were willing to fight God's battles (*cf.* Ps. 110:3) because of their confidence that God would do *what is good in his sight* (v. 13).

c. Final victory (20:1–3). This short passage is a highly condensed version of the *Ammonite* war report in 2 Samuel 11–12, which is dominated by the Bathsheba scandal. A hint of this rearrangement is found in the awkward transition between verses 1 and 2, but a more evocative allusion is preserved in the enigmatic phrase, *but David remained in Jerusalem* (v. 1; *cf.* 2 Sa. 11:1). Two purposes may be discerned in the Chronicler's version, both based on elements already found in Samuel. Firstly, although the Chronicler is not unaware that David is guilty of great sin (*cf.* 21:8), he wishes to stress Samuel's concluding emphasis in the Uriah/Bathsheba tragedy on repentance, forgiveness and restoration (2 Sa.

---

[1] For possible locations, see *IBD*, 2, p. 633.

12:13, 24–25; *cf.* Ps. 51:13–19). Guilt because of sin did not disqualify a person from playing a leading role in God's kingdom, as both post-exilic and New Testament believers continued to need reminding (*cf.* Zc. 3:1–10; 5:1–11; 1 Cor. 6:9).

Secondly, the contribution of those who shared in leadership with David is underlined, as in the account of the Philistine wars (20:4–8). Here it is Joab rather than David who 'led out the army' (v. 1, GNB), and, in the next section, David's men who defeat the Philistines. In this instance there is real irony in the fact that the incident took place 'at the time of the year when kings usually go to war' (GNB). There is more than a hint here that plurality in leadership among God's people is essential, if only to make up for the deficiencies of others (*cf.* Eph. 4:11–13; Ac. 13:1–3; Phil. 1:1).

The *crown* (v. 2) belonged either to the Ammonite *king* (NIV, NRSV, RSV) or, with some of the vss (LXX, Vulg.), to the chief Ammonite deity 'Milcom' (GNB, REB, NEB). Its chief features were (a) distinctive *precious stone(s)* and its weight (*c.* 30 kg). Hebrew syntax suggests that the crown rather than the jewel (against GNB, REB, NEB) was placed on David's head, though its heaviness must have made any act of coronation quite brief! Many Ammonites were assigned to forced *labour* (v. 3),[1] and some, like those of other subject nations, were incorporated into David's forces (*cf.* 11:26–47, esp. vv. 39, 41–47).

David's rule over Ammon seems to be part of a complex four-stage system of administration of the empire outside the land of Israel.[2] Zobah was in a straightforward state of vassalship (19:10), but control was tightened increasingly by imposing tribute on Moab (18:2, *cf.* v. 6) and garrisons or governors in Damascus and Edom (18:6, 13). Ammon was most restricted of all, apparently demoted to provincial status. The Philistines' role is unclear. Although Gath suffered a heavier defeat than all the other Philistine cities, it was allowed to keep its native ruler (1 Ki. 2:39–40). The Philistines as a whole remained subject to Solomon (2 Ch. 9:26) and did not

---

[1] MT might be read 'he sawed' (*cf.* AV), but 2 Sa. 12:31 and the generally merciful treatment of prisoners of war in the ancient Near East support the interpretation adopted here.
[2] The position within Israel was also complicated, with the Canaanite city states not fully absorbed and the northern tribes preserving their own traditions of independence.

trouble Israel again for well over a hundred years (2 Ch. 21:16).

iii. Victories over the Philistines (20:4–8)
'The Philistines were defeated' (20:4, GNB)

20:4–8 – *cf.* 2 Samuel 21:18–22

The account of David's wars is completed by three cameos taken from the Philistine wars. All three incidents are probably associated with David's assault on Gath (18:1), since two of his three opponents came from that city (vv. 5, 6, 8). The Philistine warriors are also all called 'Rephaites' (RSV) or *descendants of Rapha* ('giants', NRSV), who were one of the pre-Israelite groups in Canaan (*e.g.* Gn. 15:20) and famous for their size (*cf.* v. 6). These people were known elsewhere as the 'Avvites' (or Avvim), whom the first Philistines had driven out (Dt. 2:23, where Caphtorites, *i.e.* Cretans, certainly = Philistines), and as the 'Anakites' (or Anakim), who had also presumably been overrun by the Philistines since Joshua removed them from all but three Philistine towns, including Gath (Jos. 11:22).

This section has several links with other passages. It shares with 20:1–3, for example, the idea that David's soldiers rather than David himself are the real heroes. This emphasis on joint leadership is all the more significant since the Philistines had been Israel's most intractable enemy for decades. A link also exists with the Davidic covenant. The addition of *were subjugated* ('defeated', GNB) in v. 4 (*cf.* 2 Sa. 21:18) strongly suggests that defeating the Philistines is seen as a fulfilment of God's promises in 17:10, where the same Heb. word occurs. There is even a connection with the time of Joshua. Describing the Philistines as the Rephaites or the descendants of Rapha (vv. 4, 6, 8) identifies them as the descendants of those who had struck terror into Moses' spies (*cf.* Nu. 13:28–33; Dt. 1:26–28; 2:10–23). Only now had fear finally turned to faith, as David and his men completed Joshua's conquest at last, an achievement which was possible only because God had kept his promise (*cf.* 17:11–14; 14:17).

Yet this summit of Israel's military achievements must be put into perspective, for it does not begin to scale the peaks of even the Old Testament's hopes for David and his dynasty (*cf. e.g.* Ps. 2:8, 'I will make the nations your inheritance and the ends of the earth your possession'). Such hopes have been realized only in David's son Jesus, who became the conqueror of every opposing power and Lord of every nation, not through military force but because he was crucified (Rev. 6:2; 14:14; 19:11–16; Heb. 2:7, 9).

A major problem arises in the case of *Elhanan*'s defeat of *Lahmi the brother of Goliath* (v. 5). According to 2 Samuel 21:19, 'Elhanan son of Jaare-oregim the Bethlehemite' also overcame Goliath himself, apparently contradicting the account of David's famous victory in 1 Samuel 17. Scholars have often assumed that the Chronicler has tendentiously corrected the confusion by inventing Lahmi out of the word 'Bethlehemite' in 2 Samuel 21. Although there is no simple solution, since 1 Samuel has clearly preserved two separate accounts of Goliath's end, some features do lend support to the Chronicler's version, as earlier commentators sometimes recognized (*e.g.* Keil). Scribal corruption is certainly present in 2 Samuel 21:19, as for example in the name 'Jaare-oregim', which should be *Jair*, as here. The crucial word 'Bethlehemite' is also suspicious, since this form is used elsewhere only of Jesse (1 Sa. 16:1, 18; 17:58; MT *bêt hallaḥmî*; Elhanan of Bethlehem, 2 Sa. 23:24 = 1 Ch. 11:26, possibly a separate person, uses a different form), and may therefore be an inferior reading to Lahmi. It is therefore quite feasible to think of a confrontation between Elhanan and Lahmi, perhaps in association with David's offensive against Gath as a revenge for Goliath's death.

The duel was a recognized form of combat in Canaan and in the Philistines' original homeland in the Aegean. It had the advantage of enabling conflicts to be settled without recourse to a pitched battle and its greater casualties.[1] Finally, Goliath's weapon, a *spear with a shaft like a weaver's rod*, also has known parallels and is not the unhistorical creation which some have alleged. It was actually a javelin with a loop and cord round the shaft for greater distance and stability, and was known in the Aegean area from the twelfth century BC. Even the Old

---

[1] A. M. Snodgrass, *Early Greek Armour and Weapons* (Edinburgh: Edinburgh University Press, 1964), p. 189; T. Dothan, *The Philistines and their Material Culture* (New Haven and London: Yale University Press, 1982), p. 19.

Testament reports one in the possession of another non-Israelite (1 Ch. 11:23).[1]

E. David's preparations for the temple (21:1 – 29:30)

i. David's sin and God's grace (21:1 – 22:1)

'The house of the LORD is to be here' (22:1).

21:1–27 – *cf*. 2 Samuel 24:1–25

David's great sin (v. 8) comes as a considerable shock after the high points of covenant promise (chapter 17) and military victory (chapters 18–20). The central theme, however, is actually God's forgiving grace (vv. 15–27) rather than David's sin or the resultant judgment (vv. 9–14), and it is this to which the temple becomes a permanent witness (21:28 – 22:1).

The basic source is 2 Samuel 24, though the Chronicler has made more extensive changes than usual. Geographical, chronological, and administrative details are omitted (*cf*. 2 Sa. 24:2, 4–8, 11, 15 and 1 Ch. 21:2, 4, 9, 14), making way for two new emphases. Firstly, the Chronicler's version takes place against a more overtly spiritual background in which Satan (v. 1) and Yahweh's angel (vv. 12–30) are prominent. The post-exilic period in general saw much greater interest in unseen spiritual beings, an interest which was separately continued in both Judaism and the New Testament. The issues of sin and atonement are worked out in a wider context than that of either merely moral conflict or the fatalistic dualism of contemporary Persian religion. Though sin is a human problem, it has deeper spiritual roots which can be dealt with only through God's sovereign purpose and direct intervention.

Chronicles' second emphasis, which emerges in the additional material in 21:28 – 22:1, links the place of David's atonement with the site of the new temple. This connection is not made explicit in Samuel, and Chronicles' interest is not just a geographical one.[2] The temple stood at the actual place where David's sin had brought Jerusalem to the brink of

---

[1] Y. Yadin, *The Art of Warfare in Biblical Lands* (London: Weidenfeld & Nicolson, 1963), pp. 354–355; *idem*, 'Goliath's javelin and the מנור ארגים', *PEQ*, 1955, pp. 58–69; T. Dothan, *op. cit.*, pp. 19–20.

[2] In 2 Sa., ch. 24 is apparently located as near as possible to the account of Solomon because it anticipates the permanent institution of the altar of burnt offering in Solomon's temple (*cf*. Hertzberg, pp. 410–411, 415–416; McCarter, pp. 516–517.

destruction, and where God alone had delivered his people. It was above all a place of forgiveness, where sin and all its consequences could be removed.

The significance of David's sin has actually been increased, rather than reduced, as many writers have alleged.[1] Important material is added in verses 6–7 and in certain phrases in verses 3 and 17. Other changes have increased the striking resemblance between this incident and that of David's murder and adultery in 2 Samuel 11–12, as the following correspondences show.

(a) Only in these two incidents does David make the simple confession, 'I have sinned' (Heb. *ḥāṭā'tî*, 2 Sa. 12:13; 24:10 = 1 Ch. 21:8), which is a turning-point in both narratives.

(b) David's sin results in death for Israel (2 Sa. 11:17–26; 12:15–19; 24:15 = 1 Ch. 21:14).

(c) Prophetic disapproval is voiced (2 Sa. 12:1–4; 24:11–14 = 1 Ch. 21:9–13), and Chronicles repeats the prophetic messenger formula, 'Thus says the LORD' (21:11; *cf.* 2 Sa. 24:13) to emphasize the point.

(d) God's punishment is effected through the sword (2 Sa. 12:10; 1 Ch. 21:12, 16, 27).

(e) David is forgiven by God's word of promise (2 Sa. 12:13; 24:16 = 1 Ch. 21:15).

(f) God grants forgiveness through his covenant promises. Both the house of God (1 Ch. 21:29–30) and David's house/dynasty (2 Sa. 12:10) had been threatened directly by David's sins, but God pointedly restores both 'houses' – in 2 Samuel 12:24–25 through David's heir Solomon, and in 1 Chronicles 21:28 – 22:1 through the building of the temple.[2]

Although parts of this pattern occur already in both 2 Samuel 11–12 and 2 Samuel 24, its impact has been increased by the addition of two features not mentioned in 2 Samuel 24, *viz.* the sword of the Lord (point d above) and the permanence of atonement provided through the temple (point f above). The result is to heighten the contrast between God's wrath

---

[1] *Cf.* G. von Rad, *Old Testament Theology*, I (London: SCM Press, 1962), p. 350; O. Kaiser, *Introduction to the Old Testament* (Oxford: Blackwell, 1975), p. 177.

[2] Compare the following statement, reached quite independently: 'As David's adultery with Bathsheba is the hinge of the presentation of the reign of David in 2 Samuel, so David's census of the people in 1 Chron. 21, the presumptuous act of numbering the people of God, is the pivot of the presentation of the reign of David in 1 Chronicles' (Johnstone, 'Guilt', p. 123).

and God's mercy. Comparison with 2 Samuel 11–12 also shows the greater gravity of David's sin over against the Uriah/Bathsheba crisis: (a) David's confession is more reluctant (vv. 8, 13, 17); (b) satanic involvement is acknowledged (v. 1); (c) the sword of the LORD rather than the sword of man falls on Israel (vv. 15–16, 27); (d) many more Israelites perish (v. 14); and (e) crucially, David can no longer worship at God's sanctuary (vv. 29–30; contrast 2 Sa. 12:20).

The implications of this incident for the Chronicler's contemporaries are not hard to deduce. In the author's mind, it was not only David who needed forgiveness, for the whole of Israel's history illustrated the nation's constant unfaithfulness towards God (*cf.* 1 Ch. 10:13–14; 2 Ch. 36:14). Even after the disgrace of exile, Israel's sin and failure to please God continued unabated (*e.g.* Zc. 1:1–6; Mal. 1:6 – 3:15; Ezr. 9:1 – 10:44; Ne. 9:1–37). The Chronicler's aim is not to heighten Israel's condemnation, however, despite the magnitude of the problem. Indeed, the very opposite is true, for the Chronicler saw that in the grace of God complete atonement was always available. The temple existed as the place *par excellence* where all sinners could receive forgiveness and bring their offerings again in worship (*e.g.* Mal. 3:10; Ne. 10:32–39; *cf.* Lk. 18:13).

This willingness on God's part to forgive the sinner is now permanently affirmed through Jesus Christ, in whom all Old Testament sacrifices have been fulfilled (*e.g.* Heb. 9:14, 25–26). Jesus' sacrifice opened a way into God's heavenly temple, which is superior to Solomon's and Zerubbabel's (Heb. 6:19–20; 9:11–15, 24–28). Like the Chronicler, the writer to the Hebrews also finds significance in the place of atonement by drawing parallels between the earthly and heavenly altars. Invitations are given to both the heavenly sanctuary ('Let us draw near to God with a sincere heart in full assurance of faith . . .', Heb. 10:19–25) and the earthly site of Jesus' death ('Let us . . . go to him outside the camp, bearing the disgrace he bore', Heb. 13:11–14). The cross of Christ makes both Satan's incitements (*e.g.* Rev. 20:1–10) and the angel's sword of judgment (Rev. 6:4, 8) totally ineffective.

a. The census (21:1–6). Two of the most difficult issues in Chronicles are raised by verse 1, *viz.*, the meaning of Satan's brief appearance and of the census. *Satan* is mentioned directly only three times in the Old Testament (see Jb. 1–2; Zc.

3:1–2), and only here as a proper name (elsewhere it has the definite article, and means 'The Opponent, Adversary, Enemy'). His origin is nowhere discussed, except perhaps for a hint in Isaiah 14:12–15, and identification with the snake is not made until the late first century AD (Rev. 12:9; 20:2). The Old Testament is interested mainly in his function, which is always to oppose God, rather than his origin or his identity. His activity is actually quite restricted, and he is always power-less against God's intervention. Although he appears more frequently in the New Testament, he is equally restrained there too, as supremely expressed in his final defeat at Christ's death (Jn. 12:31; 16:11; Col. 2:15; *etc.*).

The verbs 'stood up' (NRSV, RSV; *cf.* Zc. 3:1) and *incited* (*cf.* Jb. 2:3; *cf.* Gn. 3:1–7) associate Satan's activity with what is said of him in other parts of the Old Testament. In comparison with 2 Samuel·24:1, however, a striking change of subject is immediately noticeable: 'The anger of the LORD burned against Israel, and he incited David against them.' Some writers have assumed that the Chronicler thought his source was theologically deficient (*e.g.* Myers, Rudolph), but this deals only with a possible misunderstanding of the idea of God's incitement, not with its interpretation. It is clear in 2 Samuel 24:1 that God incited David because he was angry with him.[1] This is not to be understood fatalistically, however, since according to 1 Samuel 26:19 any harmful effects of such incitement could be annulled by a positive human response. Ironically, in that context David himself advises Saul to repent if he thought that God had incited him.[2] On the same analogy, this census is to be understood as God's judgment on Israel, but the full effects could be avoided if David would only acknowledge the error of his ways.

It is into this basic theological framework that Satan is

---

[1] 'Again' in 2 Sa. 24:1 refers back to 2 Sa. 21:1, and is one of several links between 2 Sa. 21 and 24. Both chs. have a similar framework, including God's wrath and judgment, David's repentance on Israel's behalf, and answered prayer (*cf.* especially 2 Sa. 21:14 and 24:25). The fact that no direct reason is given in 2 Sa. 24:1 for God's wrath does not mean that God acted arbitrarily or unethically (see A. Schenker, *Der Mächtige im Schmelzofen des Mitleids*, Göttingen: Vandenhoeck & Ruprecht, 1982, pp. 19–20, 67–68).

[2] 1 Sa. 26:19 and 2 Sa. 24:1 contain the only two uses of the verb 'incite' (Heb. *hēsît*) with a negative connotation and a divine subject. When *hēsît* is used positively with a divine subject (2 Ch. 18:31; Jb. 36:16), it has the opposite sense of rescue or deliverance.

introduced. His role is to be sharply distinguished from God's, who remains totally in control, but who sometimes judges by handing sinners over to Satan (1 Cor. 5:5; 1 Tim. 3:20). When Satan incites, he is interested merely in his own ends. He neither cares for righteous punishment nor looks for possible repentance, since they are as foreign to his nature as temptation to sin is to God's. Satan is also not to be regarded simply as the agent of divine judgment, since God here uses his own destroying angel (vv. 15–16; *cf*. Ex. 12:23). By changing the subject of the verb *incited* from 2 Samuel 24:1, it is therefore given quite a different meaning.

Although divine judgment, human choice, and satanic temptation are not mutually exclusive, they cannot therefore be equated. Satan in fact has nothing more to contribute after verse 1 and disappears quickly from view, as in Job 1–2 and Zechariah 3. David, conversely, has a real choice about what to do. This includes a genuine possibility for repentance, as shown by both Joab's (vv. 3, 6) and his own sense of guilt (v. 8), and by his response to God's judgment in verses 9–13 (see also Jon. 3:1–9; Am. 4:6–11).[1]

Neither Chronicles nor Samuel offers any explicit reason why God .was angry with David in the first place, nor why David's *census* should be regarded as a sin. Censuses in the Old Testament were not in themselves objectionable to God, and were carried out a number of times – for military purposes (Nu. 1:3, 45; 26:2), for sanctuary taxation (Ex. 30:11–16; 38:25–28; Nu. 3:40–41), for populating the land (Nu. 26:52–55; Ne. 7:4–5), for organizing the Levites (Nu. 3:14–39; 1 Ch. 23:2ff.), and for building the temple (2 Ch. 2:17–18). This census, however, clearly displeased both man (vv. 3, 6) and God (v. 7). Schenker's analysis offers five possible explanations for this negative assessment: (a) the tribes felt a threat to their independence; (b) the charismatic ideal of God's holy war had become secularized; (c) God's blessing could not be reduced to mere statistics; (d) David failed to recognize the census as Yahweh's prerogative by not paying an expiatory ransom (*cf*. Ex. 30:12); and (e) it was an expression of human pride.[2]

It seems in fact that it was the purpose to which a census was

[1] See also A. Schenker, *op. cit.*, pp. 19–21, but with several significant differences from the interpretation offered here.
[2] A. Schenker, *op. cit.*, pp. 16–18, 64–67.

put that provides the clue to its meaning. Though the context of David's action was a military one, he seems to have forgotten that the people were not his but God's. His self-centred motive expressed itself in one or more of the following errors: (i) he did not raise the half-shekel poll-tax mentioned in the Mosaic law, an omission which might result in a plague (Ex. 30:12); (ii) he failed to recognize that God's people could not ultimately be numbered because of the nature of God's promise (v. 3; 27:23–24); (iii) whereas all other Old Testament censuses anticipated a particular God-given purpose, this one seems to have been an end in itself. Even Joab recognized that God might yet *multiply his troops a hundred times* (v. 3), and Solomon also accepted that Israel could not be counted because they were the Lord's people (1 Ki. 3:8). Ironically, David's action resulted in a severe reduction in Israel's numbers (v. 14).

Because David's command was 'abhorrent to Joab' (v. 6, NRSV, RSV) and *evil in the sight of God* (v. 7), David brought *guilt on Israel* (v. 3). None of these phrases appears in Samuel, and Chronicles' use of *guilt* (Heb. *'ašmâ*) is particularly interesting. This word regularly refers to actions which deserve God's wrath (2 Ch. 24:18; 28:10, 13; 33:23; *cf.* the cognate verb in 2 Ch. 19:10).[1]

The census numbers (v. 5) are a problem, since they do not tally with 2 Samuel 24:9. The usual solution is to assume that Chronicles' *one million one hundred thousand* for *all Israel* represents a deduction of one hundred thousand each for Levi and Benjamin (*cf.* v. 6) from Samuel's total of one million three hundred thousand for Israel and Judah, and that Chronicles' statement on Judah is a later gloss (*e.g.* Williamson, Rudolph). Unfortunately, this proposal is unjustified and inconsistent. There is no independent evidence of any textual addition, and nowhere else does Chronicles use the simplistic figure of one hundred thousand for each tribe. It is also inconsistent to assume that a glossator has deducted only 30,000 for Benjamin's omission from *Judah's* total of *four hundred and seventy thousand*. This figure could be a more precise equivalent for

---

[1] *Cf.* also Ezr. 9:6, 7, 13, 15 for a similar use. The other main group of references, in Lv. 4:3; 5:24, 26; 22:16 (*cf.* also Ezr. 10:10, 19) has the connotation of that which requires expiation and/or restitution, and makes no mention of God's anger.

Samuel's round number of five hundred thousand, but otherwise the whole matter remains an unresolved issue of scribal
transmission.[1] *Levi* and *Benjamin* may have been excluded (v.
6) because of Joab's haste or guilt or both (*cf.* 27:24). Alternatively, Levi may not have been counted for traditional
reasons (Nu. 1:49; 2:33), and Benjamin because it contained
either the ark at Jerusalem or the Tent at Gibeon (v. 29).

b. A second choice (21:7–14). David's confession (v. 8) is
stronger than in Samuel, the simple acknowledgement *I have
sinned greatly* (*cf.* 2 Sa. 12:13) being supplemented by 'the
iniquity of thy servant' (RSV) and 'I have done very foolishly'
(NRSV, RSV). The reality of judgment is not diminished by his
confession, however. David is faced with a choice of punishments all associated with breaking God's covenant (*cf.* Lv.
26:25–26), and between which there seems little to choose (vv.
11–12).[2]

Against the darkness of judgment, David's plea makes
God's *mercy* shine all the brighter (v. 13). This mercy (Heb.
raḥᵃmîm) refers to God's undeserved love arising from his
deep compassion. David's position in verse 13 is actually parallel to that in verse 1, but, where he had previously chosen to
increase God's judgment, he now falls back on the possibility
of hidden hope in God's heart. Because David's discovery is
actually based on the God's nature as a merciful God, it is in
fact a permanent hope.[3] For the Chronicler it was symbolized
by the temple (22:1; 1 Ki. 8:37 = 2 Ch. 6:28), and is confirmed
in the New Testament by the work of Christ. The Bible always
affirms that God will hear the prayer: 'in wrath remember
mercy' (Hab. 3:2; *cf.* Jn. 3:16–21).

[1] 'All Israel' (2 Sa. 24:9 has simply 'Israel') does not inevitably include the
south. Although this appears to be the only reference where the Chronicler
uses this term for the north in the account of the United Monarchy, he has
several such uses in his account of the Divided Monarchy (*e.g.* 2 Ch. 10:6;
11:13). Since 'all Israel' is in fact used for both north and south separately in 2
Ch. 10–36 (Williamson, *IBC*, pp. 102–110), it is hard to see what grounds can
be used for denying such flexibility to David's reign, especially when in this
instance the Chronicler is particularly influenced by his source.

[2] 'Three years' is correctly read in v. 12 (against MT's 'seven' in 2 Sa. 24:13). It
is also unnecessary to emend 'swept away' (Heb. *nispeh*) to harmonize with
'fleeing' (Heb. *nusᵉḳâ*) in 2 Sa. 24:13, since the Niphal of *sāpâ* is frequently used
in military contexts.

[3] *Cf.* the description of God in the *Book of Common Prayer*: '. . . whose nature it
is always to have mercy'.

The prophet *Gad*, usually known as *David's seer*, was regarded by Chronicles as one of David's historians (1 Ch. 29:29; 2 Ch. 29:25). Like Nathan, he brings news of salvation (vv. 18–19) as well as judgment (vv. 9–12).

c. God's and man's repentance (21:15–17). Much more is made of the *angel* here than in Samuel (vv. 12, 15, 16, 18, 20, 27, 30; *cf.* 2 Sa. 24:16–17). In describing him as a 'destroying angel' (v. 15), Chronicles affirms the triple reference of 2 Samuel 24:16–17, but also seems to evoke a deliberate echo of the plague of the firstborn (Ex. 12:23). Is Chronicles suggesting that the fate from which Israel had been so miraculously delivered in Egypt was about to overwhelm them after all, and under David of all people? The angel is also portrayed as *standing*, a posture shared with Satan (v. 1), and symbolizing readiness for action. In other respects, however, this angel is sharply contrasted with Satan, for the angel is a servant who carries out God's will (*cf.* Ps. 103:20–21), both in judgment and salvation. Interestingly, the angel apparently stands in two different places, *at the threshing-floor* (v. 15) and *between heaven and earth* (v. 16). This involves no real contradiction, since the word 'at' (v. 15) is sufficiently vague to allow an aerial location, and angels in any case are normally thought to have greater freedom of movement than mere humans.

The angel's *sword* is his most striking feature (vv. 12, 16, 27, 30). Though not mentioned directly in Samuel, it may well be implied by mention of the angel's extended hand (2 Sa. 24:16–17). Its presence in an alternative Hebrew MS of Samuel (4QSamª), which is clearly independent of Chronicles, confirms that it was not a creation of the Chronicler.[1] The angel's sword stands over the whole narrative from verses 16–27, as well as over Jerusalem. Compared with the swords of Israel (v. 5) or of their enemies (v. 12), its effectiveness is greatly superior, threatening Jerusalem with divine judgment. This was not the first time the angel's sword had appeared in the Old Testament (*cf.* Gn. 3:24; Nu. 22:22–35; Jos. 5:13–15),

---

[1] See F. M. Cross, *The Ancient Library of Qumrân* (London: Duckworth, 1958), p. 141; E. Ulrich, *The Qumran Text of Samuel and Josephus* (Missoula: Scholars Press, 1978), pp. 156–158.

but never before had it been turned against the Israelite nation.[1]

God's call, *Enough!* (v. 15) brings an immediate halt to the judgment. The sole reason is God's great *mercy* (v. 13), for it is said specifically that God himself 'repented of the evil' (v. 15, RSV, REB, NEB; *was grieved*, NIV; 'changed his mind', GNB). This astonishing idea does not refer to any moral change in God, but to a particular change of plan arising from his deep grief or compassion. It is mentioned especially when God withholds judgment, often in response to intercession (Ex. 32:12–14; Am. 7:3–6) or human repentance (Je. 18:8; Jon. 3:9–10). Eventually, this was recognized as an outstanding feature of his character (Joel 2:13–14; Jon. 4:2), so that what might appear as changeableness in God is actually seen to be a quality of his unchangeable nature.

David's own response (v. 17) is further repentance, finally accepting full personal responsibility for the census. As before (vv. 3, 6–8), Chronicles accentuates the point – the three phrases *Was it not I who ordered the fighting men to be counted?*, *O LORD my God*, and *Do not let this plague remain on your people* are not in Samuel. The reading, 'I, the shepherd who did wrong' (v. 17, NEB; *cf.* Williamson, Ackroyd) is now often preferred to 'done very wickedly' (NRSV, RSV, *cf.* NIV) on the basis of the LXX of 2 Samuel and 4QSam[a], and may be superior, though it is not supported in MSS of Chronicles. 'Ornan' (vv. 15ff., NRSV, RSV) is the regular post-exilic pronunciation of *Araunah* (NIV, GNB), a Jebusite name which 2 Samuel 24 was unable to spell consistently!

d. A new altar (21:18–27). Atonement in the Old Testament (and the New Testament) is God's gift, expressed through his word and enacted through sacrifice. Special attention is given to sacrifice here by God's order to build an *altar* (v. 18). The command was mediated by an angel and a prophet (v. 18) because God's fellowship with his people was not yet fully restored. Chronicles' account of how the site was

[1] The presence of this motif elsewhere in the OT alongside its appearance in the fragment of 4QSam[a], renders unconvincing P. E. Dion's argument that it is primarily employed to resolve the question of the diversity of altars as an issue of post-exilic theology ('The angel with the drawn sword [I Chr 21, 6]', *ZAW* 97, 1985, pp. 114–117). In any case, the debate about altars in Israel was certainly not confined to post-exilic times.

purchased is more extensive than Samuel's and contains deliberate echoes of two earlier passages – Abraham's purchase of the cave of Machpelah (Gn. 23) and Gideon's encounter with the angel (Jdg. 6:11–24). Like Abraham, David bought the whole site (vv. 22, 25) and paid the *full price* (vv. 22, 24; *cf.* Gn. 23:9 – this phrase is not used in the Old Testament outside these references). Abraham's purchase was the first piece of the Promised Land actually owned by God's people, and David's acquisition completes Abraham's act of faith. Gideon had received an order to build an altar while threshing wheat (*cf.* v. 20) and his subsequent sacrifice had been consumed by heavenly fire (*cf.* v. 26).[1]

In fact, David's altar was the only one in pre-exilic times which God explicitly commanded to be built (see Ezk. 43:13–17 for a later example). Whereas Gideon's altar replaced a pagan one, David's was completely new. It alone fulfilled the Deuteronomic requirement of 'the place the LORD your God will choose' (Dt. 12:5, 11, 14). David's site also had associations with another place of sacrifice chosen by God. It was known as 'Moriah' (2 Ch. 3:1), the same name given to the place where God had provided a unique sacrifice for Abraham (Gn. 22:2).[2]

God's approval of David's altar is twice affirmed with phrases not found in Samuel. Firstly, *the LORD answered him with fire from heaven* (v. 26), an answer to prayer which strikingly recalled the institution of worship in Moses' Tent (or tabernacle – Lv. 9:24; 2 Ch. 7:1; *cf.* Jdg. 6:21; 1 Ki. 18:38). Secondly, the statement *the angel . . . put his sword back into its sheath* (v. 27) shows that atonement was necessary to remove the threat of judgment and that sacrifice was essential to atonement. The various *offerings* (v. 26), therefore, included a propitiatory function, as well as signifying worship and fellowship.

A *threshing-floor* (vv. 15ff.) was a flat area just outside a town or village, usually on high ground to take advantage of the wind. In the light of Ornan's threshing (v. 20), Chronicles has added *and wheat for the grain offering* (v. 23). The price is a major problem, for Samuel has only fifty silver shekels for Chronicles' *six hundred shekels of gold* (v. 25). Rashi's guess that the figure represents fifty shekels for each of the twelve tribes

---

[1] For fuller details, *cf.* Williamson, pp. 148–149; Willi, *CA*, pp. 157–158.
[2] It is not clear whether the difference between 'Mount Moriah' (2 Ch. 3:1) and 'the land of Moriah' (Gn. 22:2) is significant.

is often mentioned, but it does nothing to explain the discrepancy in the metals. One could assume that the larger sum was for the whole site and the smaller sum for the altar alone, but no satisfactory solution is yet available.

e. A new house of God (21:28 – 22:1). A brief theological supplement (*cf.* 10:13–14; 14:17) explains why Israel's major sanctuary was transferred from Gibeon (*cf.* 16:39–42) to Jerusalem. Worship was suspended only temporarily at Gibeon (*cf.* 2 Ch. 1:3–13) because of *the sword of the angel of the LORD* (v. 30), but the consequences were irreversible. David had actually been barred from Gibeon because he *was afraid* (*cf.* 13:12) and unable *to enquire of God*. The latter phrase is synonymous with 'seeking' in Chronicles and refers generally to expectant worship. It was a fundamental requirement of God-pleasing kingship, and David's inability to seek God disturbed the pattern of his entire reign (see comment on 13:3). David therefore drew his own conclusions from this and from the special events at Jerusalem (*when David saw* ..., v. 28; *then David said* ..., 22:1), especially because *the LORD had answered him* (v. 28). Having seen his prayers answered and his sacrifices accepted, the site had already become a 'house of prayer' and a 'temple for sacrifices' *cf.* 2 Ch. 7:12; Is. 56:7). The appropriate response was to build a new *house* and a new *altar* (22:1).[1]

ii. David's initial preparations for the temple (22:2–19)
'The house that is to be built for the LORD must be exceedingly
    magnificent, of fame and glory throughout all lands; I will
        therefore make preparations for it' (22:5, RSV).
The phrase *to build the house of God*, which with small variations occurs nine times (vv. 2, 5, 6, 7, 8, 10, 11, 19), is the dominant theme of chapter 22. From now until the end of Chronicles' account of David, everything will be directly concerned with the temple. The context also shifts from David alone to David and Solomon, since the building of the temple is really a joint project.

The precise topic in this chapter is preparation and provision. The verb 'to make preparations, provide' (Heb. *hēkîn*) occurs five times in connection with the necessary materials and workforce (vv. 3, 5, 14), but the chapter is equally about

---

[1] On the syntax and literary history of 21:28 – 22:1, *cf.* Williamson, p. 151.

the preparation of Solomon, the temple-builder.[1] David's speech to Solomon (vv. 6–16), the centre-piece of the chapter, deals with three distinct but essential elements of preparation:

(a) God's preparation of David, Solomon, and Israel through his covenant promise (vv. 7–10);

(b) Solomon's need for self-preparation through obedience to God (vv. 11–13); and

(c) the provision of sufficient materials and skilled workmen (vv. 14–16).

Like the rest of chapters 22–29, this chapter appears to have no obvious source in earlier biblical material. Nevertheless, the influence of three separate parts of the Old Testament is readily identifiable. Firstly, verses 7–10 expound the Davidic covenant promise of 2 Samuel 7 (= 1 Ch. 17), in common with other passages in Chronicles' account of the United Monarchy (1 Ch. 28:2–7; 2 Ch. 6:15–17; 7:17–18).

Secondly, David's handover to Solomon is modelled on elements of Moses' appointment of Joshua (especially Dt. 31; Jos. 1). Although parallels can also be drawn with the appointment of leaders such as Saul and David, two features of the comparison stand out. The first is that Moses' and David's failure to realize fully their intentions is counterbalanced by their successors' achievement (vv. 6–9; 28:3; Dt. 1:37–38; 31:2–3). Conquering the Promised Land and building the temple were privileges too great to be entrusted to one individual, and in both instances the Bible underlines that it is God who plans the task and ensures it is carried out (*cf.* also 1 Cor. 3:6–7). The second is the repetition of certain distinctive ideas and phrases. This includes exhortations about obedience to God's law (vv. 12–13; 28:7–9; Dt. 31:5; Jos. 1:7–8), and various notable encouragements such as *Be strong and courageous* (v. 13; 28:20; Dt. 31:7, 23; Jos. 1:6ff.), *Do not be afraid or discouraged* (v. 13; 28:20; Dt. 31:8; Jos. 1:9), and *The LORD be with you* (vv. 11, 16; 28:20; Dt. 31:6, 8, 23; Jos. 1:5, 9).[2] The

---

[1] *Hēkîn*, in the sense 'establish, confirm', is also used in v. 10 of David's kingdom, but this is based on 17:11, 14, and is not relevant to the other occurrences in ch. 22.

[2] See especially H. G. M. Williamson, 'The accession of Solomon in the books of Chronicles', *VT* 26, 1976, pp. 351–361; D. J. McCarthy, 'An installation genre?', *JBL* 90, 1971, pp. 31–41; R. L. Braun, 'Solomon the chosen temple builder', *JBL* 95, 1976, pp. 586–588. Features which occur in the appointment of other leaders are the combination of private and public appointments

parallel between Joshua and Solomon is not a rigid device, since David has also been modelled on Joshua as one who completed the conquest of the Promised Land (see comment on 1 Ch. 13:5 and on chs. 18, 20). The purpose here seems to be to demonstrate that Solomon's task was no less crucial than Joshua's, and required the same qualities of faith and courage.

Thirdly, Chronicles is considerably indebted to 1 Kings' account of Solomon. Every section of chapter 22 has some association with 1 Kings, and, while full details are given below, two aspects are worth highlighting now. The basic framework for the whole of 1 Chronicles 22–29 seems to have come from 1 Kings 2:1–12, since the latter begins with David's impending death, as verse 5 here, and ends with the concluding formula to David's reign, exactly as in 1 Chronicles 29:26–30. Further, two distinctive features of Chronicles' account of these preparations are found in several places in 1 Kings, *viz.* David's own awareness of his inability to build the temple (vv. 7–9; 28:2–3; *cf.* 1 Ki. 5:3–4, EVV [vv. 17–18, MT]; 8:17–19), and his acknowledgment of Solomon's inexperience (v. 5; 29:1; *cf.* 1 Ki. 3:7). This extensive dependence of chapter 22 on earlier biblical material supports the view that David's preparations for the temple in Chronicles are historically based, and not just a piece of post-exilic tradition. In any case, the fact that Solomon began construction work as early as the fourth year of his reign (1 Ki. 6:1, 37) makes it unlikely that he could have accumulated sufficient resources without his father's previous assistance.

The Chronicler's concern for the temple will certainly have stimulated his contemporaries to consider their own attitude towards its worship and offerings, though the precise application of this material is no longer recoverable. A constant tendency to neglect or despise worship in the Second Temple is evident in the Old Testament, and Ezra and Nehemiah in particular made strenuous efforts to ensure that people, priests, and Levites took their responsibilities seriously. Both these men too made substantial provision for the temple, including precious metals (*cf.* vv. 14–16; Ezr. 8:24–34; Ne. 10:32–39; 13:10–14; *cf.* Ezr. 2:68–69; Ne. 7:70–72), and both encouraged people to prepare themselves for worship by

(Moses, Ex. 3:7–10 and 4:29–31; Saul, 1 Sa. 10:1 and 10:17–25; and David, 1 Sa. 16:1–13 and 2 Sa. 2:2–4; 5:1–3), and full acceptance by the people (see Ex. 4:30–31; 1 Sa. 10:24; 11:14–15; 2 Sa. 5:3).

obedience to God's law through Moses (*cf*. vv. 12–13, 19, Ne. 7:73b – 10:29). Malachi also expressed deep concern over these matters (*e.g.* Mal. 1:6–14; 3:6–12).

The New Testament concept of God's temple has been transformed through Jesus' incarnation. Jesus contrasted the demolition of Herod's temple (Mk. 13:1–2; Mt. 24:1–2; *cf*. 2 Ch. 7:19–22), with the resurrection of the temple of his body (Jn. 2:18–22), and Peter and Paul both saw the church as a new resurrected temple (1 Cor. 3:16–17; 2 Cor. 6:16; 1 Pet. 2:5). The church, like Solomon's temple, is being carefully prepared for God's presence (Eph. 5:25–32), and believers must continue to build it with work characterized as gold, silver, and precious stones (1 Cor. 3:10–15), constantly purifying themselves from sinful practices (2 Cor. 6:14 – 7:1). God is also preparing his church, having cleansed her through Christ's death (Eph. 5:25–27) and getting her ready to be 'as a bride beautifully dressed for her husband' (Rev. 21:2). Only in the new Jerusalem will God's plan to dwell permanently among his people (2 Ch. 6:1–2, 18, 41; 7:16), first announced to Moses (Ex. 19:5–6; 25:8; 29:44–46), be finally completed and a separate temple become superfluous (Rev. 21:1–5, 22).

a. Preparing workers and materials (22:2–5). David assembled a workforce (vv. 2, 4), together with materials of *stone*, *iron*, *bronze* and *cedar* (vv. 2–4; *cf*. vv. 14–16). The workers here were *aliens* (v. 2), *i.e.* the non-Israelite inhabitants of Canaan. David's introduction of a forced labour system, though mentioned directly only here, is already hinted at by the presence in David's 'cabinet' of an official in charge of forced labour (2 Sa. 20:24). The same official (Adoram, 2 Sa. 20:24; 1 Ki. 12:18; = Adoniram, 1 Ki. 4:6; 5:14; = Hadoram, 2 Ch. 10:18) continued under Solomon, who expanded the system. It was customary in the ancient Near East for prisoners of war and subject peoples to provide the basic labour force for major building projects. Here they acted as *stonecutters*, *masons*, *carpenters*, and skilled metalworkers (vv. 2, 15–16). Some of the materials were booty from David's wars (*cf*. 18:8, 11), others were specially provided. Particular mention is made of the *cedar* (v. 4), to which Solomon added (1 Ki. 5:6, 8–10, EVV [vv. 20, 22–24, MT]; 2 Ch. 2:8–10, 16) and which was one of the temple's outstanding features (*cf.* 17:1, 6). Provision was also made in the same way for the Second Temple (Ezr. 3:7).

5. Solomon too had to be prepared because he was *inexperienced*, as he acknowledged in his famous request for wisdom (1 Ki. 3:7). The word (Heb. *rāk*) implies someone who needs further training and instruction and who must seek wisdom to live by (*cf.* vv. 11–13; Pr. 4:3). A similar deficiency in Rehoboam's personal development was a contributory cause of the division of the kingdom (2 Ch. 13:7).

The temple owed its *fame and splendour* to more than just its architectural qualities. David envisaged its *magnificence* as an expression of the Davidic covenant (vv. 7–10; 28:1–10) and of the kingdom of God (29:10–13), while for Solomon it was the place of God's earthly residence and where he would answer prayer (2 Ch. 6:18–42). In every way, it commanded the attention of *all nations* (*cf.* Is. 2:1–4 = Mi. 4:1–3; Is. 56:6–8; Zc. 8:20–23; 14:9, 16–17).

b. Preparing the temple builder (22:6–16). David explains in three stages why and how the temple is to be built:

i. The temple fulfils God's promise (22:7–10). It will be a fulfilment of God's covenant promise to build David a dynastic house (2 Sa. 7:1–17 = 1 Ch. 17:1–15). Verses 7–10 are an exposition of the Davidic covenant and its significance for the proposed temple. David recalls his own frustrated hope about building (v. 7; *cf.* 2 Sa. 7:1–2, 5 = 1 Ch. 17:1, 4), but is answered by a word from Yahweh which seems to be subsequent to Nathan's prophecy and which is alluded to in Kings (vv. 8–10; *cf.* 1 Ki. 5:3–5, EVV [vv. 17–19, MT]; 8:17–19). Nathan's original message has been amplified in three ways – (a) David cannot build because he is a 'warrior' (28:3) who has *shed much blood* (v. 8); (b) *Solomon* (Heb. *šᵉlōmōh* – his other name was Jedidiah, 2 Sa. 12:25) as a *man of rest* is qualified to build because in his reign God *will give him rest* and Israel will have *peace* (Heb. *šālôm*) *and quiet* (v. 9; *cf.* v. 18); (c) Solomon is now identified as the anonymous 'seed/offspring' of 17:11. The Davidic covenant will therefore be fulfilled initially, but not exclusively, through Solomon – it is he who will build the house, he who will enjoy the status of God's (adopted) son, and he whose throne will be established (v. 10; these three phrases are almost identical with their equivalents in 17:11–14). Alongside this direct focus on Solomon, the words *for ever* are an unmistakable hint that both covenant and temple have an eschatological dimension that will far outlast Solomon.

David's disqualification was not because of sin, for he had fought 'before me' (v. 8, RSV; *in my sight*, REB, NEB, NIV, NRSV). It was God who had promised him military victory (14:10, 14; 17:11) and enabled him to achieve it (18:6, 13; 19:13). It has been suggested that David's wars incurred some ceremonial impurity, but the main thrust is probably to underline the contrast with Solomon's reign as one of peace and rest. The play on Solomon's name, found only here, is only the most obvious feature of this. It is equally significant that Chronicles sees Solomon's reign as fulfilling the conditions of 'rest' required in the Deuteronomic law as a prerequisite for building a temple for God's name (Dt. 12:10–11). Although other leaders made substantial contributions towards achieving this rest, notably Joshua (for *rest* as both noun, Heb. *mᵉnûḥâ*, and verb, Heb. *nûaḥ*, *cf.* v. 9 and Jos. 1:13; 21:44; *etc.*; for *quiet*, Heb. *šeqeṭ*, *cf.* v. 9 and Jos. 11:23)[1] and David (2 Sa. 7:1, 11, and comment on 1 Ch. 17:1, 10), only in Solomon's reign did Israel fully enjoy such conditions.[2] As a result, the temple represented not only God's gift of peace and forgiveness (*cf.* ch. 21) to Israel, but was a permanent symbol that God had kept his promise about the land. Verse 8 does not demean David's role in this, since his wars provided the necessary conditions for Solomon's peace. Nor does Chronicles contradict 1 Kings 5:3 as is sometimes proposed, as though only constraints of time originally prevented David from building. In fact, 1 Kings 5:3 affirms God's purpose through David to 'put his enemies under his feet', and never envisages David even attempting the task that the Old Testament consistently attributes to Solomon.

ii. Special instructions for Solomon (22:11–13). David now commands Solomon to *build the house* (v. 11). In the process, he extends the connection between temple and covenant by stressing the need to obey God's word, whether in prophecy

---

[1] For further details, see R. L. Braun, 'Solomon the chosen temple builder', *JBL* 95, 1976, pp. 581–590.

[2] The border skirmishes mentioned in 1 Ki. 11:14–28 are apparently discounted, presumably because they did not take place within Israel itself.

(v. 11) or Mosaic law (vv. 12–13). The temple is to symbolize Solomon's obedience to the Mosaic as well as the Davidic covenant. The need for covenant conditions to be properly kept does not nullify God's unconditional promise. Rather, obedience brings God's promises into effect. Biblical covenants were in fact regularly instituted through the obedient faith of a covenant mediator – see Genesis 6:18, 22 (Noah); Genesis 15:6; 17:9–14, 23–27 (Abraham); Exodus 19:5–6; 24:3–8 (Moses and Israel); Matthew 26:26–28; Hebrews 5:8–10; 10:12–18 (Jesus and the new covenant). In this case, David and Solomon complemented each other in establishing the covenant – David through his conquests and his preparation, and Solomon in his work of construction.

Verses 11–13 (with 28:10, 20) represent a genre of installation or commissioning, made up of three components, *viz.* (a) assurance of divine help (*the* LORD *be with you*, v. 11); (b) encouragement (*may you have success*, v. 11, ... *Be strong and courageous. Do not be afraid or discouraged*, v. 13); and (c) instruction to undertake the task (*build the house*, v. 11). The phraseology particularly recalls Joshua's appointment (Dt. 31; Jos. 1).[1]

The form of this genre is actually quite flexible, but more importantly, it recognizes that God's call to any task invariably includes the means to accomplish it. This latter is conveyed by the gifts of *discretion and understanding* (v. 12, NIV, NRSV, RSV), and by an assurance of God's presence. *The* LORD *be with you* (v. 11, also v. 16) is not just conventional good wishes, but a vital piece of Old Testament theology: it guarantees Solomon's ultimate *success* (vv. 11, 13) and anticipates the enabling work of the Holy Spirit in the New Testament. The fact that David's instructions are enclosed within a prayer for his son shows his own awareness that the temple could be completed only by relying on God's help.

iii. David's provision for Solomon (22:14–16). Finally, David describes the preparations of men and materials already begun, though in comparison with verses 2–4, this passage lays more emphasis on precious metals and includes a wider variety of skilled workers. Again the great quantity of

---

[1] See introductory section to this ch.

materials is consistently stressed, and in verse 16, *beyond/ without number* is better applied to the metals than to the craftsmen, as in JB. The amounts of *gold* and *silver* (v. 14) are unexpectedly enormous, even for Chronicles, far exceeding similar references to these metals in the United Monarchy (*cf.* 1 Ch. 19:6; 29:4, 7; 2 Ch. 9:9, 13). In the light of these comparisons, and the not unreasonable proportion of gold to silver here, an error in scribal transmission seems probable. 'With great pains' (v. 14, NRSV, RSV, *cf.* NIV) might also be rendered 'by my efforts' (GNB, *cf.* Keil, Rudolph), 'poor as I am' (JB, *cf.* Ackroyd), or 'in spite of all my troubles' (NEB). There is little to choose between these alternatives, though the last seems least likely. In response to David's imperative, 'you must add' (v. 14, NRSV, RSV, JB; this is preferable to the jussive of REB, NEB, NIV, *you may* . . .), Solomon acquired further materials, particularly Lebanese cedars (1 Ki. 5:1ff. = 2 Ch. 2:1ff.).

David's final command to his son is, 'Arise and be doing!' (v. 16, RSV). This raises the question whether the events of 1 Chronicles 22, 28–29 belong during the period of David and Solomon's co-regency (*cf.* 23:1; 1 Ki. 1:20, 37, 43–48).[1] Although David's physical weakness (1 Ki. 1:1–4) might seem to rule out placing the strong leadership described in these chapters in this last phase of his reign, several factors do seem to support such a reconstruction. The decisive point is that it is impossible to envisage the central role given to Solomon in Chronicles 22, 28–29 as taking place before the confused circumstances which culminated in Adonijah's failed *coup*. Solomon's future had been neglected before his dramatic coronation decisively settled the succession issue. In any case, David's activities in 1 Chronicles 22, 28–29 are not inconsistent with old age. He is described only as making speeches (1 Ch. 22:6–19; 28:1–10, 19–20; 29:1–5), praying (29:10–20), handing over the temple plans (28:11–18), and initiating the brief period of fund-raising for the temple (29:1–9).[2] To complement Chronicles' account, the earlier record portrays David carrying out his instructions in the last stage of his reign

---

[1] On the details and background of this co-regency, see E. Ball, 'The co-regency of David and Solomon (1 Kings I)', *VT* 27, 1977, pp. 268–279.

[2] 1 Ch. 22:2–4 may belong to an earlier period of temple preparations, though certainty is impossible, while 22:5 is clearly a summary of David's speeches in chs. 22, 28–29.

with customary vigour (1 Ki. 1:28–35). Also, if it is correct to regard 1 Chronicles 22–29 as an expansion of David's last words in 1 Kings 2:1–12, it is likely that Chronicles has carried over the basic assumption that Solomon has been made king. It appears, therefore, that Chronicles has made a significant contribution to the record of David's last years.

c. Preparing Israel's leaders (22:17–19). The occasion at which David addressed *all the leaders of Israel* (v. 17) is unspecified, and may or may not be part of the general assembly of chapters 28–29 (for the leaders, *cf.* 28:1, 8). David again (*cf.* v. 9) stresses in three distinct ways that the *rest* (v. 18; 'peace', GNB, NRSV, RSV, REB, NEB) which Israel enjoys is a God-given precondition for the building of a sanctuary (v. 19; *cf.* 28:1). With two of Chronicles' characteristic phrases, the leaders are challenged to participate with Solomon, so continuing into Solomon's reign the positive qualities associated with his father. They are to *help* (v. 17) Solomon, a term which strongly evokes Israel's help for David (1 Ch. 12:1, 17, 18, 21, 22), and they must *seek the LORD* (v. 19) as David had sought him (*cf.* 13:3; 14:10, 14). David explains how to seek ('devote your heart and soul'; *cf.* REB, NEB, JB) and what it meant in practice (*Build the sanctuary*). As elsewhere, 'seeking' is an act of obedience rather than a search for guidance, and David will yet again underline its importance (1 Ch. 28:8–9). The future temple will serve a double function (v. 19): to house the *sacred articles*, especially *the ark*, and to exalt the *Name of the LORD* before the people (vv. 7, 8, 10; 28:3; 29:16; *cf.* 2 Ch. 7:16; 20:8–9; 33:4, 7).

iii. The Levites prepare for the temple (23:1 – 26:32)

'These were the sons of Levi . . . for the service of the house of
the LORD' (23:24, NIV, NRSV, RSV)

The next five chapters mainly contain lists of Levites, supplemented by separate lists of priests (24:1–19) and royal officials (ch. 27). Although this may make them appear rather unattractive, they do make a distinctive and important contribution on all Israel's preparations for the temple (*cf.* the similar theme of preparation in the lists of chs. 1–9 and 15:4–10, 16–24).[1]

---

[1] For a similar view of the function of 1 Ch. 23–27, *cf.* J. W. Wright, 'The legacy of David in Chronicles: The narrative function of 1 Chronicles 23–27', *JBL* 110, 1991, pp. 229–242.

David first of all divides the Levites into four groups (23:1–6a). More details of their organization are then given. Those who were to serve in the temple are dealt with in 23:28–32, and the three remaining groups in chapters 25–26 in the reverse of the order here, according to their decreasing proximity to the temple. It is this association with the temple that gives the clue as to the nature of these lists, and this is confirmed by their over-all setting within chapters 21–29. Whereas chapter 22 was concerned with preparing the temple-builders, this section involves preparation of those who will serve in the temple.

An often overlooked but important dimension is the support provided by the royal family (23:1) and the royal administration (ch. 27). The whole project is a collective effort of royal and religious personnel united by their commitment to the Davidic covenant. Eventually, the preparations will include the whole people (chs. 28–29), so that chapters 23–27 are an important link in a chain involving all the major sections of Israelite society in building God's house.

A variety of lists have been used to achieve this purpose. It is widely assumed that the lists are the product of post-exilic temple organization, either in the Chronicler's own day or in the time of (a) later reviser(s).[1] But the material as a whole does not fit easily into this context. Although corroborative evidence for the arrangements underlying the lists is not extensive, some correlation is possible, particularly with the organization of musicians and gatekeepers in the Ezra–Nehemiah period. Unfortunately, the details in the latter do not tally with 1 Chronicles 23–27. The Hemanites, for example, the most prominent of the three musical families of Asaph, Jeduthun, and Heman in 1 Chronicles 25, do not appear among the musicians of the post-exilic period (*cf.* Ezr. 2:41; Ne. 11:17, 22). Furthermore, whereas here the musicians and gatekeepers are regarded consistently as Levites (chs. 23–27), under Ezra and Nehemiah, the gatekeepers always, and the musicians usually, were treated as independent groups (*e.g.* Ezr. 10:23–24; Ne. 7:43–45; 10:28; 11:15–19).

It is unlikely, therefore, that chapters 23–27 describe a

---

[1] For a cautious example of this kind of approach, *cf.* H. G. M. Williamson, 'The origins of the twenty-four priestly courses', *SVT* 30, 1979, pp. 251–268.

situation between the return from exile and the Ezra–Nehemiah period. Their origin must be either earlier or later. A later date might be argued for on the basis of independent evidence for the system of priestly courses (1 Ch. 24) from the second century BC on (see below for details). It might also be assumed (as is often the case) that the Levites underwent a process of expansion, gradually adding the categories of musicians and gatekeepers and increasing the divisions among the musicians. But the evidence might equally be interpreted in the opposite direction, *viz.* that there was an increasing move towards independence among the various Levitical groups. The latter view finds some support in the general lack of interest in the Levites in the Ezra–Nehemiah period, though a tendency for Levitical structures to disintegrate is evident in other periods also (*cf.* Jdg. 17–19). One must also take seriously Chronicles' understanding that the arrangements for the Levites and priests described here originated at the end of the Davidic period (*e.g.* 23:1, 6; 24:3, 6, 31; 25:1). Further, if the lists themselves are not post-exilic, there is no reason why the Chronicler himself should not be regarded as the editor. This conclusion would be consistent with two aspects of the Chronicler's style. One is his use of lists to anticipate a new section of narrative (1 Ch. 1–9; 15:4–10, 16–24), the other is his presentation of past realities as a present ideal. Even though neither the ark nor the Davidic monarchy existed in the post-exilic period, for example, the Chronicler used both to inspire his readers. By the same token, there can be no objection in principle to the Chronicler's recalling of the Levites' past as a stimulus to renewal of temple worship in the present.

This approach is not invalidated by certain inconsistencies in the lists. For example, some passages (*e.g.* 26:20–32) are only loosely associated with the framework of 23:2–6a, while others (*e.g.* ch. 27) are not integrated with this scheme at all. The lists also seem to come from a variety of dates. The Kohathites and Merarites in 23:16–23 are repeated with the addition of one generation in 24:20–30,[1] the musicians in chapter 25 seem to be taken from two separate lists (vv. 1–6, 7–31), and the list of gatekeepers (26:1–19) is at least two

---

[1] It is this factor that led Williamson to argue that the 'reviser', who in his view was responsible for several parts of chs. 23–27, lived only a single generation after the Chronicler (*ibid.*, p. 266).

generations later than the time of David. However, none of the lists need be much later than the early monarchy, and the variety of origins shows merely that the Chronicler did not harmonize the lists into a single chronological scheme.

Why did the Chronicler give such a high profile to the Levites? Three purposes may be discerned. The first is his intention to portray David as a second Moses. Though Moses had been initially responsible for organizing Israel's worship, David had to make modifications because of fundamental changes resulting from Israel's occupation of the Promised Land and the ark's arrival in Jerusalem. Like Moses' earlier instructions, David's changes were determinative for future generations. Subsequent amendments by David's successors Rehoboam (2 Ch. 11:13–14), Jehoshaphat (2 Ch. 19:8–11, Joash (2 Ch. 24:4–14), Hezekiah (2 Ch. 29–31), and Josiah (2 Ch. 34:9–13; 35:3–15), were far less substantial than those made by David.

Secondly, the Chronicler shows the contribution of each Levitical group to temple worship. The priests in their divisions (2 Ch. 8:14; *cf.* 7:2ff.), the Levites who assisted the priests (2 Ch. 8:14), the musicians (2 Ch. 5:12–13; 7:6) and the gatekeepers (2 Ch. 8:14) are all specifically mentioned in Solomon's organization of the temple. Even the treasurers (2 Ch. 8:15) and the various royal officials of chapter 27 played their part (1 Ch. 28:1; 29:6). The whole section clearly anticipates the building and the operation of the temple.

The Chronicler's third purpose seems to be associated with Nehemiah's reforms, where a similar appeal to Davidic authority is found (*cf.* Ne. 12:45–47). Nehemiah's concern for the neglect of the Levites was almost certainly shared by the Chronicler (Ne. 13:10–11; *cf.* 2 Ch. 24:4–5; Ezr. 8:15–20), though it is doubtful whether the Chronicler any more than Nehemiah expected the Davidic system to be re-created in detail. He probably had a more general aim of seeing the Levites take a more central role, as part of a renewed commitment to the worship of God.

Levites are rarely mentioned in the New Testament, and even when they do appear, association with temple service is incidental (Lk. 10:32; Jn. 1:19; Acts 4:36). Barnabas' nickname, 'Son of encouragement' (Acts 4:36), however, sums up well Chronicles' description of their role. Though some Levites expected the Messiah (Jn. 1:19), their specific role became obsolete with Jesus' opening up of a 'new and living way' into God's heavenly temple (*cf.* Heb. 10:20) and the destruction of Herod's temple. Some tasks like those of priesthood, however, became privileges to be enjoyed by every Christian (*cf.* 1 Pet. 2:5, 9), particularly in the area of contributing to worship (*cf.* 1 Cor. 14:26).

Perhaps their main significance for Christians is to emphasize that the people who serve God are just as important as the architectural splendour of the building in which they worship. In the Old Testament as well as the New Testament, God was not content with his own presence in his temple. God's desire then and now is for true worshippers (*cf.* Jn. 4:23–24; 1 Cor. 3:16; 2 Cor. 6:16), and for this, the Levites' role was vital. Their secondary or assistant leadership, comparable to the role of the deacons in the early church (Acts 6:1–7; Phil. 1:1; 1 Tim. 3:8–13), enabled and encouraged others to serve and worship God in spirit and in truth.

Chapter 23 introduces David's organization of the Levites. The emphasis on preparation for the temple continues from chapter 22, but attention now turns from the building to the temple personnel, especially the Levites. The Levites are organized in advance by David so that when the building work is completed, they will be ready to take over the dual functions of assisting the priests (vv. 28, 32) and supervising the activities of God's house (v. 4). This might include anything from the position of fabric steward to that of the worship leader (vv. 4–5, 28b–32). The key term in the chapter is *service* (Heb. *ʿᵃbōḏâ*, vv. 24, 26, 28, 32), a word which has a strong religious flavour in Chronicles. It summarizes the task of priests and Levites (*e.g.* 1 Ch. 6:32; 2 Ch. 31:16, Levites; 1 Ch. 9:13; 2 Ch. 8:14, priests; 1 Ch. 28:21; 2 Ch. 35:10, both), and is linked especially with their activity in the Tent (1 Ch. 6:48; 9:19) and the temple (1 Ch. 28:21; 2 Ch. 29:35). The Levites therefore find their true value in 'the service of the house of the LORD (vv. 24, 28, 32, NRSV, RSV), which incorporates both 'work' (v. 24, GNB) and 'worship' (vv. 26, 28, 32, GNB).

a. Solomon appointed king (23:1).

The blanket statement that *David . . . made his son Solomon king* covers a multitude of

222

sins (for a detailed account of the political intrigues, see 1 Ki. 1). This verse is not intended to be understood chronologically, since Solomon's anointing and coronation took place before the events of chapter 22 (see notes on 22:14–16). Yet it is not simply to be merged with 1 Chronicles 29:22 ('They acknowledged Solomon son of David as king a second time'). Its primary purpose seems to be to show that the organization of priests and Levites was a consequence of God's covenant promise to David. The temple and its personnel were not to be regarded as an independent religious establishment, but as a symbol of the two 'houses' of chapter 17 and ultimately of the kingdom of God.

b. Census of Levites (23:2–6a). Although at first sight, the conducting of a census seems to contradict chapter 21, one must bear in mind that it is the aim of a census which gives it validity or otherwise. Since this census enabled David to establish a pattern for worship in the temple, it is consistent with other divinely inspired censuses in the Old Testament (see further comment on 21:1–6). It is sometimes alleged (*cf.* Rudolph) that the statement that David 'assembled' (v. 2, NRSV, RSV) Israel's leaders is simply a duplicate of 28:1. This view cannot be supported, however, for not only are different words for 'assembling' used with distinctive meanings, but the types of leaders involved are not the same. Indeed, these two assemblies are part of a wider policy of four (or five?) public gatherings in preparation for the temple. In addition to the *priests and Levites* here (v. 2), there is mention of assemblies of alien workers (22:2), of all Israel's leaders (22:17, repeated in 28:1), and of 'the whole assembly' (29:1, 10). The purpose of this assembly (Heb. *'āsap*) was that the priests and Levites might receive specific instructions from the king in preparation for the temple (*cf.* 1 Ch. 15:4; 2 Ch. 29:4, 15).[1]

Those counted were over *thirty years old* (v. 3), though they were subsequently employed at twenty (see also vv. 24, 27). In view of the numbers of Levites recorded in the following chapters (*e.g.* 288 musicians, 25:7–31; ninety-three gatekeepers, 26:8–11), the figure of *thirty-eight thousand* is best understood as thirty-eight groups or clans. Three of the four

[1] *Cf.* J. W. Wright, 'The legacy of David in Chronicles', *JBL* 110, 1991, pp. 229–233.

sections (vv. 4–5) are dealt with in more detail in chapters 25–26, but in reverse order, according to their proximity to the priests (24:1–19) and to the temple. Only the first section, the *twenty-four thousand* or twenty-four clans (v. 4) are not specifically mentioned later, though their activities are probably covered in 23:28–31. It is unlikely that the function of this largest section was only *to supervise* temple activities, though that is the usual meaning of this verb (*e.g.* 1 Ch. 15:21; 2 Ch. 34:12; Ezr. 3:8–9). In this context, 'to administer' (GNB) is a preferred translation. The reading 'I have made' (v. 5, NRSV, RSV; *I have provided*, NIV) follows MT but requires the addition of *David said* (v. 4). A much simpler change is the reading of LXX (A), Vulg. *viz.* 'he made' (NEB, JB; *cf.* GNB). The terms *divided* (NIV, *etc.*) and 'divisions' (v. 6, NRSV, RSV, *etc.*), which can also mean 'allotted' and 'allotment', are one indication that the Levites' appointment to their tasks is modelled on the allotment of land to the tribes in the book of Joshua (*cf. e.g.* Jos. 13:7; 14:5).[1]

c. Clans of Levites (23:6b–23).

The Levites are divided into their three traditional clans, the Gershonites (vv. 7–11), the Kohathites (vv. 12–20), and the Merarites (vv. 21–23) – for similar lists, see Ex. 6:17–25; Nu. 3:17–37; 1 Ch. 6:16–30). Apart from the special case of Moses' descendants (vv. 14–17), each family is represented by three generations. First come the names of Levi's three sons, followed by his eight grandsons, *viz.* two sons each of *Gershon* and *Merari*, and four of *Kohath*. The third generation, however, bears little resemblance to the other lists (*e.g.* the sons of *Izhar*, v. 18, and *Uzziel*, v. 20, are quite different in Ex. 6:21–22). The names are certainly those of *heads of families* (vv. 9, 24; 'fathers' houses', RSV), but it is not clear which generation they represent. The lack of harmonization between the twenty-two families here (nine Gershonite, nine Kohathite excluding the Aaronites, and four Merarite) and twenty-four groups of priests (24:7–18) and of musicians (25:7–31) suggests they are from a different date from the main lists in chapters 23–26, and there are some indications that they may be earlier rather than later. The series of personal notes about lack of sons (vv. 11, 17, 22) points in this direction, as does the reappearance of

[1] *Cf.* Kleinig, *Song*, pp. 40–41.

some names in 26:20–32, where *Shubael* (v. 16; *cf.* 26:24) and *Jeriah* (v. 19; *cf.* 26:31–32) in particular both precede David by several generations at least. The MT of verses 9–10 has suffered in transmission. The *Gershonites* are normally divided into two families (Libni [here *Ladan*] and *Shimei*) rather than three as here (*cf.* 26:21–22), and the names in verse 9 are described as both *the sons of Shimei* and *the heads of the families of Ladan*.

There is no need to regard the note about *Aaron* (v. 13b) as a later addition (Williamson, *etc.*). The practice of annotating lists is frequent in Chronicles, and is necessary here to explain Aaron's absence from the Levitical families, and to confirm the Mosaic distinction between priests and Levites (*cf.* Nu. 4:15, 19). Verse 13 contains the most detailed list of priestly duties in Chronicles, *viz.* to *consecrate*, to 'burn incense' (RSV, JB, GNB), to *minister* to God, and to *pronounce blessings* (*cf.* 1 Ch. 6:49; 2 Ch. 15:3; 23:18; 31:2). Curiously an atoning function is not mentioned directly (*cf.* 1 Ch. 6:49; Lv. 1:4; 4:19; 9:7; *etc.*). Presumably this is included in the first two of the four activities, especially since 'to burn incense' can have the more general sense of *to offer sacrifices* (*cf.* REB, NEB). The priest has an intermediary ministry, directed towards God (in the work of consecrating, burning incense, and ministering) and man (in pronouncing blessings). It was also, like that of the Davidic king, divinely instituted *for ever*.

d. Groups of Levites (23:24 – 26:32).

i. Levites at the temple (23:24–32). Ostensibly, this section follows on from verses 2–6a, but harmonization of the two passages is hampered by two major difficulties. The Levites' age varies without explanation (*cf.* vv. 3, 24, 27), and the singing of God's praise is a task first given to one group (v. 5) and then to all the Levites (v. 30). Explanations are possible in both cases, however. A difference between the minimum age of the Levites at a census and at actual employment has an earlier analogy in the Mosaic period (*cf.* Nu. 4:34–38; 8:24). In both cases, the figures are probably best interpreted as a reduction in age in the light of actual requirements, here from *thirty* (v. 3) to *twenty* (vv. 24, 27), since nowhere in the Old Testament is it envisaged that the age at which the Levites began their service was determined by other than practical considerations. Temple service will certainly have brought increased work, even though the occasional duty of transporting the ark was now to be abolished. In fact, the Levites and their duties had suffered from long-standing neglect, both before the time of David and at various points after the exile (*cf.* Ezr. 2:40ff. = Ne. 7:43.; Ezr. 8:15–20; Ne. 13:10; Mal. 3:3, 9–10). In each case, a recruitment drive would have been essential. Reference to the *last instructions of David* (v. 27) hints that the inclusion of younger Levites took place at the very end of David's reign, after the assembly of verses 1–6a.

As for the relationship between the Levites' musical activities in verses 2–6a and verses 28–31, it is often argued that the two passages are so incompatible that verses 25–32 must be either earlier (Rudolph) or later (Williamson) than the Chronicler. It is possible, however, to be less drastic. Chronicles seems to draw a distinction between the Levites in general who led the nation in praise (*e.g.* 2 Ch. 8:14–15; 20:19; 30:22; 31:9) and the special group of Levites responsible for providing musical accompaniment (so v. 5; *cf.* ch. 25). In fact the Levites here who were *to thank and praise the* LORD (v. 30) probably represent those who administered the temple (*cf.* v. 4) rather than the Levites in their entirety. The detailed arrangements for the three smaller groups are dealt with in chapters 25–26, leaving this passage, together with 24:20–31, as the only ones referring to the activities of the largest group. For instance, the Levites' role as assistants to the priests occurs in both 23:28–31 and 24:20–31. Further, the various tasks involved in caring for the temple in verses 28–31 do not include the specific activities of the smaller groups, *viz.* acting as gatekeepers, officials and judges, and playing musical instruments.

The practical and theological reasons which explain why David amended Moses' instructions about the Levites (vv. 25–27) are based on the new circumstances in which the temple symbolized Israel's rest (v. 25; *cf.* Dt. 12:8–11) and God's fixed dwelling-place *in Jerusalem for ever* (v. 25). The association of 'rest' with David does not contradict 17:1, 10; 22:9, since the 'rest' is associated with the temple rather than David. In any case, these instructions belong to the *last instructions of David* (v. 27) when his fighting days were over. The temple would also render the Levites' transportation duties superfluous, though it would place fresh demands on their faith in God's provision and the extent of their commitment to

God's service.[1] Such obedient faith was no easier in the Chronicler's day than under Solomon, and the reality of foreign imperial sovereignty must have made many question whether God was resident in Zion at all. But true religion is not dependent on the impermanence of current political systems, and Chronicles affirms that the first priority for God's people is to organize themselves for worship.

In the Levitical duties at the temple (vv. 28–32; *cf.* 9:28–32), two features stand out: their role as assistants to the Aaronite priests (vv. 28, 32), and the variety of their service (*cf.* 1 Cor. 12:4–6). Four different kinds of activity are mentioned: (a) a fabric committee (v. 28); (b) *purification* ('cleansing', NRSV, RSV, REB, NEB) of holy things (v. 28); (c) preparation of bread and flour, especially the 'Bread of the Presence' (REB, NEB) or 'showbread' (RSV, v. 29; *cf.* 1 Ch. 9:31–32; 28:16; 2 Ch. 2:4; Ex. 25:30; 35:13; Lv. 24:5–9; and (d) the offering of *praise* twice a day (*cf.* 1 Ch. 9:33; 2 Ch. 2:4; Ezr. 3:3; Nu. 28:1–8) and on special holy days (vv. 30–31; *cf.* 2 Ch. 2:4; 31:3; Lv. 23:1ff.; Nu. 28–29). As assistants, they were active in side-rooms and courtyards rather than the main building, preparing food and offerings rather than actually offering sacrifices. The emphasis on assistance ties in with the important concept in Chronicles of 'help', which can refer either to God's help for Israel (*cf.* 2 Ch. 18:31; 25:8), or to support for Israel's royal (1 Ch. 12:1ff.) and priestly (2 Ch. 8:14, 30:16–17) leaders. There is no sense here that the Levites are being suppressed or demoted, as commentators have often supposed – on the contrary, this was their duty (v. 28), and they played a vital role, second only to king and priests.

All this is summarized in verse 32, with the Levites' having a threefold 'responsibility' (GNB, *cf.* NIV; 'charge', NRSV, RSV; Heb. *mišmeret*) towards the *Tent*, the *Holy Place*, and the *priests* (the *Tent of Meeting* is probably that at Gibeon (1 Ch. 16:39; 2 Ch. 1:3) rather than the one which temporarily housed the

---

[1] Reference to carrying the tabernacle (v. 26) rather than the ark (*cf.* 15:2; 16:14) cannot be explained simply as the dependence of a different author on P (Nu. 3–4) as against the Chronicler's more usual reliance on Deuteronomy (Rudolph, Williamson; *cf.* von Rad, *GCW*, pp. 107–109). The reason for the change is surely to be found in the context. Whereas chs. 21–29 are concerned with the whole temple and its contents, with which the tabernacle is directly comparable, chs. 15–16 concentrate on the ark without any reference to a temple.

ark (1 Ch. 16:1). 'Responsibility' is an important word for the Chronicler, who applies it almost entirely to the priests and Levites (also Nu. and Ezk. 40–48). It has a double-sided connotation, sometimes as a charge received from God (*cf.* 2 Ch. 13:11; 23:6), and sometimes as a responsibility to or for other people or places (*cf.* 1 Ch. 9:27; 25:8; 2 Ch. 8:14; 35:2). The main point here is that the Levites actually *carried out* their responsibilities (v. 32), putting into practice their obedience to God, king, and priests. No more could have been asked of them.

ii. Priests and Levitical assistants (24:1–31). Attention now moves to the *priests* (vv. 1–19), but although this is Chronicles' most extensive reference to the priesthood, the treatment of the subject is quite limited. Neither the significance nor the functions of priesthood are dealt with (these are mentioned in passing in 1 Ch. 6:48–49; 23:13; 2 Ch. 23:18; 31:2). Rather, the chapter is entirely taken up with the way in which the priests were organized for 'service' (vv. 3, 19, NRSV, RSV; *ministering*, NIV). Two aspects of this service are emphasized – that it is to be regulated in an orderly system of twenty-four courses (vv. 1–19), and that it provides a pattern to be followed by the priests' Levitical assistants (vv. 20–31).

Such a mundane subject makes it difficult for the Christian reader to adopt anything other than an historical interpretation of this chapter. The problem is compounded by the fact that according to the New Testament, priesthood is not a separate leadership function within the church. Not that the New Testament abolishes priesthood altogether. On the contrary, the coming of Christ has brought about a decisive change from which every believer benefits. For example, every believer now enjoys direct access to Jesus, the supreme High Priest (Eph. 2:18; Heb. 4:14–16; 7:25). Even more radically, every believer becomes a priest (1 Pet. 2:5, 9; Rev. 1:6; 5:10); offering sacrifices to God with their lips (Heb. 13:15) and with their bodies (Rom. 12:1).

Despite these fundamental changes between Old Testament and New Testament, 1 Chronicles 24 does have ongoing relevance for Christian thought and practice. It witnesses, firstly, to the necessity of an orderly and organized leadership (1 Cor. 14:33, 40), even though Christian leadership is based on God's gift rather than physical descent (*cf.* Acts 6:1–7; Eph. 4:11–13). Secondly, it assumes that priesthood can be exercised continuously. In Israel, God was worshipped night (*cf.* Ps. 134:1) and day (*cf.* 1 Ch. 23:30–31), giving the people permanent assurance that their sins would not bring God's anger down on them (*cf.* Lv. 10:6–7). Continuous worship is also the church's ministry, especially in the areas of intercession (*cf.* 2 Tim. 1:3) and praise (*cf.* Lk. 24:53). This ministry continues even in heaven, where God's people fulfil their priestly role as they 'serve him day and night in his temple' (Rev. 7:15; *cf.* 4:8; 8:3–4).

The chapter raises two special literary-critical problems, *viz.* the relationship between priests and Levites, and the historical development of the system of twenty-four courses. Priesthood is surprisingly dealt with here only as part of a much larger section on the Levites, and greater significance is attached to their association with the Levites than to other, more vital, aspects of their ministry. In fact, this is one of a number of passages indicating that the Chronicler's primary interest is the Levites, arising in some way perhaps from their identity crisis after the exile (*cf.* Ezr. 2:36–40; 8:15–20). Here the Levites receive a double encouragement: to accept their role as a necessary accompaniment to the proper exercise of priesthood and worship, and to see in the organization of the priesthood a pattern for Levitical structure (*cf.* vv. 5–6, 31; 25:7–31).

The origins of the system of twenty-four courses remain shrouded in uncertainty. Since the Old Testament refers to the system only here and the earliest external reference belongs to the second century BC, it is often argued that it is actually much later than Chronicles. The view of Schürer and E. Meyer (1896) has been widely accepted that the mention of Jehoiarib (v. 7) at the head of the list of priestly families is an indication of Maccabean origin, since the Maccabees were descended from this line (1 Macc. 2:1). Recent commentators have been more reticent about such a late date, but the twenty-four classes are still frequently regarded as the end of a line of development which began at the return from exile with four priestly classes (Ezr. 2:36–39 = Ne. 7:39–42) and gradually increased to twenty-one or twenty-two classes in the late fifth century BC (Ne. 10:1–8; *cf.* Ne. 12:1–7, 12–21; *cf.* Rudolph).

However, while it is very likely that the number of priestly classes did increase during this period, it is by no means clear if and where 1 Chronicles 24 fits in. Since none of the lists in

Nehemiah has twenty-four priestly families, it is possible that twenty-four was an ideal rather than actual figure even in the Chronicler's time. If this is accepted, there can be no intrinsic argument against placing the origin of the system in pre-exilic times (Myers). The chapter places the arrangement in David's hands (vv. 3, 31; *cf*. v. 6) and mentions David's contemporaries as witnesses (vv. 3, 6, 31). Historically, this is by no means impossible. Earlier parts of the Old Testament do not mention any different system, and the very numbers of priests in the first temple would have required the existence of some kind of rota (even the sanctuary at Nob had at least eighty-five priests (1 Sa. 22:18; *cf*. a similar number under Uzziah, 2 Ch. 26:17). A system of 'divisions' of the priests was also well established in the pre-exilic period (2 Ch. 8:14; 31:2; 35:1–5), and was restored in the second temple in a spirit of appeal to earlier authority (Erz. 6:18; 2 Ch. 8:14).

1–6. The priests are divided into two family groups, and preparations for the division into twenty-four courses are explained. Verses 1–2 form an historical introduction clarifying the position of the descendants of *Eleazar* and *Ithamar* (for the tragic death of *Nadab* and *Abihu*, see Lv. 10:1–5). In MT, verse 1 begins with a note rather than a proper sentence (lit. 'And to/for the Aaronites, divisions'), indicating that the chapter is appended to the wider arrangements for the Levites. Verses 3–6 explain how the division into courses was made, even though Eleazar's descendants outnumbered Ithamar's by two to one (v. 4).

The actual choice was made by *drawing lots* (v. 5). Exact procedures are obscured by translation problems in verse 6. The main alternatives are either that one lot was taken from Eleazar and Ithamar in turn with the last eight names from Eleazar (so NIV, NRSV, RSV, REB, NEB),[1] or that two were taken for Eleazar to every one for Ithamar.[2] In favour of the former is a similar pattern for the twenty-four classes of musicians, where the last ten names were taken from the single family of Heman (25:4–5, 22–31). The practice of drawing lots (v. 5) was used in certain cases as a means by which those who belonged to God allowed him to express his will for their lives

---

[1] The usual emendation, as in NEB, is unnecessary, as MT can also have a distributive sense (*cf*. Keil).

[2] Barthélemy, *CTAT*, pp. 463–464, on the basis of MT; Rudolph, by emending MT.

– *cf.* the probably synonymous descriptions of the priests as 'sacred officers' (REB, NEB; better than 'officers of the sanctuary', NRSV, RSV, *cf.* NIV) and as 'officers of God' (*e.g.* NRSV, RSV). It was particularly appropriate in this case in that the duties of individual priests were not differentiated. Priesthood was based not on ability but on representation, and even the larger clan of Eleazar held no advantage – each family was selected *impartially* ('all alike', NRSV, RSV). The use of the lot did not of course contradict the system of royal appointment (23:4–6). Rather, it enabled duties to be allocated to divisions which had already been established by the king.

Ahimelech's presence alongside *Zadok* (v. 3) is unexpected, since Zadok was usually partnered by Abiathar (2 Sa. 15:35; 17:15; 1 Ki. 4:4; 1 Ch. 15:11). Ahimelech was probably the son of this same Abiathar (*cf.* 2 Sa. 8:17; 1 Ch. 18:16).[1] Perhaps the mention of Ahimelech reflects a growing separation between David and Abiathar in the aftermath of Adonijah's rebellion (1 Ki. 1:7ff.).

7–19. The priests are divided into twenty-four courses. The nature of the list in verses 7–18 is explained in verse 19, that this is the priests' *appointed order of ministering*. The *regulations prescribed* by *Aaron* have not been preserved, but were presumably contained in a kind of priests' handbook. The names are not those of individuals but of families: Nehemiah 12:12–21 gives the actual leaders of the priestly families in *c.* 460 BC, for example. Similar lists of priestly families occur in Ezra and Nehemiah (Ezr. 2:36–39, 61–63 = Ne. 7:39–42, 63–65; Ne. 10:1–8; 11:10–14 (*cf.* 1 Ch. 9:10–13); 12:1–7; 12:12–21), but none is identical with 1 Chronicles 24. In fact, although twelve of these names are scattered throughout the Ezra–Nehemiah lists, the remaining twelve have no parallel in the Bible. *Jedaiah* (v. 7), six times, and *Jehoiarib* (v. 7), four times, occur most frequently elsewhere. The Maccabees were descendants of Jehoiarib (*cf.* 1 Macc. 2:1), and John the Baptist of *Abijah* (v. 10; *cf.* Lk. 1:5). The family of *Hakkoz* (v. 10) had difficulty in establishing their legitimate genealogy in the exile (Ezr. 2:61–63 = Ne. 7:63–65), but their inclusion here signifies either their reinstatement or at least the validity of their claim.

---

[1] Abiathar's father was also known as Ahimelech (1 Sa. 22:20), but grandsons in Israel sometimes bore the same names as their grandparents.

In later Jewish practice, the number of twenty-four courses was based on a lunar calendar of forty-eight weeks, with each course serving for a week at a time and thus twice in a year.[1]

20–31. A priestly pattern for the Levites. As with the previous section, the conclusion (vv. 30b–31) explains the purpose of the names, *viz.* that this is a further list of Levites' families. The names are actually repeated from 23:16–23, though with the addition of one further generation. It is not essential to regard the extra generation as the immediate successor to that in chapter 23, and it may be that the compiler has given representatives of these families in his own day. A further difficulty is that only the Kohathites (vv. 20–25) and Merarites (vv. 26–30a) are included, while the Gershonites are omitted. An explanation may be that in both chapters the Kohathites follow the priests, so that verse 20 simply picks up the list from chapter 23 after the note about the priests. There may also be a further connection. The *rest of the descendants of Levi* (v. 20) may have been restricted to priestly assistants, who shared responsibility for temple administration (*cf.* 23:4) alongside those mentioned in 23:28–31. An analogy for this kind of division of labour is found in the fact that the gatekeepers also included no Gershonites (26:19), and the treasurers no Merarites (26:20, 32).

The main point of the list is to show that the Levites followed the pattern of their brothers *the descendants of Aaron* (v. 31) in casting lots for their duties, to the extent of giving no advantage to the larger families (v. 31, *cf.* vv. 5–6; 25:8; 26:13).[2] Some have even suggested that the Levites as a whole had twenty-four courses (so Rudolph), but there is no other

---

[1] Apart from the references to the 24-course system in Josephus (*Antiquities* VII:365–367; *Life* 2), mention also appears in a third- or fourth-century AD fragment from Caesarea (Y. Avi-Yonah, 'A list of priestly courses from Caesarea, *IEJ* 12, 1962, pp. 137–139), as well as in several Rabbinic passages. At Qumran, perhaps in opposition to the Jerusalem practice, 26 courses were employed. This was based on the solar calendar of 52 weeks (*cf.* Y. Yadin, ed., *The Scroll of the War of the Sons of Light*, Oxford: Oxford University Press, 1962, pp. 204–206; P. Winter, 'Twenty-six priestly courses', *VT* 6, 1956, pp. 215–217). Rabbinic sources agree that the number of courses was changed more than once before it was finally fixed.

[2] The last phrase of v. 31 cannot be translated with precision, though the general sense is clear. The simplest solution is to make a slight change to the vowels of 'families', reading, 'the larger families corresponding to the smaller ones' (*cf.* REB, NEB, JB). NRSV, RSV (*cf.* GNB) reverse the first two words of the phrase.

evidence in chapters 23–27 for that view. Textual difficulties arise in verse 23 and verses 26–27. The latter has more serious implications, since a third line, that of *Jaaziah*, seems to be added to the Merarites alongside Mahli (vv. 28–29) and Mushi (v. 30a).

iii. Musicians (25:1–31). The arrangements for the *musicians*, the first of the specialist groups of Levites, are now given. Music was of the highest importance in Israelite worship, as is clear from many parts of the Old Testament, notably the Psalms. The Levitical musicians' role in leading and directing worship was crucial, for it was they who encouraged the people to worship God with conviction, harmony, and vitality. David's organization prepared for the Levites' leading of worship in Solomon's temple, as illustrated by the temple dedication service when the great Levitical orchestra and choir made their declaration: 'He is good; his love endures for ever' (2 Ch. 5:12–14; 7:1–6; *cf.* 1 Ch. 15–16).

These musicians were divided into twenty-four courses, on the analogy of the priests. The division took place in two stages, again like the priests (*cf.* ch. 24). First they were separated into their three main families (vv. 1–6), and then into their courses by the casting of lots (vv. 7–31).

The chapter's unity has been questioned, with differences in the two sections being emphasized and verses 7–31 often treated as a later addition.[1] The Hebrew word *mispār*, for example, has different meanings in verse 1 (*list*, NIV, NRSV, RSV, GNB) and verse 7 (*number*), and the names of verses 2–4 are in a different order in verses 9–31. These arguments, however, are not strong enough by themselves to require a conclusion of multiple origin. On the other hand, verses 7–31 seem to assume that each of the individuals in verses 1–6 has twelve 'sons and brothers' (vv. 9ff.) ready for service. This is probably a general description for their descendants and relatives, and suggests that verses 7–31 are from a generation or two after verses 1–6. *David*'s direct involvement (v. 1), the mention of his contemporaries *Asaph* (vv. 2, 6), *Jeduthun* (vv. 3, 6), and *Heman* (vv. 4, 5, 6), as well as the personal touches about Heman's family (v. 5), all indicate an early origin for the

---

[1] *E.g.* Rudolph; H. G. M. Williamson, 'The origins of the twenty-four priestly courses', *SVT* 30, 1979, pp. 251–268, especially pp. 255–257.

chapter. Conversely, it is difficult to tie in Chronicles' information about the three musical families with what is known about them after the exile. Only the Asaphites participated in the first return (Ezr. 2:41 = Ne. 7:44; *cf.* Ezr. 3:10), and even in the late fifth century only the descendants of Jeduthun were alongside them (Ne. 11:17, 22; *cf.* 1 Esdras 1:15; 5:27, 29). The non-appearance of the Hemanites in post-exilic events is striking, contrasting markedly with this chapter where Heman is in a position of some prominence (only he is called the *king's seer*, and he had the largest number of children, v. 5; *cf.* also 1 Ch. 6:31ff.; 15:17ff.). Since here the names of David, Asaph, Jeduthun, and Heman are confined to verses 1–6, the most likely conclusion is that the Chronicler has used a list of those who actually served in the temple, under Solomon or later (vv. 7–31), to supplement his record of David's division (vv. 1–6).

This chapter therefore probably describes an ideal structure which did not exist in the Chronicler's day. If so, he was drawing his contemporaries' attention to the organization of cultic personnel in the same way that he wrote about cultic objects such as the ark (chs. 13–16). His aim was presumably to stimulate regular musical praise as an important ministry in itself and as a vital accompaniment to the offerings of the priests. The New Testament provides no direct analogy to the place of music in early church worship, but the use of 'harps' in heavenly praises (Rev. 5:8; 15:2–4) is a sure indication that the early Christians saw their own practices in this area as a continuation of Old Testament principles. Their participation in temple worship is further confirmation of this (*e.g.* Lk. 24:53; Acts 3:1).

1–6. The musicians are divided into three family groups. David supervised the separation of the musicians, aided probably by the 'leaders of the Levites' (v. 1, GNB) rather than the *commanders of the army*. The latter would be rather out of place here, while the Levites' leaders have already been involved (23:2), and the priests' leaders assisted in setting up the priestly courses (24:3, 6).[1]

The musicians' task is unexpectedly described as *prophesying* (v. 1, *cf.* vv. 2–3).[2] The context indicates that this activity

---

[1] Heb. *ṣābā'* is also used for the Levites in Nu. 4:3, 23, 35, 39, 43; 8:24, 25.

[2] There is some minor textual support for the reading 'prophets' in v. 1 (*cf.* JB), but this is not supported by the similar words in vv. 2, 3.

involved the playing of musical instruments, and that it was carried out under the king's supervision (vv. 2, 6). Both features are unusual in Israelite prophecy. Two explanations of this Levitical prophecy are possible. Either they supplied messages direct from God in the manner of the classical prophets, for which the Levite Jahaziel (2 Ch. 20:14–17) provides an obvious analogy (*cf*. GNB, 'to proclaim God's messages'), or their praise was itself seen as 'prophecy' in that it proclaimed God's word with God's authority. Further examples of the latter are found in several of the prophetic books. In addition to the familiar 'words' from God, they include messages addressed to God, hymns and prayers of the kind that the Levites would have used in their own worship (*e.g.* Is. 12; 42:10–13; Je. 10:6–10).[1]

The Levites' use of prophecy with music is often regarded as a post-exilic continuation of the ministry of the so-called pre-exilic cultic prophets (following Mowinckel). Alternatively, it may be a direct, but non-eschatological, development of classical prophecy.[2] However, all the remaining Old Testament evidence for prophecy in Israel accompanied by music comes from various parts of the pre-exilic period (Ex. 15:20; 1 Sa. 10:5, 10; 2 Ki. 3:15). It seems more likely, therefore, that Chronicles provides an important cultic background to an element which appears only occasionally in prophetic activity.

Of the three musical families (vv. 2–6), *Asaph* has four sons (v. 2), *Jeduthun* six (v. 3, 'Shimei' must be added to MT, as in v. 17), and *Heman* fourteen (vv. 4–6), making a total of twenty-four. The sons were under the direct supervision of their *father* (vv. 3, 6),[3] who was in turn responsible to the *king* (vv. 2, 5–6). The term *seer* (v. 5) is a synonym for 'prophet' in the Old Testament, and so should be understood in the same way as the references to prophesying (vv. 1–3). Both Asaph (2 Ch. 29:3) and Jeduthun (2 Ch. 35:15) also received this title. No further details are known of the *promises of God* (v. 5; *cf*. NRSV, RSV, GNB, REB, NEB) to Heman, who appears outside Chronicles only in a Psalm title (88:1) and possibly 1 Kings 4:31. His

---

[1] *Cf.* also J. Kleinig, *Song*, pp. 153–157, 184–185.

[2] D. L. Petersen, *Late Israelite Prophecy*, SBLMS 23 (Missoula: Scholars Press, 1977).

[3] Though *'ªbîhem* (v. 6) has been taken in a distributive sense ('fathers'; so NIV, Keil), the word is singular and, apart from the last three words in MT, v. 6 refers only to Heman's family.

'exaltation' (v. 5, *cf*. NRSV, RSV, NIV) is probably indicated by the number of his children (*cf*. Ps. 127:3–5).[1]

The names of the last nine of Heman's sons (from *Hananiah*, v. 4) are often thought to be a thinly veiled fragment of a poem. Some names are certainly unusual, especially those based on first-person verbal forms (*e.g. Giddalti, Mallothi*). By some revocalization and a little redivision of the consonants, they can be read:

> Have mercy on me, O Yah, have mercy on me.
> You are my God.
> I have magnified and exalted (you, my) Help(er);
> While I sat in adversity, I said,
> 'Give an abundance of visions.'[2]

This interpretation is a real possibility, though there seems little doubt that the ancient author also accepted the names as real (*cf*. vv. 23–31). But what did the poem mean? Two commonly proposed solutions are that it is either part of a lament or a series of 'first lines' ('incipits') of the Hemanites' favourite psalms. But the final two lines seem to give a clearer clue. They amount to a request that, despite difficult circumstances, God should speak prophetically, presumably through the Levite musicians ('visions' was a technical term for prophecy).

Music (v. 6, NIV, NRSV, RSV; also v. 7) might theoretically be translated 'singing' (REB, NEB), but the context suggests otherwise. The chapter is specifically about musicians rather than singers (*cf*. 23:5 and comment on 15:16–24; 23:28–31), though the mention of prophesying shows that the musicians were as much involved in singing God's praise as their fellow Levites.

7–31. Like their superiors the priests, the musicians were divided into twenty-four courses. Presumably, each course accompanied one of the priestly courses on a regular basis at morning and evening worship. The total is given as *288* (v. 7). This appears to contradict the '4,000' of 23:5, though understanding the latter as forty (family) groups at least makes the figures somewhat more compatible. Drawing *lots* is again the

---

[1] 'To exalt him' is lit. 'to lift up his horn'. This is an idiom for increasing strength and status (*e.g.* Ps. 92:10; La. 2:17), and is never used of blowing a musical instrument (against JB, Dhorme).

[2] For variant translations, see *e.g.* Curtis and Madsen; D. L. Petersen, *op. cit.*, pp. 64–66.

method used (vv. 7–8), without privilege for age or experience (*cf.* 24:5, 31; 26:13). The names (vv. 9–31) in fact follow a fairly regular pattern, with Jeduthun alternating first with Asaph and then with Heman (vv. 9–21), and the last ten names all coming from the Hemanites (vv. 22–31). This is not totally artificial, as has been alleged. The pattern is not completely uniform, and implies a kind of 'seeding' system not dissimilar to that used for the priests (24:5). In verse 9, *Asaph* may not have been originally included (so REB, NEB), and the phrase 'he, his sons and brothers, twelve' (*cf.* REB, NEB, NIV; but not NRSV, RSV, JB) may have been added subsequently to the clause about Joseph, but the textual support for these changes is not uniform.[1]

iv. Gatekeepers (26:1–19). Chapter 26 introduces groups of Levites who have apparently ordinary tasks. They include primarily the *gatekeepers* (vv. 1–19) and *treasurers* (vv. 20–28), but also *judges* and various civil servants who worked *away from the temple* (vv. 29–32). They represent the final two groups of the four mentioned in 23:3–6a. The 'gatekeepers' of 23:5 incorporate the treasurers here (vv. 1–28), while the various officials in verses 30–32 are associated with the 'officials and judges' (v. 29; 23:4).

A very important point is made by the inclusion of these groups, even though they might seem to represent a diversion from Chronicles' main theme. As God's people pay proper attention to their status as a worshipping community, the distinction between the sacred and the secular disappears. All tasks, whether mundane or specialized, 'religious' or 'lay', have value in the eyes of God. Every Levite was as much involved in the 'service of the temple of the LORD' as the priests and their immediate assistants (*cf.* 23:24, 32). The gatekeepers were 'to serve in the house of the LORD side by side with their kinsmen' (v. 12, REB, NEB), and even the Levitical officials in Transjordan were occupied with 'the business of God and of the king' (v. 32, JB).

The arrangements described here were a preparation for Solomon's temple, and they were specifically confirmed by Solomon (2 Ch. 8:14–15). Though less prominent than some of their Levitical colleagues, from time to time the gatekeepers

---

[1] *Cf.* Barthélemy, *CTAT*, pp. 467–468.

made a vital contribution to national life, notably under the high priest Jehoiada (2 Ch. 23:4–6, 19), and in the reigns of Hezekiah (2 Ch. 31:14–19) and Josiah (2 Ch. 34:9–13). The gatekeepers were especially important to the Chronicler (*cf.* 1 Ch. 9:17–27). Comparatively large numbers of gatekeepers returned from exile (Ezr. 2:42 = Ne. 7:45) and eventually resettled in Jerusalem (Ne. 11:19; *cf.* 7:1). The detailed treatment in 1 Chronicles 9:17–27, which may well describe developments in or near the Chronicler's own time, suggests that the Chronicler saw in them an example by which others might be encouraged. The treasurers in particular were likely to have been grateful for the Chronicler's support. Apart from a temporary improvement stimulated by Nehemiah's direct involvement (Ne. 12:44–47), there was a regular shortfall in contributions for the tithes (Ne. 10:32–39; 13:10–13; Mal. 3:6–12).

The Chronicler seems to have used several lists deriving from different periods as sources for this chapter. The mention of *Obed-Edom* and his grandsons (vv. 4–8), for example, is a hint that verses 1–19 relate to the early monarchy (*cf.* 13:13–14; 15:25). Verses 1–19, therefore, may well belong to a period similar to that of the musicians in 25:7–31, *viz.* at least a generation or two after David. The position of verses 20–32 is rather different, even though *David* appears twice (vv. 26, 31). On the one hand, some of the *heads of* Levitical *families* (*cf.* vv. 21, 26) are clearly pre-Davidic, while, on the other, there are hints of Solomon's reign (vv. 31–32) if not the later monarchy (v. 27). For fuller details, see comment on verses 20–32 below.

There are substantial differences between the information about the gatekeepers and treasurers here and what is known of them in the post-exilic period. In the sixth and fifth centuries BC, the gatekeepers were always treated separately from the Levites (*e.g.* Ezr. 2:42, 70 = Ne. 7:45, 73; Ezr. 7:24; Ne. 10:28; 11:25–26; 12:47). Differences occur in both the numbers (ninety-three here as against 172 in Nehemiah's time, Ne. 11:19, and 212 in 1 Ch. 9:22; *cf.* also Ezr. 2:42; Ne. 7:45; 11:19) and the names of the gatekeepers (*cf.* the preceding references in this paragraph). The non-appearance of Obed-Edom's family after the exile is particularly noticeable in the light of their numerical supremacy here. Finally, there is no appropriate period between the United Monarchy and the Hasmonean period for the kind of extensive control over Transjordan described in verses 31–32.

For the New Testament church, Jesus' death made the role of temple gatekeepers obsolete, of course. The need for treasurers still continued, however, and they could have a significantly negative or positive influence on the church's ministry. They had the potential to devalue the priority of worship (*e.g.* Mk. 11:15–18), and one notorious treasurer even betrayed the Messiah because of his love of money (Mt. 26:14–15; Acts 1:18–19). Alternatively, financial leadership in the early church often continued the Old Testament pattern of 'service' (*cf.* 1 Ch. 26:12), as exemplified in concern for the poor and awareness of the needs of other churches (*e.g.* Acts 11:29–30; Rom. 15:25; 2 Cor. 8:4).

The gatekeepers ('*temple guards*', GNB; 'porters', AV) had no common task. Essentially their duty was to make ordinary people aware of the practical limits of holiness, for anyone entering the sanctuary unlawfully did so on penalty of death (*cf.* Nu. 3:10). They had special responsibility for the temple doors, as a safeguard against idolatrous practices (*cf.* Mal. 1:10; 2 Ch. 28:24; 29:3, 7), and also to ensure the temple's security (*cf.* 1 Sa. 3:15). The job, however, could also bring a special sense of privilege. As one of the psalmists put it, 'I would rather be a doorkeeper in the house of my God than dwell in the tents of the wicked' (Ps. 84:10).

This section is divided between the names of the family heads (vv. 1–12; *cf. chief men*, v. 12) and the allotting of each group to various stations (vv. 13–19). Three family groups are mentioned, those of *Meshelemiah* (vv. 1–3, 9; also known as *Shelemiah*, v. 14), *Obed-Edom* (vv. 4–8), and *Hosah* (vv. 10–11).[1] Obed-Edom's lack of a genealogy is a strong indication of his identity with Obed-Edom the Gittite, who was probably a Philistine (*cf.* 13:13–14; 15:25). It is less certain that he was the same as 'Obed-Edom son of Jeduthun', another gatekeeper (16:38), though both are associated with Hosah. The note, *For God had blessed Obed-Edom* (v. 5), shows that God's blessing on his household (13:14) extended to the numbers of his children

---

[1] Meshelemiah's ancestry (v. 1) should be traced back to 'Ebiasaph' (REB, NEB, JB) rather than 'Asaph' (NIV, NRSV). Although the latter is the MT's reading, it has been influenced by the association of 'Korahites' (*cf.* v. 1) and Asaphites in psalm titles. Support for the change comes from Ex. 6:24 (Abiasaph); 1 Ch. 6:37 (EVV; MT, v. 22); 9:19.

(*cf.* v. 8, and for a similar expression, 25:5).[1]

Able men (v. 7, NIV, NRSV, RSV; 'men of ability', REB, NEB; *cf.* vv. 6, 8, 9, 30, 31, 32) might be better translated, 'strong men' (*cf.* JB).[2] The job might entail removal of unwelcome people or objects (*cf.* 2 Ch. 26:16–20), and would have required some physical strength. *Shimri's* promotion (v. 10) has a parallel in Chronicles in the contrasting demotion of Reuben (5:1–2; *cf.* also 2:3). Such changes of fortune were of obvious interest in genealogical lists, but the circumstances surrounding loss of primogeniture rights were normally tightly controlled. Only serious rebelliousness against one's parents led to these drastic consequences (*cf.* Gn. 35:22; 49:3–4).[3] The total number of gatekeepers was ninety-three (62+18+13), considerably fewer than the '4,000' of 23:5, but as with the musicians, the larger number might be reduced considerably by being explained as forty clans.

Lots were cast for their duties (v. 13), this time on the basis of family groups rather than individual families as before (*cf.* 24:5, 31; 25:8). The descendants of *Meshelemiah* (= *Shelemiah*, v. 14) and *Obed-Edom* were both divided in two, through separate lines from their eldest sons *Zechariah* (v. 14; *cf.* 9:21) and *Shemaiah* (vv. 6–7, 15). The total number of positions was twenty-four, but they were not distributed equally between the twenty-four families of verses 1–12, nor do they correspond to the twenty-four courses of priests and Levites.

Guarding the *East Gate* (v. 14) seems to have been the position of greatest responsibility. This would have led directly to the temple entrance, but it also reflects the fact that in post-exilic times it was known as the 'King's Gate' (*cf.* 1 Ch. 9:18; Dn. 2:49). *Zechariah's* role as a *wise counsellor* may also indicate an official position as a royal advisor (*cf.* 1 Ch. 27:32–33; 2 Ch. 22:3, 4; 25:16).[4] The need for a separate guard at the *South Gate* (v. 15) is often alleged to reflect the plan of the

---

[1] The variation in numbers between 26:8 (62) and 16:38 (68) is explained by a difference of two generations. Interestingly, the figures represent a slight decline, without any attempt to force God's blessing into an automatic increase for each generation.

[2] For the paramilitary role of the gatekeepers, *cf.* J. W. Wright, 'Guarding the gates: 1 Chronicles 26:1–19 and the role of gatekeepers in Chronicles', *JSOT* 48, 1990, pp. 69–81.

[3] See also M. J. Selman in A. R. Millard and D. J. Wiseman (eds.), *Essays on the Patriarchal Narratives* (Leicester: IVP, 1980), p. 126.

[4] J. W. Wright, *op. cit.*, p. 76.

Second Temple rather than Solomon's. In Solomon's temple, it is argued, the south entrance was attached directly to the royal palace, making the need for a guard unnecessary (Ezk. 43:8). But Ezekiel 43:7–8 is concerned with idolatry in the temple precincts, and the structure next to the south gate is just as likely to have been a 'high place' or even a royal cemetery as part of the palace.[1] In any case, it was Ezekiel's firm conviction that the need to preserve the temple's holiness was not in any way lessened because of the proximity of royal buildings.

Neither the *Shalleketh Gate* nor *Shuppim* (v. 16) are known elsewhere, and the latter may be the result of a copyist's error. 'Colonnade' (v. 18, REB, NEB, NRSV) is the most likely meaning of 'parbar' (RSV, JB; *court*, NIV; 'pavilion', GNB). The Qumran community understood it to be an area of free-standing pillars to the west of the temple, behind the Holy of Holies, and therefore perhaps comparable to the structure mentioned here which was also on the *west*.[2]

v. Treasurers (26:20–28). These were associated with the gatekeepers because the temple *treasuries* or *storehouses* (vv. 15, 17) were situated near the gates (*cf.* 9:26; Ne. 12:25). Two separate treasuries are mentioned: the general account (*the treasuries of the house of God*, v. 20, *cf.* v. 22) which was supervised by the *Gershonites* (vv. 21–22), and a special account for *the treasuries for the dedicated things* (v. 20, *cf.* v. 26) under the control of *Shelomith*, an *Amramite* (vv. 23–28; *cf.* 28:12).

The 'dedicated things' were spoils of war (v. 27), provided by David (v. 26; *cf.* 1 Ch. 18:11; 2 Ch. 5:1), and other leaders (v. 28). The events to which verse 28 refers are not otherwise mentioned, except perhaps in the case of *Saul* (*cf.* 1 Sa. 15:21). A statement that these gifts were for the temple's *repair* (v. 27; *cf.* NRSV, RSV, 'maintenance'; REB, NEB, 'upkeep') is unexpected, since it had not yet been built. Either this is a

---

[1] See especially W. Zimmerli, *Ezekiel*, Hermeneia (Philadelphia: Fortress Press, 1983), vol. 2, pp. 416–418; G. C. Heider, *The Cult of Molek, JSOTS* 43 (Sheffield: JSOT Press, 1985), pp. 392–394.

[2] *Cf.* J. Maier, *The Temple Scroll, JSOTS* 34 (Sheffield: JSOT Press, 1985), pp. 35, 90–91. It is also preferable to accept the standard change in EVV of MT's 'Levites' to 'each day' (NRSV, RSV) in the first phrase of v. 17, with LXX. Barthélemy's arguments to the contrary are not convincing (*CTAT*, pp. 469–470).

hint of a later date for the paragraph, or the word must be understood in the sense of 'strengthening'.

The family names in the whole of verses 20–32 are based on the list of Kohathites in 23:16–20. Several details confirm 23:6b–23 as old traditional names of the Levitical groups. *Shubael* (v. 24, NIV, REB, NEB) or 'Shebuel' (GNB, NRSV, RSV, JB) appears in both lists, for example (*cf.* 23:16), but there is a minimum of six generations between him and his descendant *Shelomith* (vv. 25, 26, 28, NIV, GNB) / 'Shelomoth' (REB, NEB, NRSV, RSV, JB) who was contemporary with David (vv. 24–25). *Jeriah* also appears in verses 31–32 and 23:19, but since he is credited with 2,700 relatives by the end of David's reign, he too must belong to an earlier generation. There is a problem with 'Ahijah' (v. 20, NRSV, RSV), whose name appears nowhere else in chapters 23–27, even though he appears to be the chief treasurer. His name is usually correctly read as 'their brothers' (*cf.* NIV, *etc.*) on the basis of the LXX. It is also unclear whether *Zetham* and *Joel* were the sons (vv. 21–22) or brothers (23:8) of *Jehieli*. The most striking feature is that the Kohathites (v. 23; *cf.* 23:12–20) were active throughout Israel.

vi. Levite officials throughout Israel (26:29–32). While the *Amramites* were temple treasurers (vv. 23–28), the *Izharites* (v. 29) and the *Hebronites* (vv. 30–32) had 'outside duties' (v. 29, NRSV, RSV). Only for the *Uzzielites* (v. 23) are no details given. The *officials and judges* (v. 29) correspond to the fourth group of Levites in 23:4 (*cf.* also 2 Ch. 19:8–11). Other officials were active to the *west of the Jordan* (vv. 30–31a) and in Transjordan (vv. 31b–32). Although they were still regarded as doing the *work of the LORD* (v. 30, *cf.* v. 32), they were also royal officials in the *king's service* (v. 30, *cf.* v. 32). This was a new development, but it is unclear whether or not it began in David's reign and why the number of officials east of the Jordan comfortably outnumbered those to the west (vv. 30, 32). Is there a hint here that these Levites were part of Solomon's army of officials (*cf.* 1 Ki. 4:7–19; 9:23), and that their demands became one of the reasons for Solomon's unpopularity in the north? At no other point during the monarchy would so many administrators under Jerusalem's control have been active in Transjordan.

iv. Other leaders prepare for the temple (27:1–34)

'For the LORD had promised to make the Israelites as many as the stars in the sky' (27:23, REB).

To the modern reader, this chapter seems the most unpromising of all the Chronicler's lists and genealogies. The contents are secular rather than religious, the temple is not mentioned (in contrast with chs. 23–26), and even God makes only a single passing appearance (v. 23). The picture of order and unity is often thought to be overneat, probably deriving from a later reviser whose view of David owed more to sympathetic admiration than critical objectivity.

Pessimism of this kind, however, is unjustified. Both the chapter's arrangement and the editorial comment in verses 23–24 strongly suggest that it is part of the Chronicler's purposes. Although the temple is not mentioned directly, the chapter is in fact just as much concerned with temple preparations as the rest of chapters 23–27, except that the focus has now widened from the Levitical temple personnel to 'all Israel', a favourite theme of Chronicles. Representatives of all the groups mentioned in this chapter, such as the military officials (vv. 1–15), the tribal officials (vv. 16–22), and the officials in charge of royal property (vv. 25–31), all reappear in 28:1; 29:6. All Israel's leaders in fact (22:17; 28:1), together with 'all the people' (28:21; *cf.* 29:1, 10), were involved in the building project, and it would have been impossible for the gifts described in 29:6–9 to have been presented without the commitment of the groups in chapter 27.

Despite the success represented by these lists, the explanatory note in verses 23–24 shows that David could certainly not take all the credit (for similar notes, see *e.g.* 10:13–14; 14:17). The real author of Israel's prosperity was *the* LORD himself (v. 23). The fact that no comprehensive total of Israel's population was available (the figures in 21:5 are incomplete, *cf.* 21:6 and v. 24 here) is a clear allusion to David's earlier sin and guilt (ch. 21). In the end therefore, the temple preparations bear a sharper testimony to the reliability and effectiveness of the kingdom of God (*cf.* 17:14; 29:11, 23) than to the kingdom of David.

The chapter is constructed around four lists. They fall into two groups, two lists relating to the nation (vv. 1–24), and two to the king (vv. 25–34). The compiler mentions a source (v. 24) from which one list (vv. 16–22) may be derived, but all of them could have been originally independent of the others. Conversely, there is nothing intrinsically impossible about a Davidic origin in each case. This remains true even for the first list (vv. 1–15), which though independent of the parallel names in 11:11–31, is still rooted in Davidic soil. It is certainly much more difficult to think of the royalist character of these lists as originating in post-exilic Israel.

What, then, is the Chronicler's purpose in including them? It seems that the various aspects of Israel's political structures, including the military divisions (vv. 1–15), the twelve-tribe structure (vv. 16–22), and a single monarchial authority across the geographical regions (vv. 25–31), confirm the whole nation's readiness to build the temple. The participation of the royal officials is especially interesting, since it is notable that chapters 23–27 begin (23:1) and end (27:25–34) with an emphasis on royal commitment. The whole picture is sometimes thought to have been inspired by the vision in Ezekiel 47–48, where the temple is surrounded by the tribes in their newly organized land (Ackroyd). But Ezekiel's purpose was different, for his new temple preceded the redistribution of the land, in reverse order to the historical circumstances of Solomon's temple. A better parallel occurs in Ezra–Nehemiah, where Israel is united in practical living (*e.g.* Ezr. 10:9ff.; Ne. 3) as well as temple worship (*e.g.* Ezr. 3:10–13; 6:13–18; Ne. 8–10). Such extensive national unity is not easy to attain, however, and, in the Chronicler's view, is most effectively stimulated by committing the nation to God's covenant promises.

The New Testament church, like David's kingdom, provides the opportunity for all believers as well as the religious leaders to play a part in building the church (Eph. 2:19–22), and, as in the Old Testament, no distinction is made between the sacred and secular realms. The Lord is active in and sovereign over the whole of life, and he has given gifts to each believer to be used wherever they are appropriate (Rom. 12:3–8; 1 Cor. 14:12).

a. The divisions of the army (27:1–15). The heading (v. 1) is more easily applied to the first list than to the whole chapter, since only the army divisions are introduced by their *heads of families* (*cf.* chs. 23–26). These military leaders were directly involved in the temple preparations (28:1), and, like the

Levites, they *served the king* (v. 1; *cf.* 26:30, 32). They were probably in charge of monthly levies rather than a standing army. A more permanent nucleus for the army was provided by the Three and the Thirty (2 Sa. 23:8–39 = 1 Ch. 11:10–41), together with the Cherethites, Pelethites, and Gittites (*e.g.* 2 Sa. 15:18). Although the leaders in verses 2–15 also belonged, with one possible exception (*cf.* v. 8), to the Three and the Thirty (*cf.* 1 Ch. 11:11–31), the mention of a separate *division* for each *month* suggests these units probably enlisted in wartime only. When the army was far from home, the arrangements were doubtless adapted.

Although no other details exist for the structure of David's army, the common assumption that this arrangement is a literary creation based on Solomon's monthly supplies for the court (1 Ki. 4:7–19) should not be accepted automatically. For one thing, David's court had its own supply system (vv. 25–31), and for another, Solomon's administration and David's army had different bases. Whereas Solomon received his supplies from new geographical areas, David seems to have selected his leading soldiers for individual reasons rather than because of geographical or tribal factors. Six of the twelve commanders were from Judah (vv. 3, 7, 9, 11, 13, 15), two were Ephraimites (vv. 10, 14), one a Levite (vv. 5–6), one a Benjaminite (v. 12), and two of unknown derivation (vv. 4, 8).

Several names have variants as compared with 1 Chronicles 11:11–31, either in the spelling (*cf. e.g.* v. 15 and 11:30) or in the patronymic (*e.g. Jashobeam's* family name in 11:11 is replaced by his father's name, v. 2). Twice, a father's name has been replaced by that of his son – *Ammizabad* succeeded *Benaiah* (v. 6, *cf.* LXX, Vulg.), and *Zebadiah* followed *Asahel* (v. 7; *cf.* 11:26), who was killed before David became king over all Israel (2 Sa. 2:18–23). *Mikloth* might also be the grandson of *Dodai* (v. 4, NIV, GNB; *cf.* 11:12, where Dodai's son is Eleazar).[1] While the form of this list seems to be based on the earlier part of David's reign, therefore, it also includes amendments from his later years. The presence of a priest in charge of one of the levies (v. 5) is not surprising since priests and Levites were not exempt from military activity (*cf.* 11:22–24; 12:26–28). Whether *Jehoiada* was actually 'chief priest' (REB, NEB, JB) is

---

[1] RSV, REB, NEB, and JB have followed LXX in omitting the clause containing 'Mikloth's' name.

uncertain, since his relationship with David's priest Abiathar (*cf.* 15:11; 27:34) is unknown; others have understood him to be simply *chief* of his army division (NIV) or even 'the leader of "The Thirty"' (GNB, *cf.* 11:25). *Shamhuth* (v. 8) is the only commander not paralleled in chapter 11, but he may have been confused with one of the two 'Shammahs' (2 Sa. 23:11–12; see comment on 1 Ch. 11:11–47; 1 Ch. 11:27; *cf.* 2 Sa. 23:25). The figure of *24,000* for each of the levies is clearly an ideal or round number. It is best understood as twenty-four units, and is comparable with the figures for the Levites in 23:3–6.

b. The officers of the tribes (27:16–24). These tribal leaders are called *officers* (v. 22), but their exact status is unknown. Since tribal elders were not usually referred to in this way (*cf.* 1 Ch. 11:3; 2 Ch. 5:4), they are probably either David's appointees or Joab's assistants for the census (21:1–7; *cf.* vv. 23–24). Against the latter, however, is the fact that Levi (v. 17) and Benjamin (v. 21)are included, though they were excluded from the census (21:6). In favour of the former is that all the remaining lists in this chapter are of royal officials. If this conclusion is correct, then verses 1–22 are evidence that the move away from the traditional tribal system towards a centralized bureaucracy began in the latter years of David rather than under Solomon, as is usually thought.

It is sometimes said that the passage is patterned on Moses' census (Nu. 1:1–19) in order to show David's census in a better light (Curtis and Madsen, Williamson). Links are found in the order of the tribes and the exclusion of those under twenty (v. 23; *cf.* Nu. 1:3). But notable differences still exist in the order of tribal names (*e.g.* Asher and Gad are omitted, Aaron is unusually included together with Levi though neither are in Nu. 1, and Manasseh is divided into two). Perhaps even more significantly, whereas Moses employed leaders chosen by the tribes, David used his own army commanders (*cf.* 21:2).

A brief but important paragraph (vv. 23–24) explains why no statistics are given for the tribes as they were for the militia, and why nothing was *entered in the book of the annals of King David* (v. 24).[1] While it seems to have been normal practice not

---

[1] EVV are correct to follow LXX's 'in the book' for MT's 'in the number of', which is clearly a dittography.

to count those under twenty (v. 23; *cf.* 23:24, 27; Nu. 1:3; – the census had included fighting men only, 21:5), the fact that Joab did *not finish* the census was quite unexpected (v. 24). The point is not to transfer blame from *David* to *Joab*, but to show that behind the striking gap in official records lay the sovereign action of God. At stake was the vitality of God's promise, first made to Abraham, to make his people innumerable (v. 23; *cf.* Gn. 15:5; 22:17; 26:4). Any unauthorized census could limit Israel's faith and God's freedom. David may have realized this before the counting was finished, though there is no supporting evidence, or else God sovereignly intervened to abort the project. Support for the latter interpretation comes from verse 24 and 21:7, with the result that God's 'wrath came upon Israel' (NRSV, RSV; NEB's 'this brought harm upon Israel' is an unacceptable reductionism).

c. The officers of the king (27:25–34). These officials are concerned with the administration of royal property (v. 31b) rather than with the country as a whole. There is no sign of the much more complex arrangements introduced by Solomon (1 Ki. 4:7–19), therefore indicating a Davidic origin for this list. David's wealth was derived from a wide area, from the 'Shephelah' (v. 28, NRSV, RSV, REB, NEB; *western foothills*, NIV, GNB) to the plain of *Sharon* (v. 29), perhaps even to the Jezreel valley (*the valleys*). The officials fall into four groups: (a) two treasurers (v. 25; the same word is used as in 26:15, 17, 20, *etc.*; *cf. storehouses*, NIV); (b) a minister of agriculture (v. 26); (c) a ministry for wine and oil (vv. 27–28); and (iv) a ministry of livestock (vv. 29–31). In verse 28, 'sycomore-figs' (REB, NEB, *cf.* GNB) are meant, not the European sycamore tree.

32–34. The royal counsellors are David's personal advisers, though there was probably no sharp distinction between them and state officials (1 Ch. 18:14–17). Three are unknown elsewhere, including *Jonathan*, who is more likely to have been David's *uncle* (NIV, NRSV, RSV) than his 'favourite nephew' (REB, NEB). *Ahithophel* and *Hushai* are well known from 2 Samuel. Hushai's title, *the king's friend* (*cf.* 2 Sa. 15:37; 16:16) was of Egyptian origin and seems to have become standard under David as well as Solomon (1 Ki. 4:5). *Abiathar* the priest and *Joab*, David's commander-in-chief, were closely associated with David from his early days as a fugitive (2 Sa. 22:20; 26:6), remaining loyal even during Absalom's rebellion (2 Sa. 15:24;

18:2), until they incurred David's displeasure by supporting Adonijah (1 Ki. 1:7).

v. David's final preparations for the temple (28:1 – 29:25)

'All this abundance that we have provided . . . comes from your hand' (29:16).

29:27, 23 – *cf.* 1 Kings 2:11 – 12

Chapter 28 resumes the preparations for temple building which were left off at the end of chapter 22. It comprises three speeches by David: (a) verses 1–10, addressed primarily to the leaders and confirming Solomon as the person divinely chosen to build the temple; (b) verses 11–19, addressed to Solomon, explaining the divinely given plans for the temple; (c) verses 20–21, a final exhortation to Solomon to begin the work.

There is some overlap with chapter 22, which also contains speeches by David to Solomon (vv. 6–16) and to Israel's leaders (vv. 17–19). The major difference is that now the emphasis falls on Israel's leaders rather than on Solomon. Several of the points previously made to Solomon are now put before the leaders, but in a heightened form, as if to underline that the building work was to be as much a national enterprise as Solomon's. Even the ordinary people had a vital contribution to make (vv. 8, 21).

A distinctive aspect of the chapter is its emphasis on obedience. The latter part of the chapter demonstrates the need for obedience in carrying out the specific details of the temple plans (vv. 11–21), but the main thrust is in verse 8 which makes Israel's permanent occupation of the Promised Land conditional on their obedience to God's law. The issue of the Promised Land was certainly a vital one in the fifth century BC, since the prayers of both Ezra (Ezr. 9:10–15; *cf.* 7:26) and Nehemiah (Ne. 1:7–9; 9:33–37) also highlight the crucial importance of keeping the law. In fact, the requirements of verse 8 are a basic principle for every generation of Israelites who live in the Promised Land.

The real thread that runs through the chapter, however, is that the temple project is God's initiative. It was God who had brought Solomon to the throne (*cf.* v. 4), and who had given him the opportunity to build the temple. The temple plans too are the result, not of the designs of a powerful king or an expert architect, but of divine revelation, communicated in writing and through God's Spirit (vv. 12, 19). Of course, David and Solomon had substantial parts to play, but the real credit belongs to higher authority.

As the Old Testament temple was an outward and visible sign of the Davidic covenant, so the church as the 'temple of the living God' (2 Cor. 6:16) is the sign of the new covenant in Christ. The church too is the result of God's choice and of a plan revealed by the Holy Spirit and written down in the Scriptures. Jesus has laid the church's foundation (Eph. 2:19–20; 1 Cor. 3:10), and the building work continues through Jesus and the Spirit (Eph. 2:21–22), in preparation for the church's ultimate destiny (Eph. 5:25–27). Chronicles' reminder of the real origin and purpose of the temple is a call to put aside lesser priorities and build God's church with him. For David's generation, this resulted in a generous response and great rejoicing (29:1–20).

a. David speaks about the temple builder (28:1–10). Israel's *officials* all *assemble* in Jerusalem to hear the elderly king's plans for the temple (v. 1). How this assembly compares with others in chapters 22–29 is debatable. It is almost certainly distinct from the whole 'assembly' (29:1, 10), but might be the same as the leaders' gathering in 22:17–19. Some see it as an alternative version of Solomon's original anointing ceremony at Gihon (1 Ki. 1), but this is not supported by the details of the text. The range of leaders here is much wider, and the careful and extensive preparations of chapters 28–29 bear little resemblance to the rather impromptu attempts to install a new king (see also the discussion on 22:14–16). Of the leaders mentioned in verse 1, the tribal officers, those who served the king, the military commanders, and those in charge of royal property all occur in chapter 27, while the leading soldiers are probably those listed in 11:10 – 12:40.

The first speech is addressed primarily to the leaders (vv. 2–8) and then briefly to Solomon (vv. 9–10). David's unusual form of address, *my brothers and my people* (v. 2), identifies the king with his people, with the king like everyone else under divine orders (*cf.* vv. 7–10; Dt. 17:18–20). The main part of the speech is really a development of David's private address to Solomon in 22:7–13. Like 22:7–13, its foundation is an exposition of the Davidic covenant (1 Ch. 17). For example, three crucial issues from the earlier speech are repeated, *viz.* David's inability to build the temple (vv. 2–3; *cf.* 22:7–8),

Solomon as David's rightful successor (vv. 4–5; *cf.* 22:9), and therefore Solomon as the temple builder (v. 6; *cf.* 22:10). Some phrases also are repeated verbatim, *e.g. I had it in my heart to build a house* (v. 2, *cf.* 17:2, 22:7); *You are not to build a house* (v. 3; *cf.* 17:4; 22:8) and, *he* [*i.e.* Solomon] *is the one who will build my house* (v. 6; *cf.* 17:12; 22:10). In contrast to the hasty arrangements for Solomon's anointing (1 Ki. 1:28–53), Solomon is now deliberately and publicly confirmed as one who not merely holds the key to both houses of God's promise, but who is himself that key.

These speeches, however, are certainly not vain repetition. On four key points, David goes far beyond what was said previously.

(a) Firstly, a new dimension of the idea of 'rest' is expounded (vv. 2–3). The temple is described, for example, as a *house of rest* and God's *footstool* (v. 2, *cf.* NRSV, RSV; *cf.* Ps. 132:7, 8, 14), expressions which are found only in Chronicles (*cf.* 2 Ch. 6:41–42) and Ps. 132. Further, God's resting-place is meant, in place of the more usual symbol of the ark for Israel's rest (22:9; 23:25; *cf.* Dt. 12:8–11). Israel's rest therefore cannot be thought of apart from God's rest. As in the case of God's sabbath rest at creation (Gn. 2:1–3), God's rest represents the completion of his work. The idea of rest was so significant for the temple that even though David's role as a 'man of war' (v. 3, JB) was a vital part of the temple preparations in creating the necessary conditions for the work, it disqualified him from building the temple himself. Only Solomon, the 'man of rest' (22:9), was sufficiently fitted for the task (see further on 22:7–10).

(b) This leads into David's main theme, Solomon's election (v. 4). It is unparalleled in the Old Testament to read of the divine choice of any individual king after David.[1] Yet here, the verb 'to choose' occurs five times (vv. 4–10), three times of Solomon himself. He was chosen to sit on God's throne (v. 5), to be God's (adopted) son (v. 6), and to build the temple (v. 10, *cf.* v. 4). Divine election in the Old Testament represents selection for a specific task, clearly here to build the temple. It has little to do with a person's innate qualities or achievements. For example, whenever the corresponding verb *he was*

---

[1] See further R. L. Braun, 'Solomon, the chosen temple builder', *JBL* 95, 1976, pp. 581–590, especially pp. 588–590.

pleased to (v. 4) has God as its subject, any personal object is always described as helpless, humble, fearing or serving God (*e.g.* Pss. 44:3; 147:11; 149:4; Is. 42:1). Very frequently too, there is an element of surprise in God's choice. The mention of David's *many sons* (v. 5), among whom Solomon was by no means the eldest (*cf.* 2 Sa. 3:2–5; 5:13–16), is one instance of this. Others occur in the unsavoury circumstances surrounding his birth (2 Sa. 11:1 – 12:25) and his accession (1 Ki. 1). This divine right of kings, as it is developed here, is far from giving unqualified approval to the king's every move. Rather it confirms that despite Solomon's weaknesses, God was still working out his own purposes through him. Furthermore, Solomon's election was not an isolated act. God had also chosen his father and his tribe, *Judah* (Gn. 49:10; *cf.* 1 Ch. 2:3 – 4:23). This was of great significance for post-exilic Israel, for God's choice of David's line survived even the exile through Zerubbabel and his family (*cf.* 1 Ch. 3:19; Hg. 2:23).

(c) The sense of God's overarching purpose leads to another new feature, the reference to *the throne of the kingdom of the* LORD (v. 5; '... of the LORD's sovereignty', REB, NEB). This important idea was hinted at in 17:14 (*cf.* also 29:11, 23; 2 Ch. 13:8, *etc.*), but now it explicitly confirms the link between God's throne and David's. God's kingdom would be represented jointly by Solomon and the temple. Indeed, in the Chronicler's own time, when Solomon and the Davidic monarchy had long since disappeared, the temple remained the chief symbol of the continuing reality of the kingdom of the Lord (see further on 17:10b–14).

(d) Finally, David dwells at length on the need of the leaders (v. 8) as well as Solomon (vv. 7, 9–10) for obedience (*cf.* 22:12–13). Obedience to *all the commands of the* LORD *your God* (v. 8) was the condition for Israel's continued occupation of the Promised Land. For Solomon, the priority was to *build a temple as a sanctuary* (v. 10). These demands undermine neither Solomon's election nor God's unconditional promise (17:13–14). On the contrary, they make the promise effective. Election in the Old Testament is for service, and the way for Solomon to make his 'calling and election sure' was to *acknowledge, serve,* and *seek* God (v. 9).

What is more, Solomon would not be left to carry out the task alone, since God himself will 'seek' Solomon's heart (v. 9, EVV). God's seeking has two different senses in this verse. The more general meaning is conveyed by *the LORD searches every heart*, which may have negative as well as positive results (*cf.* 2 Ch. 24:22). However, a second and clearly positive sense is based on a promise quoted from previous Scriptures (*e.g.* Dt. 4:29; Je. 29:13–14; Is. 55:6), that God (and David!) looks for people to seek him so that he may *be found* by them. Though in other contexts this promise was an incentive to repentance, here it represents an invitation to action.[1] God's seeking also anticipates not only Solomon's own seeking, but the promise that the temple was to be a place of hope for all who seek God (*cf.* 2 Ch. 7:14; 31:21). Conversely, if Solomon did not obey, there remained the possibility that God 'will cast you off for ever' (v. 9, REB, NEB). With these promises and warnings, David finally commissions Solomon for the work (v. 10 and the fuller version in v. 20; see also notes on 22:11–13).

Solomon's response, typical of humanity, was inconsistent. Though he did seek God (2 Ch. 1:5), it was not with a 'whole heart' (v. 9, RSV, REB, NEB; *cf.* 1 Ki. 11:4, 6), and his divided devotion led ultimately to a divided kingdom (*cf.* v. 8). In a sense, his fate was little better than that which befell Saul (see comment on 10:13–14), but there were two significant differences between Solomon and Saul. Solomon was obedient in his primary task of building the temple, and his kingdom was sustained by God's covenant mercy. Chronicles highlights both features, though God's faithfulness is the more crucial (1 Ch. 17:13; 2 Ch. 6:1–11).

b. David tells Solomon God's plans (28:11–19).

This paragraph forms the chapter's focus, despite the fairly lengthy list of constructional details which have little outward appeal for most modern readers. It is all about the temple plan (Heb. *tabnît*), a word which occurs four times (vv. 11, 12, 18, 19). Two aspects of this plan are brought out. Firstly, it was given by divine revelation. This is clear from verse 19, where David is spoken of in prophetic terms (*from the hand of the LORD*

---

[1] *Cf.* the positive interpretation of 'desire' (29:18), which is identical in Heb. to 'motive behind the thoughts' here. *Cf.* also J. G. McConville's positive view of God's seeking in 1 Ch. 28:9, though he does not distinguish the different meanings of 'seek', and his use of Ps. 132:13; Dt. 11:12 is rather remote ('1 Chronicles 28:9: Yahweh "seeks out" Solomon', *JTS* 37, 1986, pp. 105–108).

upon me; *cf. e.g.* Ezk. 40:1), receiving all the details *in writing.*[1] It is also probably the sense of verse 12, where a reference to God's Spirit (*all that the Spirit had put in his mind*; *cf.* Rudolph, Myers) is preferable to 'all he had in mind' (REB, NEB, NRSV, RSV, *etc.*). The vocabulary and theology of verse 12a and verse 19 are quite similar, and together they form a kind of inclusion. 'Spirit' is used with the same sense in 1 Chronicles 12:18 (EVV; MT, v. 19), and the unusual expression, literally 'the spirit with him', may also point in this direction.

Secondly, the manner of this revelation forms a pattern similar to that for the Tent (Ex. 25:9, 40) and Ezekiel's visionary temple (especially Ezk. 40:1–4; 43:10–11). The word 'plan', for example, occurs with one exception (2 Ki. 16:10) only here and in Exodus 25:9, 40 (is *toknît*, 'measurement', in Ezk. 43:10 also in mind?). Each revelation included comprehensive details (vv. 12, 19; Ex. 25:9; Ezk. 40:4) and a command to do the work (vv. 10, 20; Ex. 25:40; Ezk. 43:11). Instructions about the temple furnishings or vessels (Heb. *kēlîm*, v. 13; Ex. 25:9), and the requirement of a full written record (v. 19; Ezk. 43:11) offer further points of contact. David therefore fulfils a prophetic ministry like that of Moses and Ezekiel.

The detailed instructions fall into three parts, concerning the temple architecture (vv. 11–12), its personnel (v. 13), and its contents (vv. 14–18). The most striking feature of its structure is the reference (v. 11) to the *place of atonement* (NIV), 'room for the mercy seat' (NRSV, RSV) or 'shrine of expiation' (REB, NEB). This term is used only here outside the Pentateuch (*e.g.* Ex. 25:17ff.), strengthening the conceptual link between the Tent and the temple. It is also a reminder that the temple was a 'temple for sacrifices' (2 Ch. 7:12), and a place of forgiveness and healing (2 Ch. 7:14). As such, it gave hope to all the guilty, including the king (1 Ch. 21; *cf.* 2 Sa. 11–12) and

---

[1] The use of direct speech in v. 19 is unexpected (vv. 11–18 are in reported speech). Since the problem recurs in 23:5, the change of person could well be original, requiring the addition in English of 'David said' (NIV, GNB). This is preferable to harmonizing the suffix, 'to him' (JB; *cf.* RSV), or positing a rare third-person-singular suffix in *-y* (W. G. E. Watson, 'Archaic elements in the language of Chronicles', *Bib.* 53, 1972, pp. 202). MT divides the verse after Heb. *hiśkîl, viz.* 'He gave me understanding of everything in the written (plan) because the LORD's hand was upon me, (including) all the working out of the plan' (*cf.* RSV). This is better than relegating *hiśkîl* to the second clause (NIV, GNB) or emending it (reading the infinitive *haśkîl*, NEB, JB).

the nation (*cf.* 1 Ch. 10:13–14; 2 Ch. 36:14, 16). Inclusion of *the priests and Levites* (v. 13) is a little unexpected, but in the light of chapters 23–26 it is not out of place (*cf.* the mention of *storerooms* in v. 11 and 26:15, 17, 20, 22). Post-exilic Israelites seem to have had a special interest in the temple *articles* (NIV, JB), 'vessels' (REB, NEB, NRSV, RSV) or 'utensils' (GNB), *cf.* verses 14–18 with 2 Chronicles 36:18; Ezra 1:7–11; 7:19; 8:24–34. They represented both continuity with pre-exilic worship and the fact that the temple was fully operational. Most of these articles are specifically said to have been completed by Solomon's craftsmen (2 Ch. 3:10–13 and 4:6–22).

Two are worthy of special comment. Mention is made fairly frequently in Chronicles of the *tables* for the 'showbread' (RSV) or *consecrated bread* (NIV) (v. 16; *cf.* 1 Ch. 9:32; 23:29; 2 Ch. 2:4; 4:19; 13:11). The bread signified God's presence and his constant provision for his people. A *chariot* (v. 18) is unknown elsewhere as part of the temple furniture, but its connection with the winged *cherubim* suggests the idea of God's mobile throne (*cf.* Ps. 18:10; Ezk. 1:15ff.).[1] The Chronicler's readers will have been greatly encouraged by these allusions to God's majesty and his provision.

c. David commissions Solomon (28:20–21).

A public equivalent of the earlier private commissioning of Solomon (*cf.* 22:11–13 and 28:10). The same basic features recur, *viz.* (a) encouragement (*Be strong and courageous, . . . Do not be afraid or discouraged*); (b) assurance of God's help (*for the LORD God, my God, is with you. He will not fail you or forsake you*); and (c) instruction to carry out the task (*Do the work . . . until all the work for the service of the temple of the LORD is finished*). Several of these phrases are closely associated with Moses' handover to Joshua, showing that God's assistance had not diminished from earlier days.

To this built-in guarantee, yet further encouragement is added. The three groups of religious leaders, skilled craftsmen, and the officials are all ready to assist, and *all the people*

---

[1] The rare word *kᵉpôr* (v. 17), translated 'bowls' (RSV, JB) or 'dishes' (REB, NEB, GNB; *cf.* NIV), has been connected with *kprt* on a twelfth-century BC alphabetic cuneiform tablet from Taanach. It probably referred to a pitch-covered basket of palm-fibre (W. G. E. Watson, *art. cit., Bib* 53, 1972, p. 195; D. R. Hillers, 'An alphabetic cuneiform tablet from Taanach [TT 433]', *BASOR* 173, 1964, pp. 45–50).

are now prepared (v. 21). No longer was the temple in any danger of being a monument to David's own achievements (*cf.* 17:4–10a). It would now represent the whole nation's response to God.

A joyful and momentous climax to David's reign is reached in 1 Chronicles 29 as the nation assembles to contribute to the temple fund (vv. 1–9) and confirm Solomon as king (vv. 21–25). At its centrepiece is a prayer of David's (vv. 10–20) which has been rightly described as 'among the most beautiful and impressive of all the biblical prayers'.[1] Its effect is to draw attention away from David, Solomon, and the temple to the God who has made all their achievements possible (*cf.* v. 14). Some of its phraseology has even found its way into the Lord's Prayer (*cf.* v. 11). The chapter ends with a summary of some of the basic facts of David's reign (vv. 26–30).

Verses 21–29 form an echo of the opening section of David's reign (chs. 10–12), and the two passages together make a large-scale inclusion. Both passages speak of God's sovereignty over Israel's monarchy, for example, though, while David received the kingdom through a change of dynasty (10:6, 13–14), Solomon's place on the 'throne of the LORD (29:23) signified the permanence of David's house. The 'all Israel' theme is also prominent (*cf.* 11:1–3; 12:38–40, with 29:21–26 where the phrase occurs four times), a unity that is strengthened by the support of former enemies (*cf.* 12:18; 29:24). Further parallels are the mention of prophetic support (11:1–3; 12:18; 29:29) and the generously provided meals joyfully consumed by the entire people (12:39–40; 29:22). While it is true that this is a very different account of David's end from that in Kings (1 Ki. 1:1 – 2:12), Chronicles' aims are also quite different. The Chronicler's purpose is to draw attention to God's sovereign control of David and Israel throughout David's reign in spite of some of his difficulties (*cf.* especially 2 Sa. 11–12; 1 Ch. 21). God's power has been made perfect in David's weakness (*cf.* 2 Cor. 12:8).

Prayer plays a key role in Chronicles, especially in its account of David. This prayer is the last in a series of three great prayers (*cf.* 16:8–36; 17:16–27), all sharing common phraseology, theology, and structure. Each has a strong note

---

[1] R. E. Clements, *The Prayers of the Bible* (London: SCM Press, 1985), p. 81.

of praise, worshipping God for his character and covenant faithfulness, and each ends requesting God to go on keeping his promises. Together with David's prayers of confession (21:17) and petition (14:10, 13), they emphasize that to be a man of prayer is an essential ingredient of kingship. They also underline that status and success are gifts of God, and that prayer is as much about praise and adoration as more personal concerns.

At the heart of the prayer, and underlying the whole of the Chronicler's theology, is the statement, *Yours, O LORD, is the kingdom* (v. 11). Chronicles makes direct reference to God's kingship only rarely (*cf.* 16:31; 28:5; 2 Ch. 13:8), but the same concept is clearly present elsewhere, especially in prayers (*e.g.* 2 Ch. 6:18; 20:6). The ideas expressed in these passages are fundamental to understanding Chronicles' interpretation of the Davidic covenant and the Davidic monarchy. Only God's kingdom and power are absolute. Solomon, seated on the 'throne of the LORD' (v. 23), and 'the kingdoms of all the other lands' (v. 30), are equally subject to his sovereign rule. Another important point is that the kingdom of God is not restricted to or confined by its human representatives. Its ground is God himself, his qualities, attributes, and actions, and its freedom and reputation remain untrammelled by the failure and even the absence of David and his descendants. Since everything comes from God (v. 14), human success and prosperity also derive ultimately from him.

A proper grasp of this truth was essential to Israel's survival after the exile. Other literature of the period makes the same point, sometimes mentioning the Persian emperors explicitly (*e.g.* Ezr. 6:14: 'according to the command of the God of Israel and the decrees of Cyrus, Darius, and Artaxerxes, kings of Persia' (*cf.* Ezr. 6:22; Is. 44:28 – 45:1). Nebuchadnezzar of Babylon acknowledged too that 'the Most High is sovereign over the kingdoms of men and gives them to anyone he wishes' (Dn. 4:17, 25, *cf.* vv. 3, 34–35).

In the New Testament, the theme undergoes further development. Jesus is revealed as the personification of the kingdom of God, uniting both its human and divine dimensions. Now he sits 'above all rule and authority, power and dominion' (Eph. 1:21), and is 'head over everything for the church, which is his body' (Eph. 1:22–23). The church, like David's Israel, must put its confidence in this kingdom, even though the kingdoms of this world seem to be more eviden and more pressing. But God's kingdom too has its earthl characteristics, such as the generous giving of his people (: Ch. 29:1–9, 17–18; 2 Cor. 8–9). Because this kingdom is more enduring, Christians are called, like the Chronicler's contem poraries, to be companions to those in 'the suffering anc kingdom and patient endurance that are ours in Jesus' (Rev 1:9). They may also wait confidently for God's intervention whether it comes in this life (2 Cor. 2:14; Rom. 6:17) or at th second coming (1 Cor. 15:50–57; Rev. 3:21–22). Both th Chronicler and the New Testament writers would testify tha to submit to the reality of God's kingdom provides a secur framework for the whole of life. Such an awareness, accordin to David, is gained most readily through prayer and praise (Ch. 16:31; 29:11).

d. David appeals for Israel's consecration (29:1–5). Th final *assembly*, this time comprising the whole people (vv. 1, ⁹ 10, 20, 25; for others, see notes on 23:2), lasted two days (*cf.* ⁷ 21). It had the dual purpose of receiving gifts for the templ (vv. 1–9) and confirming Solomon's kingship (vv. 21–25).

1–2. David first of all recalls the earlier stages of the temp preparations (chs. 22, 28). Solomon has been *chosen* (*c* 22:6–10; 28:2–7), but is *inexperienced* (*cf.* 22:5), yet the *task* great (*cf.* 22:5). David had already *provided* (Heb. *hᵃkînôtî*, al: 22:14; 28:2) large amounts of expensive materials (*cf.* 22:3– 14). Fuller details of these gifts are now given, especially tl precious metals, though the translation of some items uncertain; *e.g. onyx* may be 'cornelian' (NRSV, REB, NEB), *tu* quoise could be 'antimony' (NRSV, RSV), 'coloured stones' (NRS RSV) is normally used of cloth and only here of stones, ar *marble* is occasionally rendered 'alabaster' (JB). 'I have mac every effort (v. 2, GNB; 'so far as I was able', NRSV) is probabl deliberate echo of 'by my efforts' (22:14, GNB; 'with gre pains', NIV, NRSV, RSV). The unusual word 'palace' (vv. 1, 1 RSV, GNB, NEB; *palatial structure*, NIV) is a post-exilic word (He *bîrâ*) normally meaning 'fortress, citadel, capital', but it associated with the temple in Nehemiah 2:8 (*cf.* also Ne. 7:! Here it may either be associated with a post-exilic fortifi entrance to the temple and refer *pars pro toto* (the part for t whole) to the whole building, or it may signify that the temp was God's kingly residence (*cf.* v. 11).

3–5. David now makes further gifts from his *personal treasures* ('private store', REB, NEB). By modern standards, the amounts are extremely high, though they are not as exceptional as in 22:14. One should recall, however, that David was Israel's most successful soldier ever and that most of his wealth came from war booty (see also on v. 7 below).[1] *Gold of Ophir* was synonymous with fine gold, and was imported in large quantities by Solomon (2 Ch. 8:18 = 1 Ki. 9:28; 2 Ch. 9:10 = 1 Ki. 10:11; *cf.* Jb. 22:24; 28:16; Ps. 45:9; Is. 13:12). David's additional generosity leads to an appeal for anyone to *consecrate himself* ('give a generous offering', GNB). Chronicles uses this unusual Hebrew idiom, based on the ordination of the priests (*e.g.* Ex. 28:41; Lv. 8:33), uniquely in the Old Testament for self-consecration to God (also 2 Ch. 29:31; for a very different form of self-consecration, see 2 Ch. 13:9). It provides a fascinating insight into the extent to which Chronicles saw ordinary people assuming aspects of the priests' role.

e. Gifts for the temple (29:6–9). The *leaders* and the people (*cf.* v. 17) heeded the appeal. The leaders are those listed in chapter 27 (especially vv. 1, 16, 31), while *Jehiel* the treasurer is mentioned in 23:8; 26:21. Both the quality (vv. 6, 9) as well as the quantity (vv. 7–8) of giving is notable, with the gold and silver amounting to about half as much again as David's gifts. The inclusion of gold *darics* (v. 7), a coin first minted under Darius I (522–486 BC) and not before 515 BC, is an obvious post-exilic usage, presumably replacing an older equivalent. The amount (*ten thousand darics* = *c.* 85 kg) is apparently much smaller and more reasonable than the accompanying *five thousand talents* (= *c.* 150,000 kg or 150 metric tons!), but it is impossible at this distance to understand the full implications of Chronicles' large figures.

The fund-raising for the temple is often thought to have been inspired by a similar enterprise undertaken for the Tent (*cf.* Ex. 25:1–7; 35:4–9, 20:29; *cf. e.g.* Braun, pp. 279–280), though several significant differences show the independence of this account. For example, these gifts are made by the leaders rather than the people as a whole, the range of gifts is

---

[1] For comparison, Solomon received an annual revenue of 666 gold talents, not including trading taxes or certain other royal gifts, and the Queen of Sheba brought 120 talents of gold (2 Ch. 9:9, 13 = 1 Ki. 10:10, 14).

narrower, and the excessive giving of Exodus 36:2–7 is unparalleled. 'They had offered freely' (v. 9, NRSV, RSV) is a key
term in this chapter (Heb. *hiṯnaddēḇ*, vv. 5, 6, 9, 14, 17). Such
willingness was also characteristic of giving for the Tent (*e.g.*
Ex. 35:5, 21, 22, 29) and the Second Temple (*e.g.* Ezr. 1:6;
2:68; 3:5), but here the lack of any distinction between one's
self-offering and the offering of material things is very
striking. Such sacrificial generosity arose from a 'whole heart'
(v. 9, RSV; *cf.* 28:9; 29:19 for an identical phrase), and because
the giving was directed *to the LORD* (*cf.* 2 Cor. 8:5) and not just
to a project (*cf.* vv. 5, 17; 2 Ch. 17:6). When they saw such a
response, people and king *rejoiced* together (*cf.* vv. 17, 22).[1]

f. David's prayer (29:10–20). This magnificent prayer
demonstrates beyond contradiction that Chronicles' priority is
with the heart of worship rather than its form. Its interest is
centred not on David or the temple, but on God himself and
his kingdom. Since the prayer majors on both praise and
petition, it is difficult to categorize, except that rather like
Psalm 145 it is a psalm of the kingdom of God.[2] God's kingdom is not only an object of praise (vv. 10–13) but the source
of the wealth from which contributions have been made for
the temple fund (vv. 14–16). Even David's request (vv. 17–19)
that future generations might maintain the same attitude to
God appeals to God's sovereignty (*O LORD, God of . . . Abraham,
Isaac, and Israel*, v. 18). The language is full of Old Testament
quotations and allusions, reflecting the usage of the Chronicler's time as well as David's, but it is impossible to be certain
of the precise origin and date of every phrase.

The prayer falls naturally into three sections[3]: verses
10–13; 14–16; 17–19.

10–13. *Yours, O LORD, is the kingdom* (v. 11). The opening
hymnic section, which is very reminiscent of parts of Psalm

---

[1] For a similar view, *cf.* J. G. McConville, 'Ezra–Nehemiah and the fulfilment
of prophecy', *VT* 36, 1986, p. 223, n. 36, who also argues that since all references to *hiṯnaddēḇ* outside Jdg. 5:2, 9 occur in Ch., Ezr., and Ne., these later
passages are an application of the leaders' self-giving in Jdg. 5, rather than the
mere giving of offerings.

[2] For the significance of Ps. 145 for the kingdom of God, see M. J. Selman,
'The kingdom of God in the Old Testament', *TB* 40.2, 1989, pp. 174–175; B.
Lindars, 'The structure of Psalm CXLV', *VT* 39, 1989, pp. 23–30.

[3] For a different division of the prayer, see M. A. Throntveit, *Kings*, pp.
93–96.

145 (*cf.* Ps. 145:3–6, 11–12), praises God for who he is. It has a simple chiastic structure:

a. Praise (vv. 10b, 13);
b. God's possessions and gifts (vv. 11a, 12b);
c. The kingdom of God (vv. 11b–12a).

The central focus (vv. 11b–12a) is that God is supreme *head* and *ruler* in his *kingdom*. God's qualities are those of royalty, and it is no surprise that the phrase *Yours . . . is . . . the power and the glory* (v. 11) is directly associated with the 'kingdom' in the Lord's Prayer. This affirmation is supported by two statements, describing what belongs to the LORD (v. 11a, *everything in heaven and earth is yours*), and what the LORD freely gives (v. 12b, 'in your hand lie strength and power; in your hand it is to give greatness and strength to all', JB). It is a great encouragement to every reader that the God who possesses everything also gives freely to everyone. All is then placed firmly in the context of *praise*, especially of God's faithfulness (v. 10b) and his name (v. 13). Although the theme is not new (v. 10), it has to be freshly appreciated by each generation.

14–16. 'All things come from you, and of your own have we given you' (v. 14, NRSV). Not for the first time, a new awareness of God's nature and purposes brings a new awareness of oneself and one's actions (the questions, *Who am I, and who are my people?*, v. 14, are almost identical to those in an earlier prayer, *cf.* 17:16, 21). It is a sign of maturity to recognize that everything good, including material success and acts of human kindness, is God's gift, as the gift of Jesus supremely shows (*cf.* 2 Cor. 9:15). Even Israel's generosity was inspired by God's grace (vv. 14, 16). David confirms the point by two specific examples. Firstly (v. 15), he reminds his readers by quoting from the Psalms that they do not have rights either to the Promised Land, where they are still *aliens and strangers* (Ps. 39:12; *cf.* 1 Ch. 16:19–20 and 22:2!), or even to life itself, which remains as fleeting as a *shadow* (*cf.* Ps. 102:11). Further, these are not just matters of socio-political status or a metaphor for the general status of believers, but a recognition that a person's actual physical situation as well as his or her spiritual standing owes everything to God's generosity.[1]

[1] Against D. J. Estes, 'Metaphorical sojourning in 1 Chronicles 29:15', *CBQ* 53, 1991, pp. 45–49.

Secondly, even *all this abundance* (v. 16) of the temple gifts cannot be thought of as an unsolicited offering, for that too *comes from your hand.*

17–19. *Keep this desire in the hearts of your people for ever* (v. 18). Finally the prayer turns to petition, though it is preceded by a further statement about God (v. 17), this time based on Jeremiah 12:3. Two petitions, for the people (v. 18) and for Solomon (v. 19), aim at a single target, a right attitude of *heart* (the word occurs five times in vv. 17–19). Gifts given *willingly* and *with joy* (v. 17) come from a 'whole heart' (v. 19, RSV; *cf.* 28:9; 29:9), but such attitudes can be preserved only by God, for he also tests *the heart* (v. 17). Interestingly, 'purposes and thoughts' (v. 18, NRSV, RSV; *desire*, NIV) is identical in Hebrew to 'the imagination of the thoughts of' man's heart in Genesis 6:5 (RSV; *cf.* Gn. 8:21). Although, without God, man's inner motives are 'evil continually', even these can become pleasing to him through prayer (*cf.* the identical phrase in 28:9). Such God-given attitudes are essential for a successful conclusion of the task in hand (v. 19).

Finally (v. 20), the whole assembly responds to David's command, *Praise the LORD your God.* As on a previous occasion (16:36), they were ready to express verbal praise to God's *name* (*cf.* vv. 13, 16; 28:3), and not allow the temple to present a mute witness.

g. Solomon anointed king (29:21–25). The second day of the assembly (v. 21) centres on Solomon's *anointing* (v. 22). According to MT, this took place *a second time* (v. 22), ostensibly as a more formal sequel to the rather hurried ceremony described in 1 Kings 1:28–40 (*cf.* 1 Ch. 23:1). However, 'a second time' is omitted in LXX(A), P, and Vulg., and most commentators assume that the phrase in MT is a gloss based on a misinterpretation of 1 Chronicles 23:1.[1] Nevertheless, this view does not explain the substantial differences between the two accounts. The great public assembly and the thousands of sacrifices (v. 21) would have been impossible in the context of the ceremony at Gihon. The Chronicler was in any case not ignorant of the earlier account. There are several allusions to it, including Solomon's appointment as *ruler* (v. 22; 'prince',

[1] *E.g.* L. C. Allen, *The Greek Chronicles*, 2, *SVT* 27 (Leiden: Brill, 1974), p. 145; R. Braun, p. 288.

NRSV, RSV, REB, NEB; *cf.* 1 Ki. 1:35; see comment on 1 Ch. 11:2), and the pledged 'allegiance' (v. 24, NRSV, RSV) of all David's sons. The framework of 1 Chronicles 22–29 is also based on 1 Kings 2:1–12, and verse 23 follows 1 Kings 2:12 closely. Finally, Solomon could not have been involved in David's temple preparations unless his succession was secure (see introductory notes to chapter 22). In the light of all this, it seems more probable that Solomon was actually anointed twice (*cf.* David's three anointings, 1 Sa. 16:13; 2 Sa. 2:4; 5:3). Typically, Chronicles has replaced the rather personal account in Kings by emphasizing *all Israel's* role in the succession (vv. 21, 23, 25, 26).

Zadok's anointing (v. 22) is also a problem. Since he was already a priest in David's cabinet (1 Ch. 18:16), he is either being promoted to high priest, or being reappointed under a new king. Abiathar could not be trusted after his involvement in Adonijah's conspiracy, and his final downfall (1 Ki. 2:26–27; 35) would have only confirmed Zadok's position. Significant changes in verse 23 from 1 Kings 2:12 (*on the throne of the LORD as king in place of his father David* for 'on the throne of his father David', and *He prospered and all Israel obeyed him* for 'and his rule was firmly established') show Chronicles' interest in the theology of the turbulent events of 1 Kings 1–2 (*cf.* 1 Ki. 2:46). This recognition of the supremacy and reality of God's kingdom (see introductory comment and on 17:14; 28:5) leads to the unusual summarizing of a king's achievements before his predecessor's death (v. 25).

vi. Concluding formula for David (29:26–30)

Chronicles expands the concluding formula for David's reign in 1 Kings 2:10–12, though only 1 Kings 2:11 has an equivalent here (v. 27; 1 Ki. 2:12 is amended as v. 23 above). David's *seven*-year rule over *Israel* in *Hebron* (v. 27) follows 1 Kings 2:11 rather than the more precise details of a seven-and-a-half year reign over Judah in 2 Samuel 5:5; 1 Chronicles 3:4. David's *wealth and honour* (v. 28) and Solomon's *splendour* (v. 25) must be understood as covenant blessings arising from God's faithfulness.

Mention of the prophetic writings as a source of further information (v. 29) probably refers to the present books of Samuel and Kings, in the light of 2 Chronicles 20:34; 32:32. Prophetic interventions by these men of God are found at the major stages of Chronicles' account of David, *viz. Samuel* at the transfer of Saul's kingdom to David (*cf.* 1 Ch. 10:13, 11:3), *Nathan* in the promise of a house for David (*cf.* 1 Ch. 17:1–15), and *Gad* in the choice of the temple site (*cf.* 1 Ch. 21:9–13, 18–19). Since Israel's contacts with *the kingdoms of all the other lands* (v. 30, a phrase unique to Chronicles, *cf.* 2 Ch. 12:8; 17;10; 20:29) were also the subject of prophetic words (1 Ch. 17:8; *cf.* 14:17; 18:6, 13), verses 29–30 suggest that the Chronicler is indicating that his account of David is based on the authority of God's revelation to the prophets.